Cary D. Rostow, PhD
Robert D. Davis, PhD

A Handbook
for Psychological
Fitness-for-Duty Evaluations
in Law Enforcement

Pre-publication
REVIEWS,
COMMENTARIES,
EVALUATIONS . . .

"Finally—a handbook that covers it all in easy-to-understand language. A must for supervisors, middle managers, and command staff. The fully researched text and appropriate case studies clearly outline the pitfalls and problems associated with law enforcement personnel management. This book provides clear solutions, legal procedures, and case law studies while underscoring the necessity of hiring the best qualified law enforcement personnel. This is a viable and important addition to any criminal justice professional reading list."

Lieutenant Gary L. Hoffman (Ret.)
Law Enforcement Trainer/
Human Resource Consultant;
Co-developer of CEdAC and other
law enforcement training/education
programs

"Historically, police psychologists have walked a path strewn with anxiety-provoking land mines. Drs. Rostow and Davis provide a wealth of pertinent information in a very readable format. This is a professional guide to which we can turn in relating successfully to officers (the tightrope beween officers and administration), fitness-for-duty examinations, testing instruments, and legal precedents (ever changing and often confusing), to name a few. I can't imagine how we functioned without this reference."

Dorothy McCoy, EdD
Law Enforcement Consultant,
Walterboro, South Carolina;
Author, *From Shyness*
to Social Butterfly

More pre-publication
REVIEWS, COMMENTARIES, EVALUATIONS . . .

"Drs. Rostow and Davis have written an excellent sourcebook for one of the most difficult issues that confronts law enforcement executives on a daily basis. It provides both law enforcement executives and mental health professionals with a thorough explanation of the factors involved with fitness-for-duty evaluations. The authors offer both legal and psychological rationales for the development of a fitness-for-duty evaluation system. In addition, they have provided law enforcement executives with guidelines as to what they should expect from such evaluations, along with useful case examples. One of the best aspects of this handbook is the Appendixes, which provide extremely helpful models for the important aspects that must be part of any fitness-for-duty evaluation. This handbook is a must for law enforcement agencies and mental health professionals who are interested in performing such evaluations."

Jon H. Moss, PhD
Police Psychologist
(independent consultant),
Richmond, Virginia

"This book is an essential resource for any mental health professional who works with law enforcement officers and others in the criminal justice system. It provides a valuable framework and resource for any professional conducting fitness-for-duty evaluations. The book gives specific guidelines, procedures, and practices for conducting fitness-for-duty evaluations, as well as sample reports for the practitioner to use.

For administrators in law enforcement agencies, this book is a must! It gives the administrator the reasons and rationale for conducting fitness-for-duty evaluations, the utility and benefits of doing evaluations, the limitations of evaluations and recommendations, and a model that can be used for developing policy and procedures concerning fitness-for-duty evaluations.

In sum, this book is a needed addition to the field. It fills a void in the literature, in law enforcement, and in police psychology of an oft neglected but crucial area of concern."

Wayman C. Mullins, PhD
Professor, Department of Criminal Justice, Texas State University

"*A Handbook for Psychological Fitness-for-Duty Evaluations in Law Enforcement* is a must-read for law enforcement executives. Police psychologists, attorneys, and public sector and union grievance committees will also find this to be an important guide. It explains the referral for FFDEs, the nature and structure of FFDEs, pitfalls in providing the service, types of reports and recommendations, forensic issues with regard to them, expert witness testimony related to the challenge of a recommendation, and the implications of the Daubert decision and HIPAA for FFDEs and the expert testimony related to them.

Those of us involved in police psychology and law enforcement administration can thank Davis and Rostow for providing this comprehensive and insightful guide to the administration of fitness-for-duty evaluations."

William U. Weiss, PhD
Professor of Psychology,
The University of Evansville;
Editor, *Journal of Police and Criminal Psychology*

A Handbook
for Psychological
Fitness-for-Duty Evaluations
in Law Enforcement

THE HAWORTH PRESS
Titles of Related Interest

Introduction to Crime Analysis: Basic Resources for Criminal Justice Practice by Deborah A. Osborne and Susan C. Wernicke

The Elements of Police Hostage and Crisis Negotiations: Critical Incidents and How to Respond to Them by James L. Greenstone

Forensic Social Work: Legal Aspects of Professional Practice, Second Edition by Robert L. Barker and Douglas M. Branson

Detection of Response Bias in Forensic Neuropsychology edited by Jim Horn and Robert L. Denney

Forensic Neuropsychology: Conceptual Foundations and Clinical Practice by Jose A. Valciukas

Criminal Justice: Retribution or Restoration? edited by Eleanor Hannon Judah and Fr. Michael Bryant

Criminal Justice Politics and Women: The Aftermath of Legally Mandated Change edited by Claudine Schweber and Clarice Feinman

Current Trends in Correctional Education: Theory and Practice edited by Sol Chaneles

The Clinical Treatment of the Criminal Offender in Outpatient Mental Health Settings: New and Emerging Perspectives edited by Sol Chaneles and Nathaniel J. Pallone

How to Work with Sex Offenders: A Handbook for Criminal Justice, Human Service, and Mental Health Professionals by Rudy Flora

Older Offenders: Current Trends edited by Sol Chaneles and Cathleen Burnett

Young Victims, Young Offenders: Current Issues in Policy Treatment edited by Nathaniel J. Pallone

Kids Who Commit Adult Crimes: Serious Criminality by Juvenile Offenders by R. Barri Flowers

The Aggressive Adolescent: Clinical and Forensic Issues by Daniel L. Davis

A Handbook
for Psychological
Fitness-for-Duty Evaluations
in Law Enforcement

Cary D. Rostow, PhD
Robert D. Davis, PhD

The Haworth Clinical Practice Press
The Haworth Reference Press
Imprints of The Haworth Press, Inc.
New York • London • Oxford

Published by

The Haworth Clinical Practice Press and The Haworth Reference Press, imprints of the Haworth Press, Inc., 10 Alice Street, Binghamton, NY 13904-1580.

Cover design by Lora Wiggins.

Library of Congress Cataloging-in-Publication Data

Rostow, Cary D.
     A handbook for psychological fitness-for-duty evaluations in law enforcement / Cary D. Rostow, Robert D. Davis.
          p. cm.
     Includes bibliographical references and index.
     ISBN 0-7890-2396-2 (hard : alk. paper)—ISBN 0-7890-2397-0 (soft : alk. paper)
     1. Police psychology—Handbooks, manuals, etc. 2. Law enforcement—Psychological aspects—Handbooks, manuals, etc. 3. Police—Health and hygiene—Handbooks, manuals, etc. I. Davis, Robert D. (Robert Douglas), 1961- . II. Title.
HV7936.P75R68 2004
363.2'01'9—dc22
                                                                                                    2004000375

CONTENTS

SECTION II: THE MECHANICS OF THE FITNESS-FOR-DUTY EVALUATION METHODOLOGY

Chapter 4. Usefulness of Fitness-for-Duty Evaluations in Law Enforcement Agencies

APPENDIXES

ABOUT THE AUTHORS

Cary D. Rostow, PhD, is a licensed clinical psychologist and neuropsychologist in Baton Rouge, Louisiana. He has performed hundreds of fitness-for-duty evaluations for law enforcement agencies regarding incumbent law enforcement officers, as well as for many organizations including universities, nuclear plants, fire departments, and private industry. Brought up in an NYPD family, he received his undergraduate degree at the University of Illinois at Chicago and his MA and PhD in clinical psychology at Northern Illinois University in DeKalb. Thereafter, he became an evaluator for the Illinois Department of Public Health until 1977, when he took a position as a professor of psychology at Northwestern State University in Natchitoches, Louisiana. By 1980, Dr. Rostow was engaged in a full community-based clinical psychology/neuropsychology practice, providing services for a broad range of patients and institutions. He holds a post-doctoral MS in clinical psychopharmacology from the California School of Professional Psychology. By the mid-1990s, his interests had focused upon police psychology, and he and Dr. Davis developed a program to establish an actuarial system for the selection of police officer candidates, based upon a model in which the officers were followed for subsequent civil rights violations at work. He is a member of the Psychology Section of the International Association of Chiefs of Police, the Society of Police and Criminal Psychology, and the American Psychological Association.

Robert D. Davis, PhD, is a police and criminal psychologist in Baton Rouge, Louisiana. He earned a BS degree in psychology from Louisiana State University and a PhD in clinical psychology and neuropsychology from the University of Southern Mississippi. Following his internship and residency in forensic psychology and neuropsychology at Tulane University Medical Center, Dr. Davis began a full-time practice and continued his pursuit of educational goals, including a post-doctoral MS in clinical psychopharmacology from the California School of Professional Psychology and completion of the

Law Enforcement Basic Training Academy of Louisiana State University. His research interests involve actuarial models for the prediction of law enforcement liabilities as a tool for police candidate selection, and the development of a police-specific selection test based upon the dynamics of police culture.

Preface and Acknowledgments

Police psychology is the application of the science and techniques of the discipline and profession of psychology to **law enforcement** issues and problems. Police psychology involves a wide range of tasks, including the selection of candidates for police employment and training, the examination of **incumbent officers** regarding their fitness for duty, and consultations with police executives on the management of law enforcement agencies, as well as a wide variety of special services (criminal profiling, hostage negotiation, management of mentally impaired suspects, and psychological autopsy) useful for many law enforcement agencies. The application of psychological science to law enforcement dates back to shortly after the turn of the twentieth century when Terman and Otis (1917) attempted to use intellectual testing for the selection of police officers. Modern police psychology may date to the 1940s, when police employee assistance programs (EAPs) were introduced, and the 1970s, with the more direct involvement of professional police psychologists within standard law enforcement systems.

In the 1990s, Matrix, Inc., a professional police psychology corporation that was founded by the authors, was invited by a regional municipal insurance provider to develop a means by which the overall risk of police officer liability could be reduced using scientific psychological evaluation methodologies. Matrix, Inc., approached psychological issues in law enforcement (LE) as a risk management/liability problem which required special emphasis on the goals of ensuring that the behavior of officers conformed to the needs for public safety and to the protection of the assets of law enforcement agencies. In both selection and fitness-for-duty evaluation (FFDE) conditions, the emphasis of the authors was upon the careful collection of information and application of scientific and legal principles.

Matrix, Inc., first developed the **M-PULSE** system, a self-updating computerized selection methodology based upon statistical regression theory. M-PULSE (Matrix Psychological Uniform Law Enforcement Selection Evaluation) is an actuarial method for forecasting the civil rights liability risk of police candidates at the time of selection. Matrix, Inc., then turned to the development of a standardized fitness-for-duty evaluation and a host of scientifically driven programs for law enforcement purposes. The FFDE was seen as an alternative to either ignoring the unacceptable and impaired behaviors of a given officer or discharging all such persons without any attempt at rehabilitation or a fair opportunity to recover from the burden of impairment. This book represents the fruits of our practice of professional psychology as we have applied it to FFDEs in law enforcement psychology.

The purpose of this book is to bridge the gap between the worlds of the police executive and the police psychologist. It offers a set of understandable concepts and a vocabulary that will provide the police executive with insights into the utility, rationale, and methods of the FFDE. In addition, it offers the psychologist a sample of the challenges and forensic issues that face the law enforcement executive as a means of contributing to the professionalization of police psychology as an independent discipline. This work was meant to encourage the sharing of concerns and ideas that form the daily life of both professions, but about which there is typically little dialogue and mutual understanding. We have attempted to avoid the jargon of professional psychology where possible in order to make the work useful to a large law enforcement, legal, and public administration audience. Of course, no single book can express fully the detailed understanding of areas of work as complex as law enforcement administration and police psychology. The need for brevity necessitated that, in some sections, only a superficial description of professional methods and problems was offered. It is hoped that interested readers are able to use this work to guide themselves into a deeper inquiry of their special areas of interest.

Throughout this book, we describe scenarios and examples that have been drawn from compound professional experiences, professional literature, workshops, and presentations shared among psychologists and law enforcement professionals. The examples and scenarios do not represent the actual history of any specific person, living or dead, but are fictionalized accounts of many officer reports that have been created for teaching purposes.

We would like to thank Darlene Rostow, Miriam Davis, Jerry Cronin, Beth Caillouet, Judith Parks Levy, Dennis Dixon, Velma Alford, Amy Copeland, Ivory Toldson, Laura Cronin, and Joseph Scott for their assistance with this project. We have benefited by our association with excellent law enforcement professionals, including Wayne Hunter, William "Rut" Whittington, and Greg Phares. We have been influenced by our colleagues at the Society for Police and Criminal Psychology, the Psychology Section of the International Association of Chiefs of Police, and the Police and Security Section of the Public Service Division (18) of the **American Psychological Association.** Our thanks also are extended to the editors of *The Police Chief* magazine, *Law and Order* magazine, and *The Forensic Examiner* for providing the initial opportunities to communicate the police psychology viewpoint to law enforcement leaders throughout the world.

Cary D. Rostow, PhD

SECTION I:
THE HISTORY AND DEVELOPMENT
OF POLICE PSYCHOLOGY

Chapter 1

Law Enforcement Agencies and Police Psychology

History teaches us that men and nations behave wisely once they have exhausted all other alternatives.

Abba Eban

The first organized, nonmilitary police forces in the Western world were the Roman *vigiles.* They were created by Gaius Octavius, later called Augustus, the grand nephew of Julius Caesar, around 27 B.C. He had earlier attempted to create a permanent paramilitary unit called the Praetorian Guard to protect the life of the emperor and keep the public order in Rome. When this failed to prove useful for any of its intended purposes, Octavius recruited "urban cohorts," a civilian organization that was headed by a **prefect.** The members were originally responsible for fire safety during daylight hours and were later supplemented by nighttime cohorts, known as the vigiles (watchmen), who were also empowered to arrest lawbreakers. The vigiles were armed with clubs as well as the standard Roman short swords.The prefect of the vigiles eventually became powerful and was given the power to pass judgment on most lawbreakers, except for serious offenders, who had to be turned over by the vigiles to the urban cohort for trial.

Policing authority during the Middle Ages (sixth to fifteenth centuries) was primarily the responsibility of local nobles on their individual estates (Reese, 1987). Until the nineteenth century, England had no persons who functioned in any way as modern police or prosecutors. English nobles assigned an official, known as a **constable,** to enforce the law in a given region of the country. The constables kept the peace, as well as apprehended and secured criminals. Not surprisingly, this unpaid and sometimes distasteful job became increasingly burdensome and unpopular. Constables often tried to shift duties to others, and, as has happened at other times in history, wealthier subjects began to pay for substitutes to be constables in their stead, causing deterioration in the quality of the provided service. In general, constables played only a minor role in law enforcement. A victim of crime who wanted a constable to undertake any substantial effort to apprehend a suspect was expected to pay for this service. Although the English "parish constable" or the justice of the peace was authorized to organize local subjects of the crown to put down large civil disturbances, such a use did not include individual crimes. In eighteenth-century England, a system of professional police and prosecutors who were government paid and appointed was viewed as potentially tyrannical and far too similar to the distasteful French system (Hay and Snyder, 1994).

The royal authorities in France had organized a small police organization of about forty inspectors, created by King Louis XIV in the seventeenth century, who "watched" the general public. Many well-paid informants throughout the country supported this system by aiding in the suppression of political dissent and resistance to monarchal rule, which continued during the reigns of Louis XV and Louis XVI. The French Revolution, brought about in no small part by such oppressive measures, resulted in the creation of two separate police bodies—one to handle ordinary duties and the other to deal with political crimes.

From 1663 to the late eighteenth century, the city of London used watchmen (often unemployed or elderly men) to guard the streets at night, but they were ineffective. This realization led to a demand for a more potent force to deal with criminals and to protect the populace from common crime. The development of modern policing may be said to have begun with **Sir Robert Peal** in 1829, and the establishment the **Metropolitan Police Force** (called "Bobbies" in deference to Sir Robert) in London, England. What made the Metropolitan Police Force different from earlier systems was the development of a uniform patrol system and a set of rules of conduct, both of which were rare in earlier times. Most of their work was done on foot (in contrast with the unpopular practice of using mounted, military forces to suppress larger disorders); relations with London shopkeepers were strong; and they showed some interest in "objectively" enforcing the laws of the day. Prior to that time, watchmen and bounty hunters were looked upon with contempt by the general public because they were often mercenary, brutal, poorly educated men who engendered little respect (Critchley, 1972).

AMERICAN POLICING

In the United States, police forces developed out of a number of divergent influences. As anyone who has been exposed to cinema Westerns could attest, the **sheriff** (usually an elected county law enforcement officer) could organize a "posse" from the body of able adults in times of unusual need—a feature of the English constable model. In many states, the sheriff continues to this day to be the primary law enforcement official, especially outside of large, urban areas. In some locations, paramilitary units (e.g., the **Texas Rangers**) developed out of a need to keep frontier peace both within the community and between conflicting cultures (e.g., Native Americans and settlers) when conventional military authority was unavailable. The **U.S. Marshals,** an organization that dates back to George Washington's recognition of the need for a federal police authority, provided law enforcement to meet the demand for law and order, particularly in unorganized territories. In urban areas, a modified London model (uniformed, civilian regular officers) developed gradually in eastern cities, such as the New York City Police Department, which was established in 1844. The original New York City police "volunteers" were so independent that until 1853 officers refused to wear uniforms, which they associated with the degrading position of servants' livery. Once uniforms were adopted, the police function became primarily the maintenance of order in the streets, followed by the piecemeal development of such techniques as using informants to reveal the identity of likely criminals.

The New York City Police Department set a pattern that was distinctly American in that local politicians originally appointed the men who served in it for limited terms, a result of the American fear that professional officers could trample civilian rights. American officers also began to carry revolvers by the end of the 1850s. Originally armed only with clubs, police use of firearms developed informally and without an official order and in the absence of special training. Although some early police chiefs considered it cowardly to carry firearms, patrolmen believed the revolver equalized their struggle with well-armed thugs (Walker, 1981). Some attempts were made to continue the practice of unarmed officers (as was true of the English police), but following the **draft riots of the Civil War** in 1863, it became apparent that sidearms would be indispensable for American officers. During the 1863 draft riots, recent European immigrants in New York City rose in a civil insurrection that grew out of their resentment over conscription into the Union army. The rioters simply swept the poorly armed New York City police aside and attacked persons of wealth, government institutions, and African Americans, whom they blamed for their real or imagined suffering brought about by the Civil War. After much damage and many deaths, the federal government dispatched troops who restored order only after the considerable use of firepower. Thereafter, American police officers were generally armed and prepared for all but the most determined disorder (Silver, 1967).

Theodore Roosevelt (1906) wrote the following:

> Most of the real working-men refused to join with the rioters, except when overawed and forced into their ranks; and many of them formed themselves into armed bodies, and assisted to restore order. The city was bare of troops, for they had all been sent to the front to face Lee at Gettysburg; and the police at first could not quell the mob. As regiment after regiment was hurried back to their assistance desperate street-fighting took place. The troops and police were thoroughly aroused, and attacked the rioters with the most wholesome desire to do them harm. In a very short time after the forces of order put forth their strength the outbreak was stamped out, and a lesson inflicted on the lawless and disorderly which they never entirely forgot.

Unfortunately, by the turn of the twentieth century, both English and American police were considered by many contemporaries to be both ineffective against serious crime and to be the instruments of social repression used against the poor. This reputation sprang partly from the apparent priority given to combating the petty crimes (e.g., theft) of the poor and partly because they were thought to support those who possessed money and influence. In effect, the working classes of that era commonly believed, with some justification, that the police would not protect them from the thugs hired by the owners of factories and would not hesitate to arrest the unionized workers. To make matters worse, **corruption** was generally tolerated as an unavoidable by-product of low police salaries and the practical need to supplement incomes from available opportunities. These factors made policing a less than ideal vocation, attracting those who already had many "problems" in their backgrounds. Many early American law enforcement officers were outlaws at an initial stage of their careers (Walker, 1977).

THE FIRST AMERICAN POLICE REFORM MOVEMENT

The **first American police reform movement** (which may be described as a "militarization" reform) was undertaken in the second half of the nineteenth century. Military rank and discipline were introduced to police work following the Civil War as a means of bringing some sense of mission and control to police departments. Uniforms and military hierarchies became commonplace, perhaps accepted at that time because of the many officers who had become accustomed to such systems during the Civil War (1861-1865). The military was then seen as more orderly and efficient than many civilian organizations of that era. In addition, persons of that period expected the brute force element of military missions to also be part of police work. Some police forces were organized into "strike forces," squads, and divisions that were commanded by sergeants, lieutenants, captains, and colonels—the heritage of the original "military" reforms.

Upper- and middle-class reformers fought to eliminate political patronage and corruption by asserting impartial control over the police. They tried various schemes: **bipartisan commissions, state control** (New York was first to instigate this in 1857), **employment examinations,** and promotion by merit. The administration of police forces improved, as when Theodore Roosevelt was New York's police commissioner during the 1890s, only to slip back into older, less controlled methods of operation. This **cyclical pattern** (improvement followed by a return to the older corruption) apparently is a common phenomenon for many police reform movements. In addition to trying to reshape the police, puritanical reformers also tried to control immigrant recreational and working-class community habits by passing laws against gambling, prostitution, Sunday drinking in saloons, and any use of alcohol. Such impractical laws, contrary to the attitudes of most police officers as well as the communities served by them, served only to create new opportunities for corruption, such as covert police demands for "protection" money from saloon or brothel keepers in order to prevent raids and harassment.

Following World War I (1914-1918), the great crime wave brought about by the reaction to the **Volstead Act of 1920,** also called the National Prohibition Act (alcohol prohibition), greatly contributed to the emergence of nationally organized criminal groups. With alcohol prohibited, underworld financial opportunities emerged to provide for the public's traditional desire for intoxicants, fueling companion illicit enterprises, such as prostitution, extortion, and gambling. Al Capone, the dominant gangster of Chicago, Illinois, in the prohibition era, had an estimated annual income from the various criminal aspects of his business of over $100 million. With illegal alcohol as the driving engine behind many forms of lawlessness, criminal organizations used their seemingly limitless financial resources to bribe judges, politicians, and police. The poorly trained, poorly educated, inadequately paid police officer was often unable to stand up to the political and economic power of the criminal underworld. In this sea of disorder, the public tended to idealize a few well-motivated and honest law enforcement organizations (re-created in the movie and television dramas, **The Untouchables**).

THE SECOND AMERICAN POLICE REFORM MOVEMENT

The **second American police reform movement** grew out of the turmoil of prohibition, in which an attempt was made to "professionalize" police departments by emphasizing education and adherence to an enforceable code of rules and ethics. The reformers, many of them graduates of the burgeoning American universities, called for merit-based hiring and promotion, **civil service** "guarantees" of security, and transparent codes of conduct. One hallmark of this system was the idea that only persons who had spent considerable time at lower ranks (**"seniority system"**) should become eligible for a higher rank. At the time, this reform was seen as a means of ensuring fairness and competency in the law enforcement command structure by guaranteeing that most commanders would have performed many basic law enforcement jobs, and were not simply "political appointees." To this day, one of the issues in police administration is the question of whether better-educated individuals should be **"laterally promoted"** (moved to positions of command ahead of less well-educated, experienced-in-rank officers) rather than "working their way up" through the ranks (Reese and Goldstein, 1986). **Merit hiring** and the selection of officers by competitive examination rather than the chief's personal choice was expected to reduce the **nepotism** and corrupt financial and political advantage by which jobs had been awarded previously (the **"spoils system"**). Although employment tests had been part of the earlier reforms, they were offered originally only to those who had already been personally selected by influential political figures. In a mutually contradictory way, the older **patronage**-based hiring systems were both the strength (because it engendered support among powerful voting blocks) and weakness (because it led to unfair hiring and enforcement performance) of early police departments. However, in the long run, the second wave of reforms appeared to encourage the recruitment of highly educated and personally capable candidates, who in turn brought a new level of innovation and competence to modern police agencies.

Demands for improvements in police efficiency and community-police relations seem to be a recurrent problem in urban policing. An **enforcement-priority model** (reducing crime by making arrests) has sometimes conflicted with the **community-based model** (reducing crime by improving both the served community and police relations with the community) of policing. The second American police reform movement, which created greater independence and capability in police agencies, may also have introduced new problems, such as increasing the social distance between police officers and many constituent groups of the community. The Los Angeles Police Department (**LAPD**) under Chief **William Parker** (1950-1966), earned a reputation for professionalism and proficiency, dramatized in the television series **Dragnet.** However, LAPD Chief Darryl Gates, a successor to Chief Parker and supporter of the independent, professional police department concept, suffered from accusations of insensitivity to racial and cultural minorities when using Chief Parker's basic approach. For example, he was said to have refused the demand to prosecute officers who were accused of brutality by minority community leaders because he believed it would undermine the authority and crime-suppression capability of the LAPD. Such attitudes were said to have contributed to the civil disorders of the late 1960s and engendered hostility between the police and sections of the community that they served.

The second wave of American police reformers appeared to split into two, sometimes warring, camps. Some saw technology, as well as improved administration and training, as part of their drive for better police effectiveness and crime control. Other reformers became more concerned with the dangers of excessive police power and the questionable treatment of suspects. In the early twentieth century, these civil libertarians were few but conspicuous, such as New York's Mayor William Gaynor (1909-1913) and Toledo's Mayor Samuel "Golden Rule" Jones (1897-1904). Concern about police practices reached the national level when President Hoover's **Wickersham Commission (1931)** published its exposé of police brutality and third-degree interrogation methods, which were said to involve beatings and torture. Not until the 1960s did the U.S. Supreme Court begin to regulate police behavior by imposing standards for evidence gathering and for the protection of suspects' rights during interrogation. This type of reform was closely associated with the civil rights movement of the 1960s, along with other reforms in voting rights and fair employment standards. Such changes increased police resentment toward the courts for frustrating law enforcement work with legal technicalities.

THE THIRD AMERICAN
POLICE REFORM MOVEMENT

The **third American police reform movement,** known as community policing, was more closely associated with social science research and professional psychology than were the earlier movements. The relationship between the physical decay of declining inner-city neighborhoods and changes brought about by crime, drug abuse, and economic problems had become a political issue by the 1960s. The general spirit of President Lyndon Johnson's Great Society social programs involved the use of the legislative and economic power of federal government to improve the condition of socially and economically disadvantaged persons. By 1973, the **President's Commission on Law Enforcement** recommended that police officers must develop professional discretionary methods that addressed the basic causes of crime in communities rather than the crimes themselves. Some police departments attempted to establish a vital, interactive relationship with patrolled neighborhoods, so that crime and disorder (gangs, vacant buildings, drug use centers) could be addressed at their origin. Officers were encouraged to hand out business cards, attend community meetings, and meet civic council representatives in order to become trusted members of the community. Police worked with other municipal service departments to meet these ends, for example, by having the housing authority clear abandoned buildings used as crack houses. Even less directly apparent methods, such as police officers helping communities clean up vacant lots, repair buildings, and perform other services that improve the quality of life in the community, have been attempted in the theory that good neighborhoods attract good people (Wilson and Kelling, 1982). Such improvements may have inadvertently undone the effects of some parts of the earlier reform movements by reintroducing elements of community influence to police work. For example, it may become difficult for officers within this model to arrest community political leaders, even when faced with evidence of criminal conduct, because of the impact of such an arrest upon the community.

The need to balance fairness and concern for community residents with the clear need to enforce laws independently is a significant police challenge. One response was to enlist minority group members into police agencies through special recruitment and affirmative action programs. Unfortunately, as with their European (Irish and Italian) predecessors in ethnic neighborhoods, those interested in joining police departments may not be more sympathetic to members of their own group of origin than others have been. Programs for moving officers out of patrol cars and onto the streets (such as the **Kansas City**

Preventive Patrol Experiment in 1972) was one such effort to reduce mutual antagonism between the police and the policed (Kelling, 1974).

U.S. POLICE STRUCTURES

The United States has no comprehensive national police authority, but the federal government has had a rudimentary enforcement system since 1789. The **U.S. Marshals Service,** which has the power to apprehend persons committing certain federal crimes, was the most important police agency in the western territories until they became states. However, few crimes were specifically federal until the **Reconstruction Era** (1865-1877), during which time the Marshals Service enforced federal civil rights laws. The **Bureau of Internal Revenue** was created out of a need to fund the Civil War by collecting excise taxes on alcoholic beverages. The **Secret Service,** also created as a federal detective agency, concentrated on the suppression of counterfeiting and the protection of U.S. presidents. The **Comstock laws** of the 1870s, which outlawed distribution of obscene material (mostly birth control information) through the mail, resulted in the creation of the **U.S. Postal Inspection Service.** The Bureau of Immigration and Naturalization was created in the 1920s with a mandate to secure U.S. borders.

By far the most famous federal police agency is the **Federal Bureau of Investigation (FBI).** From modest beginnings in 1908, the bureau emerged during the 1920s under **J. Edgar Hoover**'s leadership as a police agency for the investigation of political radicalism, domestic espionage, and other federal crimes. In the 1930s the FBI became part of popular culture when it received publicity for tracking down gangsters (such as John Dillinger, a famous 1930s bank robber) and developing standards for local police forces through its training schools, crime labs, and uniform crime reports. Hoover made the FBI very much his own organization—an instrument of immense personal power and occasional abuse. Although feared by many as excessively influential, the FBI has usually enjoyed widespread popular support.

EARLY POLICE PSYCHOLOGICAL TESTING

Historically, few guidelines existed for hiring or examining police officers. Officers often served at the pleasure of the chief of police and had few protections or requirements for service. In the United States, recruiting in many cities was limited to men of Irish descent, excluding women and members of other racial and ethnic groups. This was motivated by the fact that Irish immigrants spoke English and, therefore, had no language barrier and could begin police work immediately upon arrival in the United States. In addition, officer candidates were frequently recruited from among military veterans, although this often meant that applicants had little formal education or civilian experiences. By the twentieth century, most police departments had developed a civil service system in which the personal selection of recruits by police chiefs also had to achieve minimal scores on standardized testing, predominately of the "cognitive" (general information) variety.

Psychologists first became involved in police selection in the early twentieth century. **Lewis Terman** and his associates at Stanford University believed that general intelligence (and something they called **"moral integrity"**) was essential for a successful police officer. Using an early intelligence test, the **Binet-Simon Scale,** they determined that an intelligence quotient (IQ) of eighty (about the tenth percentile of the general population distribution) represented the minimum standard intellectual level needed to become a police officer (Terman and Otis, 1917). Today, intellectual or cognitive testing is a controversial area of police selection. Intellectual tests have been used by some departments to exclude highly intelligent applicants under the theory that they would not be happy limited to police work. A more serious potential problem is that traditional intelligence testing yields scores which tend to be higher for applicants of European and Asian backgrounds than for those of other ethnic cities, perhaps creating a discriminatory impact. Any test that affects the selection of persons in racially "protected" categories (usually groups believed to have suffered historical discrimination) may violate complex civil rights statutes and regulations. The **U.S. Department of Justice (DOJ)** has employed the so-called **four-fifths rule,** which proposes that any selection procedure may not be considered legal if it adversely impacts upon disadvantaged communities greater than majority communities at a level of 20 percent (i.e., not greater than four-fifths or 80 percent).

The quality of police officers in U.S. society emerged as a concern during the civil unrest of the 1960s. The **National Advisory Commission on Civil Disorders (1968)** determined that methods were needed to detect and avoid the selection and retention of police officers whose duties would be hampered by personal prejudices. The recommendation was that law enforcement departments use psychologists or psychiatrists to examine applicants and administer batteries of psychological examinations to determine the fitness of candidates. At the time, this idea was considered a great leap forward, but the development of technology for locating "personal prejudices" never appeared as a high priority within the funding or research communities, and little progress was made toward this lofty goal.

Following initial hit-and-miss psychological efforts (such as Terman's early testing), a qualified sense that psychological sciences could be useful in many areas of work was widely held. By the 1960s, most police psychologists seemed to have been involved in training, disciplinary methods, and related issues, with little effort given to developing scientific interview and testing methodologies for use with individual officers in selection or fitness situations. Although some police psychological assessment studies appeared in the psychological journals, most showed little scientific rigor. The practice of impressionistically "reading" psychological test profiles, a method that had been developed originally to diagnose mental illness with clinical patients, was often employed. In other cases, the identification of traits that were thought desirable or undesirable in police officers became the focus of some research, often with limited success. Kent and Eisenberg (1972) reviewed twenty-nine contemporary assessment articles and concluded that psychological testing for police selection "bordered on charlatanism." In 1982, Mills and Stratton found little support for the way that the traditional MMPI (Minnesota Multiphasic Personality Inventory) was used in screening new officer applicants with the Los Angeles Police Department. Cunningham (1986) reported that early testing tended to focus on low-probability behaviors (such as the presence of serious mental illness in office applicants) and showed this was unlikely to yield strong, meaningful findings since the target behavior was so rare, even if the basic scientific design for the study was valid. With poorly developed and occasionally inappropriate psychological testing, little optimism or utility was seen for most police psychology selection procedures by the early 1990s (Kurke and Scrivner, 1995).

Most reviews of police research literature (Geller and Toch, 1996) have tended to concentrate upon the usefulness of administrative methods (e.g., supervision techniques) over individual officer psychological approaches. Most of the research tended to be fragmentary, involving small numbers of officers in simple statistical comparison studies. It was not until the late 1980s that large numbers of officer test results were compared using longitudinal methods (Hiatt and Hargrave, 1988; Bartol, 1991). In these studies, statistical techniques using multi-factorial methods revealed that **index scores** (weighted combinations of test and nontest factors) showed some real promise in selecting officers who would demonstrate an enhanced risk of liability for undesirable behaviors.

DEVELOPMENT OF PROFESSIONAL POLICE PSYCHOLOGY AND EAPs

An important element of the practical beginning of police psychology may be seen in the development of **employee assistance programs (EAPs).** In general, an EAP may be described as an employer-sponsored clinical program of counseling that is designed to address behavioral problems noted in the workplace. These plans were seen as a method to deal with employee problems before the employee had to be discharged, thus saving the employer and employee unnecessary expense and stress. Beginning in industrial settings as early as the 1920s, reportedly impaired employees would be offered social services (counseling, referral to medical or legal specialists) that they may not otherwise be able to find or afford. A specially prepared counselor would receive reports concerning employee problems from important others (supervisors, family, etc.), assess the employee, and offer short-term counseling. If unable to deal directly with the impairment, the EAP counselor would make a referral to an appropriate provider (e.g., an outpatient alcohol treatment clinic) for limited intervention, and would monitor progress of the employee. In some cases, the employer would create a division of the agency staffed with mental health employees for this purpose, or in other cases an outside company would provide this service under contract. On occasion, unions might have taken the initiative to provide such services for their members. The payoff for the employer was to have a more productive workforce and reduced health-related costs because of focused treatment delivery. Aided by the now defunct **Law Enforcement Assistance Administration,** discretionary funds were set aside for psychologists and other mental health professionals to develop such programs. Most law enforcement EAPs focused predominately on assistance with alcoholism difficulties, with the Boston Police Department leading the way. The Los Angeles and Chicago police departments established counseling facilities for their officers in the 1970s. By 1986, most large police departments had some form of EAP system in place.

The creation of law enforcement EAPs was not only important in providing direct assistance to officers; such programs also introduced psychologists into law enforcement agencies so that they could contribute their talents in other ways. By the early 1990s, Blau (1994) reported that police psychologists were involved in officer recruitment, selection, fitness-for-duty evaluations, the establishment of special testing units, critical incident counseling, stress prevention and inoculation, individual and family counseling, direct operation assistance, hostage negotiation, psychological profiling, investigative hypnosis, psychological autopsy, and management consultation. Police psychology had become a profession within many law enforcement settings.

SOME CONTEMPORARY ISSUES IN POLICING

Police Unions

The earliest strike conducted by government employees in the United States was the **Boston police strike of 1919** (Russell, 1975). This strike began when the Boston police commissioner refused to permit the police to affiliate with the American Federation of Labor

(AFL). For a brief period, the city of Boston was the scene of widespread, opportunistic rioting, which began after a majority of Boston's officers left their posts. Future U.S. president and then-governor of Massachusetts Calvin Coolidge ultimately ended the strike by bringing the state militia into the city and taking charge of the police force. **Samuel Gompers,** the president of the AFL, wrote a letter (September 14, 1919) asking Calvin Coolidge to reinstate participants of the Boston police strike. Coolidge wrote back, "The right of the police of Boston to affiliate has always been questioned, never granted, is now prohibited. There is no right to strike against the public safety by anybody, anywhere, any time." Since that time, a mixed relationship has existed between unions and police executives. Unions have been an important influence in building officer morale and in creating political support for police agencies. The legacy of the Boston police strike may be characterized by the conflict between the need for police to protect the public and their desire to achieve certain occupational or financial goals.

Many police unions have appeared in U.S. police departments in recent years, in spite of a general decline in the influence of unions in many employment sectors. Critics of this trend argue that union affiliation weakens official authority in maintaining discipline and that unionized police forces are less likely to be neutral in controlling disorders which occur during labor strikes. Others argue that management deficiencies often justify the need for unions and that unionization will lead to greater officer job satisfaction and increased tenure. However, because police are public employees, some laws restrict their right to strike or to participate in other job actions, although this has been challenged frequently. The trend seems to be for police unions to engage in compulsory or binding arbitration when labor disputes arise.

Unions appear to have a mixed relationship with police psychology. In some locations, unions may contract with psychologists to provide members with employee assistance programs or individual therapy services. In other settings, unions may view police psychologists as "management" and may take an antagonistic position regarding such services as FFDEs. In some jurisdictions, an order for an officer to submit to a FFDE may be grounds for a grievance which alleges that the FFDE referral was unfair or unjustified. This union position may be more ambivalent when some members wish to have a fellow officer examined (for reasons of safety or efficacy) and others do not wish any officer examined as an antimanagement policy.

Restraints on Police Methods

Police continue to rely on investigative methods, such as interrogating and detaining suspects, which may open questions of appropriateness and constitutionality. These activities and the searches and arrests that result have received the scrutiny of the courts. In recent decades, the Supreme Court has imposed conditions on police methods, such as the requirement that immediately after arrest a person must be informed of his or her rights, including the right to counsel and the right to remain silent. The Court has also restricted the use of evidence obtained illegally, such as information from unauthorized wiretapping.

Issues that arise from the conflict between the demands for conformity to civil rights regulations and case law, and the culture in which the police must operate on a daily basis, have become important aspects of police psychology. The place of the police psychologist in assisting in the counseling and training of officers regarding cultural conflicts and their impact on officer conduct may be of cardinal importance in the future development of psychologist-police executive relations.

Police and Civil Disorders

The policeman isn't there to create disorder; the policeman is there to preserve disorder.

Former mayor of Chicago, the Honorable Richard J. Daley, during the civil disorders associated with the Democratic National Convention in 1968

The police are the sole governmental mechanism (aside from the militia or National Guard) that can prevent or control acute civil disorder. In recent times, authorities have also recognized the importance of preventing police action from precipitating civil disturbances, as well as the need for police to engage in positive community-related activities to alleviate tensions. No issue provokes more intense controversy within minority communities than that of the use of deadly force. Some police officials and minority community leaders believe that a police officer should use a firearm only in defense of a life (either that of the officer or of another person) which is in immediate jeopardy. Others think that existing state laws, many of which permit an officer to use any force necessary to arrest a suspected felon who may do major harm if uncaptured, should not be limited by social policies. Police psychologists may expect to play an increasingly important role in the development of standards of deadly force for police officers as well as contribute to the understanding of a specific incident of the use of force by an officer undergoing an FFDE.

Civilian Review Boards

In the nineteenth century, complaints regarding police officer conduct were heard by the chief and one or two senior officers. By the early twentieth century, larger departments created **complaint review boards (CRBs)** that were composed of nonuniformed, senior officers. This method came under criticism because of the feeling among community advocates that the attitude of such bodies was disposed too favorably to the officers' viewpoints. By the early 1960s, mixed CRBs appeared that were composed of both law enforcement executives and civilians (community leaders and academics) or of politically appointed, prominent civilians without police members (Walker and Bumphus, 1992).

Officers and police executives complain that **civilian review boards** undermine police autonomy, generate officer antagonism, and reduce morale (Snow, 1992). CRBs often function independently of the police department and have many divergent methods of operation. Some of them are simply complaint collection agencies that may recommend policy change, whereas many others operate as mediation centers. Some conduct hearings only following an **internal affairs (IA) division** inquiry. Others hold informal reviews of officer conduct regarding a set of particular complaints but do not conduct their own investigations. Some CRBs try to carry out limited investigations of complaints, and many have subpoena power to call witnesses and conduct hearings. The future of CRBs is currently uncertain.

Some operate as an **officer-involved shooting board (OISB),** which is involved only in excessive force complaints or when deadly force is used. Others act as an appeals board for employees who have been disciplined or fired.

Police psychology, with its emphasis on objective and scientific examination, seems to have much to offer in the elaboration of the CRB model or as part of the team that creates and evaluates "officer conduct" examination models. Future development of the FFDE procedure may be associated with applications originating with CRBs.

Chapter 2

Police Culture
and Assessment/Therapy Issues

If something is stolen from you, don't go to the police. They're not interested. Don't go to a psychologist either, because he's interested in only one thing: that it was really you who did the stealing.

Karl Kraus

The educational and training demands placed upon medical and behavioral professionals (psychologists and psychiatrists) are such that persons successful in meeting the criteria for inclusion (licenses, degrees) are limited only to those who have been devoted to the educational process. The hurdles to graduation from advanced professional schools and the requirements of licensing tend to produce a more verbally expressive person than is typical in general society. Mental heath providers must be adept in dealing with the social milieu of the culture in which they work. They must adjust their therapeutic work to the circumstances, experiences, and viewpoints of persons who are members of the social groups that they serve. Often, the population that the therapist serves is not the same as that to which the therapists belongs.

The **treatment provider** who has vainly urged a working-class adolescent to stay in school can attest to this difficulty. The youth may not have the books, computer and Internet access, parental assistance, and peer encouragement needed for academic achievement. The therapist at first may tend to dismiss the youth as lazy and unfocused. This conflicting worldview may be made infinitely more difficult by language, race, age, ethnic, and gender differences between the provider and the patient. Some social, occupational, and educational group members (even therapists) may look upon those who hold different social memberships with anger, distaste, or misunderstanding. Such differences in behavior may stem from the wellspring of differential, shared systems of beliefs held by reasonably cohesive occupational, social, religious, and political groups. Such belief systems are generally known to social scientists as culture.

CULTURE

Culture may be defined as a connected system of acquired values, beliefs, and rules of conduct that defines accepted behaviors, goals, and material and intellectual skills in any given social group, whether formally or informally structured. As used by anthropological researchers, cultural differences are thought to distinguish societies (such as tribes in preindustrial parts of the world) from one another. Culture is based on the uniquely human capacity to classify experiences, encode, and teach abstractions to others. It appears to describe how certain values (e.g., aggressiveness in the face of frustration) or definite interests (e.g., musical preferences) occur within occupations, neighborhoods, and juvenile gangs, to name a few examples. The process by which established group leaders and members (e.g., **field training officers [FTOs]** or senior police commanders) induce or compel a younger generation (recruits or supervised trainees) to reproduce and embed the culture in their way of life is difficult to quantify. Culture appears to exist frequently at an unspoken or unconscious level, or at least tends to be so pervasive that it escapes everyday reflection.

Everyone lives within a cultural context—Pennsylvanian coal miners, Native Americans, Cajuns in Louisiana, and New York gang members. Each culture has its own recognizable informative style which shapes the behavior of its members, their political judgment, and their morals in both formal and informal ways. Technical education, religious beliefs, and daily social intercourse are all means of cultural transmission. Throughout history, human culture has become more elaborate and differentiated, sometimes making human groupings appear alien to one another in the way they conduct civil affairs, war, and educational experience. Police all over the world have developed variations on a central police or law enforcement cultural theme, based upon shared experience, attitudes, and beliefs that have been handed down from one field supervisor to another.

An understanding of police or law enforcement culture is vital to the police psychologist, both in terms of the assessment and the treatment of law enforcement clients. This chapter deals with a number of specific police/psychological assessment and treatment cultural issues, including the law enforcement EAP, post-traumatic stress disorder, and general police culture in the counseling context.

POLICE-SPECIFIC PSYCHOLOGICAL ASSESSMENT, TREATMENT, AND EAP

Employee assistance programs were developed originally in industrial settings, such as geographically remote construction sites, where access to mental health providers was limited or where the employer needed to quickly intervene with common problems of the workforce (e.g., alcoholism) for economic reasons. Often known as **occupational alcoholism programs (OAPs),** these early programs attempted to reduce the misuse of alcohol and controlled substances within the workplace. They were run by peer (fellow nonprofessional employee) or professional counselors who were paid by the employer and who received referrals from supervisors when an employee appeared intoxicated or dysfunctional at work. The counselor might offer advice, call on a family support system, or refer to an outside professional for brief intervention. If more intensive therapy was required, the employee would be referred by the OAP to an outside treatment system, although this eventuality was expected to be infrequent if the OAP was working well. As a result, the employer was often able to keep valuable employees and maintain a full workforce. Over time, marital difficulties, emotional issues, legal problems, and health problems were added to the substance abuse focus of these programs, and the more appropriate designation of employee assistance program came into common use.

In 1970, **Public Law 91-616,** also referred to as the Comprehensive Alcohol Abuse and Alcoholism Prevention, Treatment, and Rehabilitation Act, mandated and funded alcoholism treatment programs for public employees. As funds ran out for such programs in the 1980s, the employee assistance program replaced alcoholism treatment programs for public employees with an emphasis upon general prevention of the need for extensive professional intervention by the use of crisis counseling and targeted referrals for assistance. As in the private sector, stress-management features were added to substance abuse treatment programs. In some cases, attempts were made to defend the cost-efficiency of EAPs to senior managers by expanding them to include new employee screening programs to find more stable workers. Some law enforcement organizations expanded EAP services to include psychological FFDEs. In addition to the ethical issues that such mixed EAP/treatment/FFDE service raises (e.g., is the EAP a health service for the officer or a means of protecting the public?), mixed plans are especially troubling in LE settings in which suspicions of compromised confidentiality are common.

Indeed, the natural suspiciousness and financial concerns of many LE executives seemed to have motivated many LE EAPs to transform themselves into peer-oriented programs, in which an officer receives counseling only from other (more or less trained) officers. Although this model offers the comfort of reassuring the officer that he or she is speaking to persons of similar background, it may place pressure on the **peer counselors** (who are often also serving officers) to report alarming information discovered in EAP counseling to LE executives. Thus both confidentiality and technical expertise, compared to the use of trained professionals, may be compromised in order to have the counseling remain within the confines of the "blue brotherhood" (Crank, 1997). Of course, there are advantages and disadvantages to both professional and peer methods, and only research into eventual issues of effectiveness will resolve the question of ultimate preference.

Internal and External EAPs

By the early 1980s, LE EAPs appeared to have evolved into three general organizational forms:

- *External programs,* which may be defined as EAP services that are provided by outside mental health providers (not employees) who have only contractual ties to the employing LE agency

- *Internal programs,* which may be defined as EAP plans in which employees of an LE agency (professional or peer) provide the basic counseling services to agency members
- *Hybrid service model programs,* in which some services are provided internally (e.g., stress counseling by a peer counselor), whereas others are provided through external service contracts (e.g., alcoholism treatment by specially trained providers) with outside professional providers

Many officers will not share their personal or social problems with independent, outside mental health professionals. Law enforcement officers may believe such persons cannot be helpful because "civilians do not understand" police work or cannot appreciate the pressure under which the officers serve. In any form of counseling, LE officers also may be concerned that the information divulged in therapy may be used against them or that such information may inhibit promotion or appointment to highly sought-after assignments. A major source of distress for the officer is the idea that an LE officer who talks to a police psychologist will be ridiculed or rejected by peers and supervisors as a "nutcase" or "damaged goods." In the *Lethal Weapon* movie series (starring Mel Gibson and Danny Glover), a mentally ill officer is teamed with a partner who must suffer the miseries associated with a lunatic partner. It is a comic masterpiece, but it is also a nightmare scenario for serving officers who may visualize themselves in the "crazy" officer role and an object of ridicule and derision. Many LE officers will resist any suggestion of weakness or contamination inherent in a psychiatric label, no matter how serious their difficulty or misery.

Law Enforcement EAPs

The Fairfax County Police Department outside of Washington, DC, was among the first to have an internal, full-time EAP program for police officers (Banks, 1992). Attempts have been made by many departments to contract with mental health clinics and local community mental health centers to provide uniform, external mental health services. Gentz (1986) reported that difficulties have arisen in using outside providers, often involving confidentiality, ethics, clinical neutrality, and proper procedure, especially when the EAP counselor suspects that an officer is violating departmental regulations. Indeed, just the fact that an officer has been referred by an LE executive for mental health services may taint that officer in a way which may damage his or her career, since others may assume that the officer is mentally impaired and unreliable.

Yet outside law enforcement authorities, such as the Department of Justice, often look upon the law enforcement EAP as an important element in reducing internal departmental tensions and improving the quality of police services. For example, in the consent decree between the Department of Justice and the Pittsburgh Police Department (*U.S. v. City of Pittsburg,* 1997), the Department of Justice proposed the following:

> The City shall continue to provide an employee assistance program ("EAP"). This program shall at a minimum provide counseling and stress management services to officers. This program shall be staffed by sufficient licensed and certified counselors who are trained and experienced in addressing psychological and emotional problems common to police officers. The City shall publicize the availability of these services to all officers. The City shall authorize officers to attend counseling without any adverse actions taken against them. The City shall refer officers to, but not require their participation in, EAP counseling where the City believes an officer's job performance may benefit from EAP services. These provisions are separate from any counseling the City may require as part of its "Track III" mandatory counseling program.

Clearly, the DOJ values the EAP approach to better police performance within the civil rights umbrella.

SPECIAL ISSUES OF PSYCHOTHERAPY IN POLICE SETTINGS

Post-Traumatic Stress Disorder

When reading about police officer experiences on duty, frequent references are made in the popular press to **post-traumatic stress**

disorder (PTSD). This psychiatric syndrome has a dramatic history and has been the exclusive topic of many books and professional journals. Although a deep discussion of it is beyond the scope of this book, a general understanding of PTSD can be useful to the LE executive and may provide a base for certain decisions that may be required in the course of supervisory duties. Of course, PTSD is only one of a great many possible difficulties that are routinely suffered by both officers and the general public, and in no case can this concept account for every officer's problems.

The Case of Officer Louis

Louis and his partner reported to the house of a well-known resident for what appeared to be that person's nonemergency request for assistance. They did not expect trouble but were greeted by a gunshot blast from the open front door that fatally injured Officer Louis's partner. A second shot tore into Officer Louis's left leg.

Reeling backward, Officer Louis drew his firearm and rapidly returned fire. He saw his nine-millimeter rounds strike the head of his assailant about nine feet away, causing it to burst open and spray the hallway with blood and gore. Officer Louis lay helplessly in front of the door for almost twenty minutes before paramedics arrived. After several months of recovery, Officer Louis returned to work. He complained of poor sleep and a "fear" that he had never experienced in earlier police work. He was sometimes paralyzed with indecision and other times overwhelmed with a sense of physical illness. His wife left him several months later, complaining of his violent temper. He dropped out of the department's softball team, which he used to love, and annoyed the **personnel division** with repeated calls inquiring about his retirement benefits. Finally, Officer Louis was seen visiting his former partner's gravesite at times that he was scheduled to be on patrol.

Officer Louis appeared to be in need of assistance. Following a traumatic event that involved actual death or serious personal injury, an officer and his or her department may expect that a PTSD response is possible. The more appalling the event (and here we had the death of a partner and an injury that appeared to be very serious at the time it occurred), the more likely the accompanying fear, helplessness, or horror will be. The memory of the event may be experienced through intrusive and distressing recollections of the event, including distracting daytime thoughts and recurrent nightmares that interrupt sleep. He or she may feel that the traumatic events are recurring (as in flashback episodes) and may report a feeling of unreality or "dream state" while awake.

Officer Louis may become very upset when in situations that remind him of, or resemble some feature of the traumatic event, such as approaching a dark house or receiving a "calm" (as in the night he was shot) request for assistance. At such times, he may begin to shake or sweat or report that his heart is racing. Even movies that depict police officers in ambush situations may bring on an attack of nausea and make it necessary for him to leave the theater. Remote references to the event (such as seeing his former partner's widow in public) may bring about similar emotional reactions.

Officer Louis may refuse to talk about that evening and may become unreasonably angry when it is mentioned. Any social event involving police officers (such as a softball game) may be avoided, and he may become something of a hermit. He may mention that he and his wife (or children or siblings) are "just not as close" as they once were or that he has separated from them. Officer Louis's sergeant may report the smell of alcohol on Louis's breath when he reports for his shift. Officer Louis may admit that he is no longer good company, often forgetful, unreasonably angry, and "jumpy." He may feel as if he failed his partner in some way ("I should have covered the door better"), a matter of regret and guilt for him. In private, he may admit to thinking about retirement, an anticipation that leads to some depression.

Acute stress disorder refers to a similar disturbance that develops within the first month after exposure to an extreme trauma and lasts for up to four weeks. The more extreme the trauma, the more likely it will result in a long-term problem. Dreamlike states and memory problems are warning signs of a serious psychological difficulty. If the symptoms persist for more than one month and are associated with problems functioning as an officer, the diagnosis of post-traumatic stress disorder may be assigned. The officer's attitudes and ideas about his or her job and people in the environment may appear to change for the worse. Substance abuse often follows, especially involving "downers," such as alcohol, marijuana, and sedative-hypnotic drugs, which appear to calm his or her mental state.

Police Culture and Police Psychology

Although a matter of some dispute, it has long been proposed that police have a unique culture (Dunham and Alpert, 1988). The debate does not appear to question the existence of such a **police culture,** but whether its values are shared with similar socioeconomic cohorts (e.g., industrial workers). The need to account for cultural variables in psychological services in regard to such populations as African Americans, Hispanics, Asian Americans, and Native Americans has been long accepted as a principle of professionalism (Juarez, 1985; Sue and Sue, 1987). It is reasonable that cultural concerns should be an important issue in the diagnosis and treatment of law enforcement personnel.

Cultural Diversity

In the past, police departments were composed predominantly of white males, particularly those of Irish or Scotch-Irish descent (Skolnick, 1994). This trend, which dates to the earliest police departments in the United States, has left a legacy with modern departments, even those whose members are no longer predominantly Irish in heritage. It was a staple belief of the police culture that "proper" police agents were male and of Western European background and that others did not have the "appropriate" attitudes or physical abilities. Only since the turn of the twentieth century have female, Eastern and Southern European, Hispanic, Asian, and African-American officers been included in the mix of law enforcement providers in any numbers. Given the emphasis on teamwork in police operations, problems associated with this emergent **cultural diversity** have become topics of interest. Some modern police departments may be predominantly staffed with Hispanic or African-American officers as a direct reflection of the communities those departments serve. Allegations by some officers that the members of the "other racial group" enjoy some type of preference appear to be a recurring police theme and a focus for understanding the officer's personal perceptions. Recognition of the role played by cultural or historical conflicts may be an important element in designing a stress management program to treat the officer's individual difficulty. To ignore or disparage such concerns may invite a rift to develop between the therapist and officer that may cripple any attempt at **therapeutic alliance.**

A common complaint among officers who are members of the majority racial community is that the fairness training that many officers receive seems to promote the concept that minority persons are "no different" from everyone else. Yet when the officer verbalizes standard police concepts (e.g., commenting that a minority community is a "high-crime area"), the officer may be labeled as racist by those who are offended by this observation. The officer may express confusion because he or she is only sharing an observation that may have been applied to any neighborhood, regardless of racial composition. Yet holding essentially the same standards of conduct in a different context (commenting on minority behavior compared with majority community behavior) may result in sanctions or disciplinary proceedings for that officer. The officer may report a sense of betrayal and frustration, as if the officer views himself or herself as a victim of deception. The "fairness" notion may seem to some officers to contain the contradictory ideas that some persons are special and are entitled to preferential treatment. The officer may share with the therapist that if persons in a certain predominately minority neighborhood commit a higher proportion of crimes than is true of others, "why can't I say so?"

Law enforcement culture does not seem to hold the same view of the disadvantaged status of certain group membership (racial, medical, and cultural) that is held by the general culture. This problem can be seen in rough treatment directed occasionally to mentally handicapped (developmentally disabled or psychotic) witnesses or suspects whom officers may refer to derisively as "noncooperative" or "smarter than they let on." The appreciation of LE cultural influences is important in conducting a meaningful FFDE, as well as in counseling or treatment settings. Ideations that appear to point to paranoid belief systems may have their roots in prosaic cultural influences, including training with hardened field supervisors and discussions with fellow officers (including minority officers who may be less inhibited in racial stereotypes than majority officers). This is not to justify such conceptions among officers but to alert the service provider to the dangers of overpathologizing such a finding, as well as to account for the enduring tendency for some officers to cling to antidiversity notions, even in the face of punishment.

Conservatism

Politically, police officers tend to be more conservative than the general population in many communities that they serve. Although it is a complex issue, the conservative viewpoint, in contrast with the liberal viewpoint, tends to stress traditional religious attitudes and gender roles, and the idea that associations among persons from different backgrounds should be voluntary. Governmental overcontrol and intrusiveness may be seen as the primary difficulty in modern society, driven especially by an aggressive **political correctness** in which conservative beliefs are criminalized or otherwise punished. In the officer's world, political correctness portrays the criminal perpetrator as the victim of social injustice and the officer as the force of oppression. To the officer, a cultural war is under way in which the forces of chaos and disorder are beating at the door of orderly civilization and moral tradition.

Minority groups, women, persons with economic difficulties, and disabled persons are liable to be seen by many white male officers from a conservative viewpoint. A tendency exists among these officers to view liberal values as methods by which criminals escape responsibility and destructive conduct is excused. Much of the traditional hostility to the judicial system stems from this viewpoint (e.g., the hostility to the **Miranda warning** and the **exclusionary rule**). To the great consternation of the officer, legal technicalities are used as tools to restrict and punish him or her in the central job of keeping the peace. When citizens are distressed, they demand performance of officers as evidenced by the suppression of crime and blame the police for the observed failure of the social and economic system. Small legalistic failings, often the result of fearful, near-combat conditions in which many urban officers work, may result in the suspect going free in spite of clear guilt; at the same time, the officer may be punished and reviled.

The mental health community is often seen as part of the liberal, politically correct community, a view that may assist in keeping the officer away from the assessment or therapy office. In a popular joke, a social worker (or any mental health provider) comes upon a man who has been beaten and left unconscious in the street. The social worker is described as waving a clenched fist skyward, proclaiming, "We must immediately find the man who did this and offer him help." The idea that the victim and those who protect society get little attention while criminals receive all manner of benefits is galling to the LE officer and contributes to the idea that psychological concepts are unfair, absurd, and to be avoided.

In FFDE circumstances, contempt for the **fitness-for-duty evaluation provider** may be interpreted as an attempt to conceal a problem, when it may more clearly reflect an irritation directed toward the courts and senior LE executives who are seen as intruding improperly into the life of a dedicated public servant. Psychologists sometimes attempt to describe this viewpoint in the language of mental illness ("the officer is in denial"). This is probably not a useful framework for understanding the officer and may complicate communication between both the officer and provider or the provider and LE department. A more constructive alternative may be to describe the FFDE in terms of discipline and command authority, which may be seen ultimately as positive conservative values by the officer. For example, the psychologist may redefine the discomforts reported by officers while submitting to the FFDE as "doing one's duty" and demonstrating professionalism.

Hypermasculinity

Police have been described as living in a "male-value" culture in which physical effectiveness, vitality, and masculinity are highly prized (Martin, 1997). Despite the growing number of women in police work, it is not hard to see that traditional masculine values have inhibited the acceptance of females in law enforcement. Female officers are seen as less effective in situations of maximum physical effort or struggle, such as the much feared, although infrequent, **life-and-death incident.** In such an incident, the physical strength, courage, and aggressiveness of an officer and his or her partner makes the difference between being killed by an assailant or living to see another day. Women and "soft" men are seen as reluctant to use force, and this attitude (regarded as **politically correct**) is seen as "costing someone their life" in traditional police culture. In a similar vein, the alternative and less demanding physical training rules, often modified for female cadets at training academies, are seen as proof of the unnecessary danger that officers must experience because of the liberal political system's obsession with female inclusion.

Some male officers behave crudely toward certain female law offenders whom they encounter (e.g., prostitutes and female drug addicts), which may be a means of expressing their distaste for the "unfair" advantages that they envision are given to women. A reluctance to arrest male domestic offenders may be noted by some officers and may stem from a disinclination to believe that men can actually be treated fairly in a domestic justice system which they believe gives any female party to a conflict an automatic legal advantage. It may be helpful to encourage the male officer, in certain counseling or assessment settings, to acknowledge that police are no longer the **grunts** (foot solders) of earlier eras but disciplined professionals who can adjust to the demands of their jobs. The psychologist should be careful to avoid shaming or denigrating the male officer for holding hypermasculine views, and instead lead him to a more general understanding of his professional role.

Mission

The **mission** (a fundamental purpose by which the officer is sent into the field to perform a service) of the LE officer is often seen as part of his or her culture. Burke (1969) described a collective mentality in which LE officers view themselves as guardians of morality, whose duty it is to protect civilized society against "the scum of the street." This mission-oriented rectitude may be observed by the provider in evaluation or counseling as a tendency to see any action as justified (e.g., planting evidence) so long as the target of the activity is one of the "bad guys" (see **innocent and vicious**). The concept of mission has been shown to be of practical benefit in many groups, such as military and religious organizations, because it provides cohesion and focus under trying and dangerous conditions.

This mission mentality may have practical and morale-building value in the often underpaid and alternately boring/threatening world of law enforcement. Care should be taken not to overrespond to the actions or statements that flow from the mission, but to offer a pro-spective in which mission limits are defined by structured **rules of engagement**. In such a view, the therapist may define the mission as "doing one's duty" and not as the more elusive and potentially dangerous "cleaning up the streets." A "clean" arrest (one that occurs within the legal rules) that will withstand examination may be presented to the officer as the actual mission goal. A "dirty" arrest can be represented as sloppy and undisciplined (a violation of both the mission and a basic conservative tenet). This reconstructed mission objective may be presented as more important than credit for a conviction per se, although there is no doubt that as long as promotions are tied to actual convictions, the drive to make an arrest regardless of merit will always play a part in LE work. Convictions which are contaminated by an act that may later be labeled as an example of brutality or bias may be presented to the officer as destructive of the mission. The support of LE executive and supervisory officers regarding this restructure of the mission statement cannot be overestimated.

Pragmatism

Officers tend to be philosophically practical and functional, and may be said to have little use for theory or abstractions in general (Swidler, 1986). Consequently, a tendency exists to resist innovation, experimentation, or theory-driven solutions to problems. Law enforcement executives often reinforce this attitude, describing the positive virtue of pragmatism as a willingness to "do what it takes" to obtain desired results (such as a drop in crime rates). The pragmatic attitude may lead officers to take a number of undesirable profession positions, as seen from the traditional mental health viewpoint. For example, officers may reject working with physically smaller male or female officers because they are presumed not to offer the same level of mutual protection as male officers of greater size. The maintenance of exclusively pragmatic attitudes may result in confusion. Lower-level commanders may stress results by whatever means necessary, whereas higher-level commanders may deplore the injuries that the same high-risk methods inevitably produce. This inherent contradiction is a major source of stress for street officers.

In evaluation or therapy, psychologists may note **perceptual rigidity** as a common feature of officer response, with the officer confused and angry that compliance with one set of commands may result in criticism and punishment from a different supervisory level. A shift in focus from dogmatic compliance with immediate supervisory demands to a form of conceptual understanding of the system in which they operate may be helpful. For example, the therapist may point out that the field supervisor and the district commander may have different priorities and responsibilities, both of which are legitimate. The officer has the task of borrowing values and goals from both sets of leaders and working out a useful compromise. Open communication between the psychologist and LE executives may also be useful in reducing the conflicting demands placed upon line officers.

Prejudice

Most street officers have developed some form of prejudicial attitude toward minorities (Skolnick, 1994). When an officer's psychological difficulties appear to be interwoven with certain biases or prejudices, the need for training may often be an important part of the treatment recommendations for the officer in therapy. Prejudice appears to grow jointly from the attitudinal transmission of values of fellow officers and supervisors and from the direct experiences of police work. A familiar story is that of the young officer, fresh from the academy, who is mocked when he is reluctant to **roust** a group of Hispanic gang members along with experienced officers. The use of racial epithets and prejudiced assumption may be resisted at first, but the new officer is likely to be isolated and may even be seen as weak if he does not exhibit enthusiasm for the sort of prejudice common in his department.

Suspiciousness

Suspiciousness is the hallmark of many police officers (Rubinstein, 1973). Almost everyone is viewed with skepticism, including fellow officers, stemming from a generalization that the entire justification of police work involves detecting hidden or covert misconduct. Therapists and FFDE providers may be disconcerted when first encountering this quasiparanoid cultural attitude. The psychologist may note that the officer expects submission and compliance when a person is accused of a violation of a criminal or traffic regulation. Yet that same officer expresses outrage and suspicion at being cited for violations in his or her own professional life, as if the power of the state is misapplied when it impacts him or her.

Furthermore, police encounters are predicated on danger, unpredictability, and the potential for violence, which contributes to the officers' suspiciousness, isolation from the community, and even officer cohesiveness. Officer groups often have their own **stratification** (hierarchy) and social systems, which promotes a set of expectations and beliefs that appear alien and incomprehensible to civilians. Submission or deference may be shown to officers who have had certain experiences (shot a suspect, survived an internal affairs investigation) rather than those of superior rank. Some superior officers may be denigrated as mere political appointees. Officers have been known to decline promotions because the new assignment would place them in a situation in which they would lose status in the eyes of fellow officers (e.g., a desk job).

Force Is Righteous

An officer may be required to use force without fear or be shunned by fellow officers (Crank, 1997). This puts officers in an impossible dilemma in which the legal and administrative rules that are concerned with the use of force may not match the realities of the street. For example, an officer may feel compelled to join his or her comrades in shooting at a suspect solely because he or she would not want to be seen as weak or an outsider. This officer may feel shame or distress but may not be able to verbalize it to the therapist because he or she views himself or herself as caught in an unresolvable dilemma.

In another case, the officer may be referred to therapy because, in his or her view, the "system has failed" and the officer has become obsessed with the idea of administering **informal justice** on the street. Related to the issue of the mission, it emphasizes the idea that the only way to control street chaos is with displays of power. As a therapy issue, this perception may be unique to law enforcement and its examination may be central to therapy. For example, only the therapist may be able to sympathize with the dilemma of the officer caught between demands of his or her peers and superior officers and those of the legal system. His or her administrators and peers are unlikely to be supportive, and family and friends may appear bewildered by the officer's anguish.

Unpredictability and Uncertainty

These two states are the center of daily street police work. Riding the edge between the fear of death and injury on one hand and the boredom of the routine "waiting for the call" on the other may be strangely attractive to some officers. This issue is poorly understood and difficult to define in therapy, and is the core of many problems reported by troubled officers. Cullen and colleagues (1983) refer to this as the **paradox of policing** and view it as important in understanding stress and depressive symptoms in officers.

In an example of **unpredictability and uncertainty,** the officer may report the recent onset of problems with heightened arousal and increased agitation, such as may occur in an anxiety disorder. Medical leave that has been granted to this officer only increases his or her sense of irritation and foreboding. He or she may report a sensation of worthlessness and boredom connected with "letting down" (abandoning) co-workers and missing the action of the job. The paradoxical nature of the need for danger and the fear of injury may be the focus of this officer's symptoms and may be seen following FFDEs, in which the officer responds poorly to counseling and medications while on medical leave.

Seduction

Seduction is a shadowy part of police work that is seldom presented to mental health professionals in direct terms. It involves the "sometimes attractive" opportunity to become part of the underworld, an ill-defined but potent criminal society as may be organized around the illicit drug, auto theft, or prostitution rackets, to name a few common situations. It is a part of society that is distant from most civilians, but in which some LE officers become deeply embedded as a normal part of their work. Many officers may observe that the **bad guys** disproportionately enjoy many of life's rewards. The ease with which an officer could obtain cash and drugs is part of the seduction, but more often it involves the somewhat less risky opportunity for sexual exploitation. Although most officers find it difficult to openly rationalize drug dealing, the "consensual" opportunity for sexual favors (for female drug addicts, for example) is often seen as "just part of the job."

For example, Barker (1978) reported that LE officers in a small southern town believed that an average of about 32 percent of all fellow officers experienced sexual activity while on the job. This was not only thought to be an outgrowth of contact with prostitutes and drug addicts but was also made possible because of a diverse cross section of women seeking the protection of officers to avoid more dangerous or disreputable men. Some women seek sexual relationships with officers because of the expectation of potential favors that might be available to them on a number of levels (assisting with minor legal scrapes, dealing with aggressive acquaintances, etc.). Other female sexual partners may be drawn to the abstract "power" of LE officers. Seduction of and by all types of persons represents misconduct in LE settings and may become the basis of both the corruption of the officer and the origin of many complaints of sexual abuse against male officers. Failure to acknowledge the destructive effects of the seduction opportunity is among the most transparent illusions in police work.

The Innocent and the Vicious

These constructs are part of the social imagination within police culture. In actual police work, the "cleansing" act of arresting a felon in connection with criminal conduct is a rare event. Most police-suspect interactions (Van Maanen, 1978) have to do with dealing with persons who display suspicious resentment of police intrusion into their affairs (the vicious). These parties may include gang members, loiterers, those disturbing the peace, and those in shady situations. This is justified as necessary to protect law-abiding citizens (the innocent) who are often the victims of robbery, assault, and criminal conduct. Officers may conceive of this conflict as a moral issue. In time, many other noncriminals, even other LE officers (and their police psychologists), may be defined as "vicious," as when the officer's actions draw the attention of a police psychologist for an FFDE or an internal affairs investigator for a criminal investigation. Such officers may appear to be clinically paranoid and may pose serious management problems from the viewpoint of the LE **police executive.** The identification of officers who are moralistically rigid and noncompliant is an important police psychology function. Such officers may articulate the idea that street officers must compensate for the "failure" of the criminal justice system to rid the community of evil and destructive criminals. One may see this when a visible stigma (e.g., wearing gang colors) marks the suspect as a danger to society, justifying immediate and extralegal actions directed at gang members, street punks, or other vicious persons.

Deception

In the end, many police officers wish to be invisible to administrative control and personal accountability, just as many professional criminals seek invisibility from LE investigators. The courts and LE executives who demand transparency are often seen as unrealistic regarding the reality of street work (Rubinstein, 1973). Officers are endlessly told what *not* to do rather than what they *should* do, leaving a feeling of unappreciation and chronic failure. Some LE officers believe that they will inevitably make a mistake and will be punished out of all proportion to the importance of the error. Everything the LE officer says or does can somehow be used against him, while the excessive "rights" offered criminals makes them invulnerable. Lying, therefore, becomes a way of life for some, a necessary self-protection and part of the reality of professional law enforcement. Initial contact with troubled street officers may reveal a disturbing tendency to fabricate elements of the events that may have led to the therapy referral. Clinically challenging this pattern in an atmosphere of trust is an important part of any psychological reconstruction with officers (Chevigny, 1995).

Bullshit

Bullshit is the general term for the bureaucratic regulations and rules thought to have been invented by police supervisors to control officer behavior. Many officers will advise cadets not to trust supervisors, but to be concerned with their own interests (Reuss-Ianni, 1983). Since the LE executive is almost never able to know much about the activity of individual officers, bullshit is the unavoidable by-product of remote efforts to control law enforcement officers through fixed rules. Bullshit includes unnecessary paperwork, educational or training requirements (often at the officer's expense), and rules that prevent promotion or advancement for seemingly little reason.

Fury directed at bullshit might be the most apparent element of evaluation and counseling for many LE officers. As a practical matter, progress in mentally directing the officer away from the obsession with bullshit may be a fair, informal measure of progress in counseling. The goal of this aspect of counseling is to encourage the officer to embrace the regulatory process as tolerable. Leading the officer to see the need to prove effectiveness and probity (as demonstrated by regulations and paperwork) to retain public support against the bad guys may be a useful tool. The insistence of the officer on directing the theme of therapy toward complaints about bullshit is a mechanism that inhibits progress toward more fundamental clinical goals.

MENTAL HEALTH PROGRAMS

Psychological evaluation and intervention programs are common in many law enforcement agencies. In 1987, White (personal correspondence) surveyed 366 community municipal and county police agencies and found 65 percent of them provided some form of mental health programming. More than 70 percent of the agencies offering services responded that mental health services were available not only to sworn officers and other employees, but also to employee family members. Family problems may exist at very high base rates within police officer households. Most research (Bell, 1988) indicates that the impact of police work on the families of officers is particularly significant when adolescent children are in the home. An old joke told by LE officers involves a playmate saying to another, "Does your father work?" The reply is, "Nah, he's a cop." Marital problems are also common because of the long and unusual hours of separation of the police officer from his or her family as well as a potential problem of unusual sexual opportunity.

Alcoholism and drug addiction are common problems in the general society as well as in the law enforcement community (Machell, 1989), although the recent use of urine drug screening has had some impact in reducing overt abuse. Drugs are easily available to many police officers as a normal part of their work, and abusable substances may help them deal with stress in a way that has traditionally been difficult to detect. Seafield 911's (1991) training manual reported a significant number of supervisor observations that were related to frequent substance use. This included the officer's temporary absence from his or her assignment, observations of drinking during lunchtime, red and glassy eyes, inappropriately loud talking, hand and arm tremors, and lateness for work.

Police psychology has evolved as a useful tool in the administration of law enforcement departments and agencies. The need for special psychological or emotional assistance for officers should be clear from the nature of police work (i.e., some exposure to violence, death, crime, and misery) when compared with most civilian forms of work. For the police to be able to protect the public, the public must trust and support those who wear the badge and must agree to submit to police authority (e.g., allow officers to stop their vehicles, enter their homes with warrants, and take them into custody). The abuse of such trust undermines the authority of law enforcement agencies, as when an officer commits a criminal act (e.g.,theft, corruption, or use of authority for personal gain). In some cases, inappropriate or inefficient officer behavior may be the product of mental or emotional illness rather than criminal intent, in which case the police psychologist may play a useful role in both protecting the public by identifying such officers as well as assisting the officer in securing treatment or other benefits. The following chapter deals with the issue of police liability for violation of civilian rights and introduces the methods for examining individual officer conduct.

Chapter 3

Law Enforcement Liability and Police Psychology

Decency, security and liberty alike demand that government officials shall be subjected to the same rules of conduct that are commands to the citizen. In a government of laws, existence of the government will be imperiled if it fails to observe the laws scrupulously. Our government is the potent omnipresent teacher. For good or ill, it teaches the whole people by its example. Crime is contagious. If the government becomes a law breaker, it breeds contempt for the law; it invites every man to become a law unto himself; it invites anarchy. To declare that in the administration of criminal laws the end justifies the means—to declare that the government may commit crimes in order to secure the conviction of a private criminal—would bring terrible retribution. Against that pernicious doctrine this Court should resolutely set its face.

Supreme Court Justice Louis Brandeis
Olmstead v. U.S. (1928)

A police department would be of little use if it could not be free to enforce the law. How could laws be enforced fairly and uniformly if industrial, ethnic, political, or social group leaders could demand that their members be given immunity from arrest, or that new officers be hired only from their membership? Where preferences have existed in the past, such as was given to Irish officer applicants in large U.S. cities in the nineteenth and early twentieth centuries, social unrest inevitably resulted. In large part, the professionalization movement (see Chapter 1) was an outgrowth of attempts to reform politically motivated preferential law enforcement and officer recruitment. The freedom of the police officer to decide to act or refrain from acting when faced with a particular law enforcement situation lay at the heart of the notion of **discretion.**

Unfortunately, the issue of discretion for police officers has been a cardinal problem from the time of earliest police organizations, touching upon the abuse of power, accusations of corruption, bigoted or biased conduct, and related complaints. As early as the 1820s, some juries had become convinced that the London Metropolitan Police were little more than instruments of oppression, and exonerated several rioters in that era in spite of police testimonial evidence. In a more recent example, the videotaped assault of **Rodney King** in 1991, an African-American motorist who was beaten by officers following a flight to avoid apprehension, released a pent-up rage in the Los Angeles African-American community. A white jury subsequently acquitted the officers of the use of excess force, confirming in the minds of many in the minority community that the police were permitted to mistreat their members with impunity. In the riots that followed, many innocent persons were assaulted, including a well-documented, horrendous attack upon a white truck driver, **Reginald Denny.** A predominantly black jury exonerated the assailants, apparently because of the belief that the police testimony was suspect and unfair, even in the face of clear documentary evidence of the crime. In many ways the King and Denny cases, and related events, illustrate the conflict between independent police discretion and the conflicting demands made by important components of society. It has been a basic principle of law to consider the interest of society to be best served by the use of civil authority to ensure disinterested and equal treatment of all persons regardless of background. The application of this principle has been difficult in reality.

The struggle between objective, disinterested law enforcement and the needs of community members to view themselves as entitled to special treatment is an ancient conflict. In American history, many powerful **political machines** existed for decades by offering special privileges (jobs, intervention with authorities) to their supporters, who were often recent, poor European immigrants. Many knowledgeable citizens during the Prohibition Era would easily have been able to name police officers that they thought would be able to provide special services in return for money or other favors. Even some cops on the beat would expect an occasional gift from a restaurant or grocery owner in return for ignoring a minor infraction or offering extra protection. In part, this was seen as a compensation for the very low pay that officers received, but at another level it was often seen as a privilege of those who were either above the law or whose personal sacrifices for the sake of society earned them special privileges. The tolerance for minor corruption or even the uneven enforcement of rules by law enforcement officials was seen as a fair exchange for the inexpensive safety and security that was afforded by police forces of that era.

THE CIVIL RIGHTS ACT OF 1871

Public attention became focused upon the actual conduct of individual police officers in the 1960s to a degree that had not been known previously. With the emergence of the civil rights movement, the fair and unbiased treatment of racial and cultural minorities within the United States became an international cause. The Kennedy administration, in support of the **civil rights movement,** found a tool to accelerate the end to the racial segregation of that era: a remnant of the Reconstruction period of American history called the **Civil Rights Act of 1871** (Kappeler, 1997).

The post–Civil War military occupation of the former Confederacy was difficult to administer given the resistance by powerful groups, most of whom had been associated with the dominant antebellum social structure. During that era, the federal government attempted to institute full citizenship for persons who had been deprived of civil rights within the states that had been in rebellion. In some localities, state or local officials, resentful of the loss of their local autonomy to federal intrusion, placed roadblocks in the path of recent civil equality for former slaves and African Americans in general. For example, local political officials attempted to block the expansion of voting rights by using such tools as **poll taxes,** literacy tests, and police interference with those attempting to vote. As military occupation came to an end in the early 1870s, Congress attempted to prevent state, municipal, and local authorities from suppressing the full participation of new citizens. Congress passed the Civil Rights Act of 1871, currently codified in federal law under the title of **42 U.S.C. 1983,** or simply **Section 1983,** in an attempt to preserve political changes within the South initiated during Reconstruction. The Civil Rights Act of 1871 gave persons whose constitutional and federally guaranteed civil rights had been violated an active means of redress by lawsuit in federal court. Under this law, the defendants are usually state or municipal law enforcement officers who can be punished civilly if they violate the federally protected rights of any person. In most cases, the defendant must be said to have acted **under the color of law** (*Lugar v. Edmondson Oil Co,* 1982) to be held accountable under this section. In other words, a government agent, such as a police officer, must have violated constitutionally guaranteed civil rights of the plaintiff while acting for the state, county, city, and not as a private citizen, to be held answerable. Once the conditions of the law are met, however, the results may be draconian. For example, settlements leveled against any individual may be unlimited and cannot be discharged by bankruptcy, as may be the case in ordinary civil lawsuits. It may be noted that related **Sections 1985 and 1981 of Title 42 of the U.S. Code,** although used less frequently, also cover civil liability. Section 1985 imposes liability for conspiring to interfere with civil rights. Section 1985 includes but is not limited to all public officials acting in the line of duty, and many nongovernmental parties may be charged under this section. Section 1981 imposes liability for interference with the exercise of civil rights and is also not limited to police or other government agencies.

In extreme cases, police officers can be held accountable under federal criminal law. Title 18 of the U.S. Code, Section 242, allows for a criminal liability (not just civil liability) for deprivation of civil rights. Penalties for violations may include fines of up to $1,000 and one year imprisonment. If death results from the offense, a sentence of life may be imposed upon any person who under color of law, statute, ordinance, regulation or custom, willfully subjects an inhabitant of any state to the deprivation of any right protected by the Constitution of the United States.

MUNICIPAL LIABILITY

In 1978 (*Monell v. Department of Social Services*), the Supreme Court expanded the application of Section 1983 to cover a new form of civil liability, described as **municipal liability** or **police executive**

liability. Under this doctrine, the plaintiff must show that the state or municipal policymakers had established a procedure or custom that infringed upon the constitutional rights of a plaintiff. Thus the lawsuit may target the directors or policymakers of a municipality or state agency, and not just the individual officer, who in many cases may just be carrying out the unlawful procedure or policy of his or her department. Since most police officers subject to Section 1983 lawsuits possessed little in the way of financial resources, opening the entire agency and its members to such action greatly enhanced the potential financial motivations of plaintiffs and their attorneys. Municipal liability made the policymakers accountable under Section 1983 by introducing a principle known as **deliberate indifference.** This doctrine expressed the idea that any supervisory official could be held accountable for action or inaction in the training, supervision, or control of subordinates (*People v. Slaughter,* 1990). The financial burden of an adverse ruling can be thus generalized from the individual (the law enforcement officer) to his supervisors (the sergeant, lieutenant, captain, and the like, limited only to "the highest levels of state government"). Moreover, no direct action in the injury-causing events is necessary for this liability to attend. In other words, once a custom or policy has been put in place, all policymakers may be punished if the policy is found to be unconstitutional.

CASE LAW

In the Western District of Louisiana, a federal lawsuit (*Lewis v. Goodie,* 1992) illustrated how a Section 1983 lawsuit may work. In this case, a police officer committed a number of civil rights violations in his official capacity. These included violent and abusive actions against persons simply because of their race. The police chief was shown to have been aware of these problems, but did not attend meetings to review the officer's behavior, keep records of the complaints against the officer, or assign any member of his staff to conduct a thorough investigation. The court noted that the officer had not received any psychological services (no screening or fitness-for-duty evaluation was conducted) when it should have become apparent that the officer was operating outside of allowable parameters. This decision, along with many others, is emblematic of a major problem for police departments and the risk management/liability insurance providers for those departments. The chief and other policymakers within the department had to face considerable financial loss.

Law enforcement agencies and individual officers and commanders share a clear liability risk. In *People v. Slaughter* (1990), a police officer became involved in an argument with two citizens and eventually shot them. The victims sued the city, claiming the police department was negligent in its screening and selection procedures. The jury, and later the appellate courts, supported the judgment against the city. In a separate case (*City of Greenwood v. Dowler,* 1986), a judge found that a policeman frequently works alone, wields great authority, and carries lethal weapons, making law enforcement ill-suited for a person with questionable mental stability

In a recent case, a frustrated motorist named Joey Waits sprayed a Chicago officer with water from a squirt bottle. Arrested the next day, he was taken to a local police station in handcuffs, where he claimed that he was struck about his face and head with an open hand fifteen to twenty times and then kneed in the groin while being subjected to antigay epithets. For trial purposes, the defendants hired a psychiatrist to examine the plaintiff and produce a twenty-two-page report that referenced a past history of the plaintiff and his sexual and psychological issues to prove that the event was not as emotionally traumatic as had been claimed. A rebuttal psychologist testified that the event and its aftermath caused Waits to lose sleep and to suffer from a lack of concentration. After three days of deliberation, a federal jury in Chicago awarding Waits $15,000 in compensatory damages and $2 million in punitive damages in his excessive force suit. Most of the punitive damages were imposed on a sergeant who witnessed the beating but did nothing to stop it (*Waits v. City of Chicago,* 2003).

In an extension to the principle of municipal or police executive liability, the Supreme Court ruled, but with a six to three majority, that single officer misconduct did not constitute a Section 1983 violation (*Board of County Com'rs of Bryan County, OK v. Brown,* 1997). Here a deputy injured a woman sleeping in the passenger seat of her husband's truck following a reported high-speed chase. The driver reportedly violated traffic laws and was pursued from Oklahoma into Texas by a Bryan County, Oklahoma, sheriff's deputy named Burns. After stopping the vehicle, the driver's wife was pulled violently from her husband's truck and injured so badly that she required multiple surgeries to her legs. Upon investigation, it was discovered that the deputy had a colorful criminal history and almost no training or experience. A relative of the sheriff, Deputy Burns had a record of nine moving violations (including DWI) and a conviction for assault and battery. In fact, a warrant had been issued for his arrest for parole violation at the time he was hired. The federal court ruled that the sheriff's hiring decision was legal and that the sheriff did not authorize Burns to use excessive force. Under these circumstances the Browns must show that the sheriff deliberately took action, which was the moving force behind the constitutional violation. In order to succeed in such a claim, the plaintiff must also prove that the particular constitutional harm suffered was a plainly obvious consequence of the hiring decision. The Court demanded a link between the ignored information on hiring and the specific injury suffered by the plaintiff. The Court's majority did not find the link and remanded the case to the state court.

The state court, however, held that the failure to conduct a good-faith investigation of the prospective employee amounted to the sheriff deliberately closing his eyes to the applicant's background. The court found that such indifferent behavior cannot be tolerated when the prospective applicant will be employed in a position of trust and authority (*Brown v. Bryan County, OK,* 2000). In spite of the principle that the behavior of an individual, errant officer is not sufficient to evoke the federal principle of municipal liability, district courts may still find for liability on other principles. The *Brown v. Bryan County, OK,* litigation series appeared to signal a change in general judicial attitudes regarding the responsibilities of law enforcement officials to select and supervise their officers. When reasons to envision a connection between the officer's misconduct and failure to train, supervise, or select regarding predictors of a specific violation exist, a hardening of judicial views toward lax law enforcement administration may be expected. Such indifferent supervision may only be made worse when the policy or violations appear to compound the lack of training/selection with instructions that cause harm. For example, if a policymaker advised or directed officers to forcibly enter a premise, contrary to law (*Pembaur v. Cincinnati,* 1986), the lack of additional safeguards (such as officer training or multiple supervision) may be considered by the court to increase the gravity of the violation.

The Supreme Court has not eliminated the possibility of liability for hiring decisions, but it sets a very high standard of culpability. If hiring practices are appropriate in general and screen out potentially bad officers, the chance of liability is extremely remote, even if some bad individuals make it through the screening process.

FAILURE TO DISCIPLINE

The failure of the LE executive to investigate complaints about employees and take remedial action can be a basis for lawsuits (Ross, 2003). An attempt to act against a troublesome employee can be a difficult problem, especially given the many protections that employees can assert in federal law as well as contractual, civil service, and union considerations. Yet the supervisors retain potential liability risk when they fail to identify misconduct or tolerate harmful behavior. In *Hogan v. Franco* (1995), a supervisor's inattention to misconduct rose to the level of deliberate indifference. In *Vann v. City of New York* (1995), an officer who was subject to extensive discipline for misconduct was returned to duty without any consideration of the use of a method to track future violent misbehavior. The court found the supervisor to be deliberately indifferent. In many such cases, the use of an FFDE can play an important part in supporting a viable defense against accusations of failure to discipline and negligent retention.

EXPERT TESTIMONY BY THE FFDE PROVIDER

The department may require the expert testimony of the police psychologist to defend against Section 1983 or related claims of deliberate indifference (see Chapter 10). This may be an important issue if the LE executive is challenged legally to prove that an officer has been properly trained or selected or supervised by a plaintiff who claimed a civil rights violation at the hands of this officer. Such testimony may also be required when an officer who was deemed unfit for duty by an FFDE later challenges that finding in court as a violation of his employment rights. In both cases, the allowable testimony of the FFDE provider may be a critical element in the case outcome. For such reasons, it is highly desirable that the police psychologist (or FFDE provider) develop conclusions in a manner that is likely to meet the requirements of **Federal Rules of Evidence (FRE)** 702 and related case law (such as ***Daubert v. Merrill Dow Pharmaceuticals, Inc., 1993,*** and ***Kuhmo Tire v. Carmichael, 1999***). Police psychologists must have a working understanding of this principle if they are going to participate in the judicial process.

The cost of civil liability is no small matter. A survey of 215 departments connected with the National Institute of Municipal Officers revealed $4.3 billion in pending liability, whereas others have estimated that 39,000 municipal governments could expect as much as $780 billion in potential liability (Kappeler, 1997, p. 8). It is quite clear that a major difficulty in this country must be addressed if law enforcement organizations are to continue to survive as viable economic entities. On August 31, 2000, *The Los Angeles Times* reported that police misconduct led Judge William J. Rea of the federal district court to cite the city of Los Angeles for a RICO Act (Racketeering Influence and Corrupt Organizations Act) violation, increasing all lawsuits stemming from the Ramparts Division scandal by threefold (to an estimated $200 million in additional costs) (Rosenzweig, 2000).

DUTY TO WARN

All executives who refer officers for FFDEs should be aware of the concept of **duty to warn,** which refers to the responsibility of a medical or mental health professional to breach confidentiality (see Chapter 13) if an identifiable person is in imminent danger. In situations in which clear evidence of immediate danger to specific persons exists, the professional must attempt to determine the degree of seriousness of the threat and notify both the person in danger as well as others who are in a position to protect the threatened person from harm. In one well-publicized case, an officer told a psychologist during an FFDE that he was planning to kill at least nine police executives in his department. The psychologist sought to consult with the attorney of his licensing board (to explore the legal issues in breaching confidentiality), a process that caused him to wait several weeks before notifying the department. The officer was eventually let go and later successfully sued the psychologist for professional negligence and **defamation** of character. Although this was an anomalous case in many ways, the delay in reporting the threat and the fact that the officer had received clinical services from the same clinic in the recent past appeared to have played a major part in the verdict by demonstrating that no pressing emergency existed to justify the disclosure (*Garner v. Stone,* 1997).

LIABILITY FOR THE CERTIFYING PROVIDER

After Officer Miguel Diaz-Martinez of the Bayamon Criminal Investigation Corps (CIC) in the Commonwealth of Puerto Rico attempted to park in a space reserved for judges, Security Officer Grancid Camilo-Robles told Officer Martinez that he could not park there. Officer Martinez responded by pushing, slapping, arresting, handcuffing, and threatening Camilo-Robles with a gun. The investigation that followed revealed that shortly after Martinez joined the police department, he had been suspended for assault. The court counted at least eighteen disciplinary infractions involving violent and/or threatening behavior. In 1989, Martinez assaulted his wife and then held several officers hostage with a shotgun. Thereafter, Martinez was committed to a psychiatric hospital and diagnosed as schizophrenic. Following the hospital discharge, the police psychologist recommended that he be separated from the force and given a civilian position. Martinez was suspended in 1990 and medically discharged in 1991.

Martinez appealed his termination and was reinstated in 1993. Shortly thereafter, he assaulted a civilian while on desk duty. Despite this incident, Drs. Guillermo Hoyos and Hector O. Riviera Gonalez examined Martinez and found him free from mental illness and fit for duty without restrictions. The day after his return, Martinez was involved in an altercation with two innocent persons that resulted in injury and death. Thereafter, the department confiscated his weapon. When Martinez returned to desk duty, he threatened to kill a fellow officer. The doctors reexamined him and found him ready for unrestricted active duty and fit to carry a weapon. The department re-armed him.

Camilo-Robles sued high-ranking officials and two psychiatrists who worked for the police department for depriving him of his civil rights by their deliberate indifference in carrying out their supervisory responsibilities (with the result that Martinez, a demonstrably unstable officer, was allowed to remain on active duty). In deciding the issue of qualified immunity, the court noted that although the FFDE examiners did not have official authority to rearm Martinez, they were aware that their certification would return Martinez to active duty. The court held that they

> eschewed easily accessible steps to forestall the rearming of Martinez and instead certified his fitness for unrestricted active duty. Because this is an adequate showing of causation to support a denial of qualified immunity, the psychiatrists' fallback position avail them naught. (*Robles v. Hoyos*, 1998)

THE RIGHT TO OFFER OPINION
OF MENTAL HEALTH BEFORE EMPLOYMENT

In a case regarding the authority of a mental health provider to produce an adverse opinion regarding a non–law enforcement employment applicant, a psychiatrist who examined an applicant was sued by the applicant for erroneously diagnosing him as psychologically unfit (*Lambley v. Kameny*, 1997). The court dismissed the claim based on the medical malpractice tribunal's finding that the plaintiff's offer of proof was insufficient. The appeals court held the applicant's claims that the psychiatrist was negligent in his examination and the diagnosis of the applicant was within the medical malpractice tribunal's jurisdiction. Thus, an adverse opinion itself was lawful without a showing of malpractice in some manner.

In a separate case, officer applicant Rosario brought a civil rights action (*Rosario v. City of New Haven*, 1998) claiming that she was denied her due process rights under the Fourteenth Amendment when she was rejected for consideration as a police officer based on the results of a psychological evaluation. The court held that the plaintiff must demonstrate by a preponderance of the evidence that the testing procedures or the results obtained were arbitrary, conscience shocking, or oppressive in a constitutional sense. The tests were often used for the purpose of preemployment screening of police officers. The plaintiff failed to demonstrate by a preponderance of the evidence that the written tests produced arbitrary, capricious, or irrational results, and her suit was dismissed.

In general, the courts have indicated a need for departments to take actions to prevent commissioned officers from violating constitutional protections or rights and have acknowledged that police psychologists and other mental heath professionals may play a part in that effort with some confidence. Some pitfalls in the use of examining professionals may be noted, and capable LE executive and police psychologist may work to avoid such situations.

One such method of LE executive and behavioral health professional cooperation in the improvement of departmental functioning is that of the fitness-for-duty evaluation (FFDE). The following chapters are intended to address a detailed understanding of the rationale for and the mechanics of the FFDE. FFDEs can be a source of cost-effective management within a law enforcement agency that assists in reducing liability risk as well as a method to improve the humane treatment of impaired officers.

SECTION II:
THE MECHANICS OF THE
FITNESS-FOR-DUTY
EVALUATION METHODOLOGY

Chapter 4

Usefulness of Fitness-for-Duty Evaluations in Law Enforcement Agencies

Set your expectations high; find men and women whose integrity and values you respect; get their agreement on a course of action; and give them your ultimate trust.

John Akers

THE CASE OF OFFICER BOB

Bob, an unmarried officer with the Anywhere Police Department, has been the recipient of a number of female citizen complaints regarding minor violence (arm twisting, questionable handcuffing, and pushing) as well as "screaming" vulgarities. He had also been caught by a video camcorder seeming to beat and kick a handcuffed and subdued suspect without apparent reason. The department had received complaints of sexual battery, stalking, and intimidation by the officer's off-duty female acquaintances on a number of occasions. He systematically denied the validity of all complaints, claiming to be dumbfounded at the "lies" others tell about him, or he attributed complaints to others' "jealousy" of his authoritative abilities in law enforcement. He is now angry, showing contempt for his supervisor and reporting to Internal Affairs that the problem lies in his supervisor's "interpretation" of the complaint situation.

Historically, Officer Bob's actions would be referred to as **behavior unbecoming an officer,** a term that usually refers to distasteful or inappropriate officer behavior, but in more recent times, may be viewed as disturbed or mentally ill conduct. Indifference toward the behavior of officers who appear to be disturbed is not a good option for any LE agency. Law enforcement executives have a duty to take reasonable precautions in hiring, supervising, and retaining officers to assure the public that those entrusted with the power to take life or freedom, under color of law, are psychologically fit and do not represent a threat to any person because of mental impairment. This principle is fundamental in a free society that expects its members to both submit to police authority in the person of a commissioned officer and to trust that officers will protect them from harm. Although officers are, of course, subject to all the same mental and physical disorders of any person, the LE executive has a duty to determine that officers are not an irrational risk of injury to others and that they are capable of performing their duties with customary care and conscientiousness. In *Bonsignore v. City of New York* (1982) the wife of a police officer was shot by her husband, who then turned the weapon on himself. The wife sued the city of New York for negligence in allowing her husband to carry a gun. The court held that, to avoid liability, a department has to show that it has taken reasonable precautions in hiring and/or retaining officers who are psychologically disturbed. Unable to do so, the jury found against the city. The plaintiff was awarded $500,000 in compensatory and punitive damages. Later appeals affirmed the right of the jury to assign financial damages for negligent retention.

To make matters even more serious, the doctrine of **executive immunity** (the legal standard by which government officials are seen as immune from civil liability for all actions taken in good faith) may not be invoked to protect an agency from claims such as negligent retention. In other words, the LE executive is normally immune to legal claims that arise in the course of his duty. This is the case because it would be impractical to have representatives of the executive branch of the government expend energy and resources to defend claims that are the inevitable result of normal (good-faith) police work. An LE executive that learns of the irrational nature of an officer's conduct and does nothing about it is not covered by this immunity doctrine and the LE executive may therefore be held liable. In *Davis v. Hennepin County* (1997), a county social worker in Wisconsin alleged that a corrections officer had systematically harassed her. Approximately two years and three formal complaints later, the county ordered the corrections officer to undergo a psychological fitness-for-duty evaluation. The officer subsequently resigned. The social worker sued the county for negligent retention (among other claims), and the county sought legal protection under the doctrine of executive immunity. The court held that official immunity may not be invoked to protect an agency from claims over which they have considerable control, such as the negligent retention of destructive or defective personnel.

The case of Officer Bob represents an authentic dilemma for police executives, particularly if the officer is a valued member of the agency and typically a good employee. Finding, selecting, hiring, and training police officers is an expensive and time-consuming job—a fact that often results in officer position vacancies throughout the country. If the LE executive does nothing and simply prays that Officer Bob's behaviors will not lead to serious adverse consequences, the executive may be taking a considerable risk. As previously described, LE executives must create a means of managing the difficult officer or they may suffer substantial financial liability (*Lewis v. Goodie*, 1992; *Brown v. Bryan County*, 2000). The courts have held that LE officers can be held to a standard of behavior that is much higher than the general public, because only LE officers in our society have the authority to deprive persons of life and liberty "under color of law." Our civil society places a generally high premium on such rights and does not easily tolerate distasteful or uninviting conduct in commissioned officers that may result in the loss of constitutionally guaranteed rights. To make matters worse, if the plaintiff in any current or future lawsuit can show that Officer Bob's potentially irrational conduct was ignored by his departmental policy makers, even unrelated criminal prosecutions may be jeopardized because the criminal defense attorney might assert that the department has a policy of ignoring inappropriate officer behaviors (Chin and Wells, 1998). The LE executive will need to make a choice from among several methods to deal with Officer Bob or the executives may risk eventual problems and expense.

LAW ENFORCEMENT EXECUTIVES' CHOICES

The law enforcement executive may ask his or her internal affairs or personnel or health and safety divisions to proceed with a disciplinary or termination process based upon Officer Bob's performance. The exercise of this option emphasizes the perspective that the officer will be charged with a violation of the regulations or codes of the department by demonstrating "behavior unbecoming an officer," insubordination, or a related charge of unseemly conduct. However, the department will lose an experienced and possibly recoverable officer who may represent a significant recruiting and training investment by proceeding in this manner. The departmental personnel authority could be asked to dismiss Officer Bob following an investigation, or in some cases Officer Bob may be suspended, fined, or otherwise punished. This disciplinary process may not resolve the LE executive's problems. If the charges are deemed insufficient for discharge, the law enforcement executive may be required to return the officer to active duty, leaving the department without a solution in regard to his discreditable behavior. Administrative punishments may be unlikely to have a substantial impact upon Officer Bob's long-term behavior and may even provoke additional undesirable conduct (such as anger or passive-aggressive actions) and clearly will not address the causes of the officer's actions.

Officer Bob may be referred to the available employee assistance program or to a mental health provider (such as a psychiatrist, psychologist, or social worker) for assessment, counseling, or for other treatments (see Chapter 2). However, in such a circumstance, a **doctor-patient** relationship may be the result, creating a legally enforceable confidential alliance between the mental health provider and the officer (see Chapter 13). In such a case, the department may not be able to obtain vital and relevant information from the treatment provider, no matter whether the therapist is an EAP or independent provider. Even nonspecific statements of violence (those that do not name a possible victim) or irrational conduct may be protected under the **rule of confidentiality** (the professional and legally enforceable requirement that no element of Bob's treatment be revealed to others without his express permission). This has always been a standard of practice in mental health work, but the introduction of the Health Insurance Portability and Accountability Act of 1996 (HIPAA) and related legal disability protections (see Chapter 13) makes this problem nearly insurmountable. The provider may legally and ethically be unable to interact with LE supervisors about any precise issue of treatment, including the goals, problems, or even any nonspecific threats the officer may make (*Garner v. Stone*, 1997). In any case, the therapist's ethical standards compel the therapist to place the patient's well-being first and honor requests made by the patient, such as to withhold certain medical record information from others. More important, the provider may either be under increasing pressure to release Officer Bob for reasons that are unconnected with issues of liability (such as payment for treatment or patient resistance to continued counseling) or focus on issues preferred by the patient (e.g., the "lies" of others). In fact, most treating professionals are completely autonomous service providers who design their treatment around personal difficulties that often appear to be totally unrelated to the reasons for departmental safety concerns. In Officer Bob's case, an independent treatment provider may elect to focus therapeutic attention on Officer Bob's relationship problems rather than his job-related threats of violence or resistance to supervision. To complicate matters further, some communities may be without treatment providers who are even vaguely familiar with police culture and the dangers of police misconduct. In such cases, a treatment provider may release an officer to duty following brief general counseling or the medication management of some symptoms, without targeting the officer's sexual or aggressive behavior. A return to duty under these circumstances may leave the department vulnerable to questions of permitting a menacing situation to continue and placing the public in danger.

EAPs are common in law enforcement settings (see Chapter 2). Although EAPs show clear advantages in terms of a timely, low-cost, and available response to the officer in need, the fact that the EAP is a contractor for the employer may create confidentiality difficulties when compared with independent mental heath providers. Information obtained within an EAP may not necessarily remain confidential when it impinges upon workplace needs, reducing the credibility of the intervention program with potential users. For example, a psychiatrist with a drug rehabilitation program informed an employer that an employee was being removed from a program because of the employee's threats to kill his supervisor. The employer fired the worker, who then sued the psychiatrist and the agency that operated the rehabilitation program, alleging the disclosure led to his dismissal and violated 42 U.S. Code §290dd-2, which protects the identity of persons in drug treatment. The district court concluded that the statute was not intended to protect drug rehabilitation patients from all kinds of damaging information but only from information that reveals their status as drug rehabilitation patients (*Chapa v. Adams,* 1997). It is not clear that treaters will be able to communicate information of this variety in the future.

THE FFDE OPTION

Finally, the LE executives may request a **fitness-for-duty evaluation,** which has a number of significant advantages over the alternatives, but which is often poorly understood by police executives and mental health professionals who are not police psychologists. A description of this methodology is the topic of many of the following chapters of this book. In general, the FFDE is a specialized mental health examination designed to inform the LE executive responsible for the officer's supervision of issues of mental impairment that may impact upon the ability of the officer to perform his duty in a safe and effective manner (see Appendix A). Although many state and local laws affect FFDE procedures, LE administrators, as a rule, have a right to order an officer to submit to an FFDE. For example, an Illinois appellate court (*Conte v. Horcher,* 1977) held that an LE executive has a right to order an FFDE on public policy grounds alone. In this case, a police lieutenant had allegedly used excessive force against a suspect taken into police custody. After the incident, the chief ordered the lieutenant to undergo a psychological FFDE, and the lieutenant refused. The court held that a department has the authority to order fitness testing to protect the public interest and the efficiency of the department, and to keep informed about the officer's ability to perform his duties. In some states, general preference is given to FFDEs as a means of ensuring that armed officers are examined prior to being returned to duty following certain forms of leave. For example, Wisconsin allows administrators to require psychological FFDEs prior to allowing an officer's return to duty following leave that appears to imply psychological disturbance (*Brown Co. Sheriff's Dept. v. Brown County Sheriff's Dept. Non-Supervisory Employees Association,* 1995).

Ordering a police officer to submit to a psychological FFDE when defendable reasons exists for such an examination appears to be an acceptable and widespread public policy methodology. For example, the Seventh Circuit Federal Appeals Court upheld a warden's order to a corrections officer that the officer submit to a psychological FFDE (*Flynn v. Sandahl*, 1995). In a Massachusetts case, the police chief was supported by the court in his demand that required a reinstated detective to submit to a psychological FFDE before allowing him to carry a firearm (*Kraft v. Police Com'rs of Boston*, 1994).

In general, the concept of FFDEs seems well supported in most judicial settings when a sound argument can be made that it is meant for the safety of the public, or to ensure the adequate functioning of the agency. General and nonspecific inquiries into the mind-set of the officer may be met with greater resistance, especially in the absence of complaints of unacceptable conduct that threatens others or disables the agency. The defensibility of the FFDE is largely dependant on the reason for evaluation rather the specific methods employed in the process itself. In combination with other methods of approaching potential police misconduct (e.g., IA investigations), the FFDE seems to be an important element in the armamentarium of the police executive.

Chapter 5

Defining the Fitness-for-Duty Evaluation

A people that values its privileges above its principles soon loses both.

Dwight D. Eisenhower
Inaugural Address, 1953

As regards law enforcement work, a fitness-for-duty evaluation is a specialized inquiry conducted under the authority of a police or security agency by a specifically qualified mental health professional in response to complaints of an officer's reported inability to perform official duties in a safe and effective manner because of impaired or deviant behavior. Be aware that the term *FFDE* may also be used in non–law enforcement contexts, such as referring persons for civilian assessments of violence or danger (e.g., such as a workplace threat). The term may also find usage in regard to the medical (nonpsychological) ability of a person to perform work (e.g, such as a pilot's visual capability following eye surgery). However, with commissioned law enforcement officers, psychological FFDEs are often conducted for purposes of estimating the risk that an officer's reportedly abnormal (disturbed or impaired) behavior represents to his or her department, supervisors, and fellow officers, as well as the community in general. This liability may involve **positive risk** (what the officer may do that is potentially damaging), such as threats of harm against others, irrational acts, racist or sexist conduct, explosiveness, or aggression. Positive risk is familiar to the general public from the popular media's description of the "out-of-control," "mentally unbalanced," or "dangerous" officer. However, liability may also be of the **negative risk** variety (what the officer may neglect to do), such as involving dereliction of duty, distractibility because of substance abuse, or rejection of supervision needed to conduct the normal operations associated with his position. Officers who are referred to as unresponsive, insubordinate, or disheveled may represent a high negative risk. Such officers may hide from supervision or from demanding job assignments. Regardless of the nature of the risk, each such officer may exemplify a serious problem for his or her department or agency, introduce inefficiency, place the public in jeopardy, and create reputational and financial liabilities for his or her LE executives and the responsible political authority.

WHO MAY OFFER THE FFDE SERVICE?

Where possible, only specifically trained and licensed mental health professionals should conduct FFDEs. Many excellent general medical and mental health providers will agree that FFDEs are such specialized and sensitive assessments that only qualified providers should attempt them. This is not a trivial concern since the LE executive may make a convience-based decision to employ community providers in an FFDE task, a choice that can be inappropriate and create more problems than it solves. Since FFDEs are highly focused evaluations that are often time-limited, subject to likely challenges, and infrequent in typical clinical settings, a reliable assessment method must be used that is appropriate for law enforcement officers. The only tools that are common to the model FFDE situation are the **clinical interview** and psychometric tests (sometimes called **standardized tests**). Interviews in the hands of a gifted and experienced examiner are a powerful tool, but they are subject to some obvious limitations. First, the examiner's impressions are always limited to his or her experience and training, a situation that can lead to biases and distortions in impression formation that may affect FFDE conclusions. For example, the examiner's experience may not be very broad in a given issue (e.g., customary officer conduct), and common officer behaviors may be misunderstood as serious mental illness, leading to inappropriate recommendations. In contrast, psychometric tests (see Chapter 8) have the advantage of a controlled method of administration and published, scientifically obtained norms with which the officer can be compared objectively to those who suffer a variety of mental problems, giving an additional certainty to the conclusions of the FFDE examiner. Standardized, psychometric testing also provides indicators of distortion and bias in the form of **validity scales** that may provide valuable additional information.

With rare exceptions, licensed psychologists should administer psychological testing because they are members of the traditional discipline that trains extensively in **psychometrics.** However, even if a psychologist is a licensed therapist or diagnostician, he or she should also be thoroughly familiar with the police psychology literature as well as personnel and civil rights issues before he or she proposes to perform specialized services in law enforcement.

POSITIVE RISK

The Case of Lieutenant James

James, a married lieutenant with the Anytown Police Department, has been working for the past year on special assignment within a local resort hotel. In spite of having been disciplined for accepting alcoholic beverages from that facility while on duty, his superiors considered him to usually be a good officer. In recent times, some complaints have been received from female employees who have reported some oblique propositions of a sexual nature, often accompanied by fantastic and bizarre claims of exceptional sexual capability, along with offers to exhibit intimate body parts. He had apparently ignored earlier supervisory warnings about nonprofessional deportment of this sort, but continued his occasionally overly familiar and raucous relationship with hotel employees. A recent complaint involved a report that Lt. James offered that he could "protect" a cashier from possible accusations of theft (some recent, unrelated arrests had been made) if she were to become sexually active with him. In addition to reports of unwanted touching of female employees, a number of witnesses reported that Lt. James had made explicit demands for sexual favors. Lt. James was then referred for an FFDE.

Lt. James appeared to be a positive liability risk because his distasteful and grossly inappropriate behavior had been gradually introducing active elements of chaos into his law enforcement assignment. His actions were working to undermine the respect others have for his police department, as well as evoking fear that he may misuse his authority if he were frustrated. In an ordinary employee such conduct would not be tolerable, but in an armed and commissioned law enforcement officer the implications of the misuse of power and the offer to shield some persons against appropriate law enforcement action appeared to be a public safety issue. Lt. James's behavior involved the classic issue of sexual harassment, but with a twist that implied a particularly alarming feature in the form of the "offer of protection" to those who would entertain his requests. The pattern of growing impropriety in a workplace setting, which involved his official position, made his conduct a clear job-related issue. None of his behavior seemed straightforwardly criminal since most incidents were based on innuendo and statements whose meaning could be contested. The **reason for referral** (to inquire into the possible psychological explanation for his conduct) appeared to be proper and justified by the situation. For Lt. James's supervisor, there were indications of behaviors that were impairing the officer's effective performance of his job, but the supervisor had no clear understanding of their nature. The referral may be understood as implicitly compassionate for the officer, in that surface events may be masking a potentially treatable problem, reducing the department's possible need for a disciplinary solution. If such were the case, appropriate action may yet preserve the officer's career, which would appear, perhaps even to Lt. James, to be in jeopardy at the time of referral.

In the FFDE interview, Lt. James appeared to be relaxed and showed little anxiety. At times, when speaking of the possibility of losing his job, Lt. James appeared somber and mildly downcast. He denied all indications of mental impairment or illness (such as depression or anxiety symptoms). When given psychological tests to measure emotional difficulties, Lt. James produced a classic **fake good** profile (unreasonable claims of perfection and lack of simple life difficulties on testing).

When asked his version of events, James reported that he did not recall touching the waitresses or requesting sexual favors, although he reluctantly admitted that he had "asked for dates" in the past. He represented himself as someone who had "slipped" into thinking of himself as a hotel or resort worker rather than a law enforcement officer. He envied male employees of the hotel who could take advantage of the "free" atmosphere associated with friendly female employees, alcohol use, and the party milieu of a resort. He complained that he felt deprived of the fruits of being an important person in an exciting place because of the unnecessary and outdated departmental regulations that were inhibiting his "style." He denied that he had offered to expose his private parts, and emotionally denounced the multiple witnesses regarding his behavior as "conspirators, whores, and liars." The line between his professional police responsibility and his desire to enjoy his position had apparently begun to fade in his mind. His personality structure, driven by a **narcissistic entitlement,** had overwhelmed his promise to uphold his duties as an officer. Lt. James had exhibited small lapses of responsibility early in his assignment, such as accepting gifts of alcoholic beverages and flirting overtly with employees. The penalties of his being caught could be mitigated by claims of misunderstanding and misinterpretation, followed by periods of time during which he took pains to avoid violations of the code of conduct. But his social/professional boundaries had begun to weaken and the risks involved in rule violations seemed more exciting as time passed and he got away with further indiscretions. In a disappointing epilogue, he seemed to express reluctantly a sense of betrayal directed at the female employee who had "turned him in," although as an officer he knew that it was her duty to do so.

During the dismissal hearing, IA established the facts of his conduct beyond a reasonable challenge. Lt. James did not claim mental impairment, and the psychologist did not propose any such explanation based upon the FFDE. A mutual agreement was struck in which all parties concluded that Lt. James was unable to resist the temptations that were placed before him and the departmental executives elected to discharge him. It was an unfortunate case of human weaknesses overwhelming professional duty.

NEGATIVE RISK

The Case of Officer Susan

Officer Susan of the Anytown Police Department had been assigned to the white-collar crime division for more than five years. During the past decade, she had suffered a number of marital and financial setbacks, and had been issued a DWI. She had been compelled by the court to seek treatment for alcoholism and anxiety disorders. She has recently been requesting a good deal of sick leave time, primarily supported by nonspecific letters from a local psychiatric provider. Officer Susan had reported a regular need for psychotropic (antidepressant) medications, without which she could not function at work. Still, she had been seen falling asleep at her desk, and had been unresponsive to colleague questions. The overall quality of her work had fallen into the unacceptable range and co-workers had begun to complain that she was not pulling her weight in her assignments. When asked by her supervisor about the reasons for her poor work performance, Officer Susan offered an elaborate set of conspiracy theories involving many senior officers (including the chief, whom she had met only a few times) and attributed her mental health problems to the destructive effects of the supposed collusion.

Officer Susan did not appear to be engaging in harmful, aggressive, or sexual conduct, but she seemed to be unable to muster the attention, energy, or focus required by her job. Her conduct has had a negative effect upon her department by forcing others to cover her duties and reducing the efficiency of her agency, upon whom the community relies to meet their public safety needs. Her complex psychiatric difficulties appeared to be tenacious and impervious to a variety of treatments over the years, and she had required many extended periods of medical leave. By her own admission, a variety of emotional problems squarely blocked her ability to achieve recognizable and adequate levels of job performance in any contemporary assignment. When disciplined, she claimed that the department was solely responsible for her stress and had caused her psychiatric difficulties. Officer Susan stated that she was entitled to medical leave, special accommodations, and transfer to new assignments whenever she felt it necessary. In time, she had failed at most available departmental assignments and was nowhere welcome for reassignment.

Consistent with Officer Susan's admissions of severe anxiety and depressive difficulties, she produced an FFDE psychometric profile that was typical for persons who suffered from significant mental illness. No attempt was made on her part to minimize or attenuate her symptoms in psychometric testing. Psychotropic medication use did not appear to sufficiently reduce the reported severity of her problems, and her level of claimed difficulty was such that she appeared significantly impaired. Upon interview, she appeared depressed. Her stories had a mildly persecutory resonance. Officer Susan claimed that each of her supervisors over many years would abuse, mistreat, and frustrate her, apparently without reason. In her eyes, she had been an above-average officer, plagued by bad luck that was made worse by the lack of fair play by her supervisors and her department. She claimed that her DWI citation was the work of a malicious and envious senior officer. She claimed that she had been "tricked' into earlier treatment because of a "rigged" Breathalyzer that had falsely indicated that she was intoxicated at the time of her arrest. At the same time, she blamed her admitted overuse of alcohol on the pressures of her work. She reported that she had suffered personal losses and had received no expected assistance from her department, which in her eyes was an insult that she should not have had to tolerate. She felt that her department's "poor response" to her misfortune was the real culprit in her occupational failures, aggravating and magnifying her emotional problems. Officer Susan reported that her supervisors had failed to train or support her appropriately, and any shortcomings regarding her capability was their fault.

The FFDE report concluded that Officer Susan was not currently fit to continue as a commissioned officer, and suggested a temporary accommodation in a less demanding assignment, if available. In addition, therapy was recommended to address the problem of impaired job performance (see Chapter 9). A follow-up (posttreatment) FFDE to measure improvement was recommended. Officer Susan's response was an initial rebuke. She admitted significant problems but felt that they were all irrelevant regarding her work performance. If only her supervisors would treat and train her better, no further therapy, medication, or reevaluation review would be needed.

However, as time passed, Susan chose to take the position that she was best served by accepting the concept that she required treatment. By pursuing treatment, she was able to demonstrate that she could become a useful and effective officer. She threw herself into the recovery process, obtaining high-quality medication consultation and accepting psychotherapy treatment with a well-qualified psychologist. In the end, a good officer was returned to duty, a matter of importance to her department and to the officer herself.

Chapter 6

Developing a Fitness-for-Duty Evaluation System

America's greatest strength, and its greatest weakness, is our belief in second chances, our belief that we can always start over, that things can be made better.

Anthony Walton

It is vitally important that the law enforcement executive and his or her department develop a detailed working relationship with the fitness-for-duty examiner well before any officer is referred for this service (Rostow and Davis, 2002). No fixed and immutable rules govern the manner in which an FFDE program is administered within any given agency. In a sense, all FFDE programs should be custom designed for each department that intends to employ an FFDE system. All LE FFDE programs must be constructed to meet the needs of the department and the working realities of that specific law enforcement and general communities in which it is embedded. The LE executive should not expect optimal operation from static, turnkey procedures adapted from other FFDE programs. All departments have specific strengths and weaknesses that should be reflected in their FFDE procedure. Such issues as expense, departmental structure and traditions, union agreements, and historical problems may all play a role in the department's specific FFDE system.

In general, two methods of organizing the administration of the fitness-for-duty examination exist. Some larger law enforcement agencies acquire police psychologists as departmental employees **(internal providers),** some of whom may plan and conduct the FFDEs. Other departments may contract for the design and delivery of FFDE services with independent, professionally qualified **external provid-**

ers. Another important dimension within the FFDE procedure is that of designing the procedure to be either mandatory or optional on the part of the officer. Some departments conduct the FFDE as a mandatory procedure (refusal may be grounds for dismissal), whereas others may offer options to the officer, such as in the selection of disciplinary proceedings as an alternative to the FFDE. In any case, the FFDE process should be the product of full disclosure and scrutiny by all stakeholders before it is introduced into the official agency personnel or civil service code, union agreement, or disciplinary system. There are likely to be as many distinctive procedures and methods as there are unique agency customs, traditions, and circumstances. All important stakeholders should understand the need for an FFDE procedure to both protect the rights of the officer in question and provide a degree of safety and confidence for the public in the integrity and proper operation of the law enforcement agency. In the absence of such awareness, the FFDE procedure may become a battleground for contentious misunderstandings.

FRIEND OF THE CHIEF

The Case of Dr. Freud

When the Anytown police chief experienced a family problem some years ago, he contacted a local psychologist, Dr. Freud, who proved helpful in assisting the chief's family. Now the chief considers Dr. Freud to be a good friend and "as good as anyone else" in the delivery of all forms of clinical service. When an officer in the Anytown Police Department appeared to have psychological difficulties, the chief asked Dr. Freud to examine the employee. The psychologist accepted the case in the standard clinical fashion, as he would with any troubled person who applied for assistance. Dr. Freud did not demand a clear statement of the reasons for referral and tried to be helpful by working several informal "treatment" sessions into the assessment process. A report was returned to the department that described details of the officer's confidential and embarrassing personal and family issues, which was inadvertently circulated to departmental clerical employees before appearing on the chief's desk. Dr. Freud's report contained a great deal of technical jargon, did not clearly state whether the officer was fit for duty, and proposed complex diagnoses. The exact purpose of the assessment, the role of the provider, the issues of confidentiality, and the boundary between treatment and assessment functions were unclear.

The problems with Dr. Freud's approach to the FFDE are common and represent some of the more egregious errors in poorly constructed FFDE procedures and methods. In a sense, no FFDE system existed at all in this example, only a collection of good intentions and a clinical model of service that did not fit the circumstance to which it was applied. Although a good general mental health clinician, the psychologist seemed to have little specific idea about how to proceed, either in conceiving of the purpose of the service or integrating procedures into the process to avoid foreseeable abuse or difficulty. The sound clinical reputation of the FFDE provider was no longer a relevant consideration when the FFDE task became that of assessing liability or risk in law enforcement, in contrast with the provision of treatment services. The reasons for the psychologist's participation in the FFDE and the goals of the FFDE task appear not to have been clear to the examined officer, the chief, the departmental executives, or the FFDE provider at any time before or during the process. The FFDE provider should have anticipated and addressed the scientific, administrative, and **forensic** difficulties of the FFDE, but had little specific experience with this sort of problem. The LE executive had not required Dr. Freud to demonstrate that the psychological FFDE procedure was a rational and technically satisfying methodology.

The law enforcement executive must have reason to believe that the FFDE examiner is knowledgeable about most areas of the FFDE process. That is not to say that the examiner should substitute for the departmental attorney, internal affairs officer, commander, and personnel department director or risk manager. Such other parties must play their part as well, but the role performed by the police psychologist should touch upon the full array of FFDE elements in a way that compliments the contributions of other professionals. It is the joint responsibility of both the police psychologist and the LE executive to consider the myriad laws and professional practices that may complicate any FFDE. The FFDE must be based on sound administrative and scientific rationales, and must fit into the other departmental procedures (e.g., disciplinary and supervisory methods, as well as training) in a predefined and nonconflicting manner. Issues of the purpose of the evaluation, the adequacy of evidence to justify the referral, the issue of confidentiality, and the likely objections and protests regarding the process must be understood by the LE executive and the police psychologist.

Where the FFDE provider is an outside consultant (external provider), the contract between the provider and the agency must clearly identify the department as the provider's legal client, not the officers who are examined by the provider. An officer who is a "client" or "patient" of the FFDE provider may be entitled to special rights that may supercede departmental needs for information that is connected with personal conduct or behavior. With the department as the identified client, the FFDE report should be the property of the department and the provider should be the record custodian of the administrative materials collected by the examiner, an aide in protecting this information for agency purposes.

A preestablished agreement concerning the nature of observations and complaints that will be appropriate for FFDE officer referrals must be established by consensus among all parties well before the first officer reaches the FFDE provider. This may be accomplished through a policy entry in the departmental code of conduct, personal regulation, civil service manual, or even as a contractual part of a union agreement. It is advisable that a letter of guidance (see Appendix C) and other necessary correspondence be designed well in advance of the referral. The nature of the administrative organization for the FFDE should be reviewed thoroughly and accepted by all central parties early in the FFDE developmental process.

GENERAL FFDE GOALS

Fitness-for-duty evaluations should be conducted in ways that are well understood and accepted by the law enforcement executives of the specific agency for whom they are conducted. In general, referrals should be made only for specific, current problems that are connected with officer behavior and recorded from observations by his supervisors, fellow officers, and civilians in the community or in some cases by the officer's family and friends (see Chapter 11). Effort should be expended to develop rules that are meant to avoid officer referrals that are characterized by general claims of misconduct ("he acts crazy") or glib, imprecise claims of medical or psychological impairment ("she is paranoid"). Only concrete behavioral reports and observations (e.g., documented instances of threatening fellow officers, civilian complaints of brutal conduct) will prove useful and defendable as a reason for an officer's FFDE referral. Similarly, long-term personality problems ("he was always like that") are usually not appropriate reasons for officer referrals, since the officer has presumably been employed without exceptional difficulty for a sizable time interval, making sudden objections to that conduct difficult to support. However, a recent change in the preexistent personality pattern ("she always had a temper, but now she has begun to physically attack others") is clearly an appropriate reason for referral. An attempt should always be made to anchor the reason for referral to job-related issues and to consequently avoid making referrals that are not clearly bound to law enforcement performance (see Chapters 11 and 12).

The communication of adequate documentation between the FFDE provider and the LE executive well before the officer's evaluation is scheduled is strongly advised. This **documentary examination phase** may give the FFDE provider and the law enforcement executive a basis for the analysis of job-related complaints prior to the officer's appearance in the FFDE provider's office, so that the issues to be explored may be clarified. For example, a report by a supervisor regarding an incident of violence can be better understood by the examiner who has obtained and read on-site reports of the occurrence written by fellow officers, civilians, and supervisors. The divergent viewpoints of third-party observations may not have been covered sufficiently in the original verbal or summarized written report from the supervisor to the examiner. As addressed previously, the FFDE methodology should not be a convenient substitute for a proper, although often contentious, administrative process (e.g., discharge or demotion) or criminal prosecution. For example, inappropriate sexual acting out among a group of officers (e.g., at a convention) may result in a complaint against an officer whose behavior may have been indistinguishable from a dozen others who were present at the time. The police psychologist may advise the LE executive that an FFDE that is limited to the targeted officer is disputable after considering multiple reports of the behaviors of others who were also present. Either all of the officers should be appropriate for referral, or the entire matter may be best placed into the hands of IA for individual or group disciplinary action following an investigation. If non-FFDE procedures are more appropriate in a given case, the documentary examination phase is one place where the FFDE provider may suggest the redirection of the officer to alternative methods.

If an officer's conduct is serious enough to suspend the officer from duty, that decision should be made immediately and the FFDE should then be used to advise the chief in the postsuspension interval. The practice of allowing officers who are suspected of impaired conduct to continue in customary LE duties until it is convenient to conduct an FFDE is inappropriate. Seldom do reasons exist to tolerate a dysfunctional officer when supporting information suggests immediate danger or functional incapability. Finally, the FFDE is not meant to "punish" officers, but is a means to protect the public and to afford the examined officer an opportunity for treatment or other actions that may be connected with potentially remediable psychological problems.

ADMINISTRATIVE CONFLICT OF INTEREST

Two **conflicts of interest** are of concern in the FFDE context: the **administrative conflict of interest** and the **clinical conflict of interest.** An administrative conflict of interest is created by a professional's relationship with an employer (or his or her representative) that creates an impression of possible bias when evaluating another employee in which pressures may exist to support the preexistent views of that employer. A clinical conflict of interest is the appearance of bias created by a conflict in the responsibilities created by the incompatible roles of a professional who is expected to both evaluate and assist the officer in treatment.

Officers Frick and Frack

While on patrol, Officers Frick and Frack of the Anytown Police Department began to argue about a small debt. They continued to loudly disagree after they stopped at a local restaurant, creating a disturbance that included pushing and verbal threats of violence. Both were referred for FFDEs. The chief informed the FFDE provider that he had always disliked Officer Frick and would be "very disappointed" if Frick was found fit for duty. In addition, the FFDE provider had treated Officer Frack for an anxiety difficulty several years before. The FFDE provider declined both referrals and recommended that the chief either refer to another FFDE provider or consider a disciplinary/administrative solution to the reported behaviors.

To avoid an administrative conflicts of interest, it is recommended that the FFDE service be performed by a professional contractor who is either not an agency employee or who is insulated from the supervisory system that is responsible for the referral of the officer for examination. In some cases, when the department employs psychologists, the department may prefer to use those professional employees as FFDE providers. This preference can be a problematic choice when the supervisor believes the officer to be unfit and the FFDE provider is expected to concur. Failure to concur with the supervisor's opinions may result in unpleasant consequences for the internal provider. It is self-evident that the FFDE should be as free as possible from the pressures of the administrative system, so that the FFDE provider may offer an independent, professional opinion without experiencing adverse consequences. Where such insulation is not in place, the FFDE provider may be reluctant to contradict the officer's ultimate supervisor. Any appearance of a failure to form independent professional opinions by the FFDE provider may create substantial credibility and defensibility problems. Worthwhile FFDE recommendations are those based upon available professional and scientific standards of practice and must not be based upon factors that stem from political or economic pressures.

In clinical conflicts of interest, any prior relationship with the referred officer or with someone close to the officer (e.g., spouse, sibling, or parent) may create the appearance of prejudice or violate the confidentiality of the original interaction. This problem may be encountered more frequently in small communities (because few people are served by few providers) and in internal provider situations. In departmental EAPs or treatment programs, the FFDE provider may have had contact with the referred officer at an earlier time. Both the department and the provider are best advised not to have that particular FFDE provider examine the officer because any finding will be subject to claims of bias and unfair procedures by the officer and his or her legal counsel.

Finally, a secure official file location should be established within the law enforcement agency to ensure that officers' fitness information, in the form of official reports, remains confidential. This file should be secured separately from standard personnel or internal affairs records to protect the confidentiality of sensitive information and prevent record misuse that could defame or injure the officer. In no case are clinical notes or psychometric testing to be stored with the FFDE report, but such sensitive material must be stored in a nearly inaccessible location and under rules that are identical to sensitive medical records, regardless of whether the department has internal or external providers perform the FFDE (see Chapter 13).

Chapter 7

Forms and Styles for the Fitness-for-Duty Evaluation in Law Enforcement

> Nearly all officers worked for departments that used criminal record checks (99%), background investigations (98%), driving record checks (98%), and medical exams (97%) to screen applicants. Psychological (91%), aptitude (84%), and physical agility (78%) tests were also widely used.
>
> Law Enforcement Management
> and Administrative Statistics (LEMAS)
> Local Police Departments, 1997

OFFICER INSTRUCTIONS

In the general FFDE model procedure, the officers referred for the FFDE should be informed in writing to report for the examination during a specific appointment at the office of the FFDE provider. The officer should not be required or encouraged to disclose or discuss the nature of the potential disability to the chief, supervisors, or other agency personnel. The officer should be discouraged from revealing details of his suspected psychological or medical problems to departmental personnel outside of the FFDE, since such discussions may violate the officer's rights of privacy and can lead to destructive misunderstandings. Only commanders or managers who are part of the officer's supervisory system should be informed of the reason for the FFDE or that the FFDE referral has been initiated. Other personnel, particularly anyone who is not in a supervisory, internal affairs, or risk management role regarding *this specifically referred officer,* including ordinary clerical and support staff, should not have access to either the reason for referral or even the fact of referral. In certain departments, this may mean the creation of a "secured" and independent administrative and clerical system for FFDE purposes.

It is advisable that the officer be given a written summary of the reason for referral, preferably in general terms. In some departments, the officer may be given verbal reasons for referral. However, this practice may lead to the officer discussing confidential or protected details of his mental or physical condition with a supervisor and therefore should be discouraged. For example, a written statement may include an indication that the FFDE is meant to inform the chief of issues that are related to the officer's "loss of temper" on a given date. Such a reason is acceptable both because it is not transparently pathological and because it is anchored to some event about which the officer is familiar. Some examples from the original complaints or investigation that led to the FFDE may add clarity to the reasons for FFDE referral. For example, the officer may be given a statement that reads, "The events of last Saturday have raised questions about your professional conduct that the chief wishes for you and Dr. Freud to discuss." To avoid unpleasant conflict once in the FFDE situation, an additional statement may be added, such as, "Dr. Freud is our police psychologist and will ask that you complete some questionnaires and psychological tests. The chief asks that you participate fully in any tasks that Dr. Freud asks you to do." In other circumstances, a more general reference to the reason for referral may be offered, such as, "Dr. Freud has been asked to professionally inquire into the reported conflicts between yourself and department personnel over the past year."

It is often advisable to cite preestablished violations of departmental regulations, which may have been made known earlier in a letter of counseling or disciplinary hearing, and tie these instances to the reason for the FFDE. For example, the order to report for the FFDE may state that the referral was being made in accordance with "the departmental rules of misconduct in connection with the findings of the disciplinary committee [or the letter of counseling] regarding the events of March 30." In some instances, the reason for referral may cite a series of difficulties, noting that the FFDE examiner may discuss with the officer "the circumstances and reasons behind the ten complaints made by motorists in connection with the issue of your rudeness (i.e., behavior unbecoming an officer)."

The FFDE referral letter should also be nonspecific with regard to suspected causes of the difficulties (e.g., suspected alcohol abuse or paranoid disorder) in order to enhance the possibility that the examinee will participate in an unguarded and open manner. In some cases, alerted to concerns about a possible illicit drug use, the examinee may "shut down" any discussion of substance use. Although such a confrontational or defensive strategy may be understandable in certain criminal investigations, an adversarial FFDE would likely result in a meaningless outcome. In such a case, the department and the officer may lose the chance for the officer to arrange for his or her recovery and remain an active employee.

OFFICER PERSONAL INFORMATION

The officer should be informed that the examination might touch upon a broad range of issues in many parts of his or her life, including behaviors or events that may be embarrassing or personal. Although such a wide range of topics may be necessary for the provider's professional examination, the bulk of such material will not be forwarded to the officer's department. A good rule of thumb is that the only information that is included in the report sent to the LE executives is that which has job-related significance (such as facts to explicate the issue of dangerousness). The officer should be told that the department is entitled to and requires any information that may touch upon his or her ability to perform his or her essential job duties or any information that may indicate danger or risk to the department, fellow officers, and the public. Where permitted, the officer should be told to expect to give consent for the FFDE (that is, to cooperate to the best of the officer's ability), but that the officer may refuse or discontinue interviewing, testing, and evaluation, and elect instead to submit to the prescribed administrative procedures of his or her department. The alternative procedures should be spelled out clearly in the letter of referral and in the departmental conduct code (e.g., "refusal to submit and comply fully with the FFDE will result in a dismissal hearing [within forty-eight hours of refusal] regarding conduct unbecoming an officer, Civil Service Code Number 1234"). The officer may be warned that certain medical or psychological legal protections (see Chapters 13, 14, and 15) might be lost upon the officer's rejection of the FFDE option, because such a refusal implies both that the officer denies that he or she may be handicapped and that the officer has rejected examination.

In departments in which the FFDE is a mandatory procedure, the option of refusal may be absent and the additional charge of insubordination may be added to those infractions that have already been cited when an officer refuses either direct or indirect cooperation. A voluntary, if not enthusiastic, compliance is necessary if the FFDE is to be productive and advantageous. In both the mandatory and optional case, the officer is essentially making the choice between submitting to an independent professional evaluation or refusing that opportunity (actively or passively) and confronting directly the accusations that form the basis of the complaints against him or her. The selection of the administrative alternative may carry with it a direct risk of disciplinary outcome or discharge. A compelled or mandatory compliance is worthless if the officer is evasive, untruthful, distorts his or her responses or denies any form of difficulty (in the face of obvious problems in personnel or work history). In the case of such an officer, it may be better for all concerned to avoid the FFDE and move directly to an adversarial methodology (e.g., civil service discharge hearing) in which the officer is either cleared of misconduct or is subject to discipline or discharge.

DIRECTIONS FOR AN FFDE APPEARANCE

In the officer referral letter, there should be precise directions (in some cases including both a map and written steps) regarding the location of the provider's office and the precise appearance time for the FFDE. The officer should be told to report for evaluation in a timely fashion and in civilian clothing and to be prepared to spend a full day at the examiner's office, as is required by the FFDE provider. The officer must bring positive identification, such as picture ID (commission card, driver's license, passport, etc.). Many FFDE providers may collect photographs and fingerprints at the examination site to ensure the identity of the examinee. The officer is to bring any needed equipment, including eyeglasses, hearing aids, medications, lunch, and other items that are necessary in a situation that requires prolonged sitting, speaking, and writing within a fixed location. The possession of illicit drugs or alcoholic beverages in the examiner's office or parking lot is prohibited. Drugs or alcohol that are consumed prior to reporting for examination and results in the appearance of intoxication, will cause the examiner to discontinue the examination and report to the referring LE executive that the FFDE could not be completed for such a reason. Some FFDE examiners may require officers who appear intoxicated to submit to a urine drug screen before continuing with examination.

The officer must be instructed not to bring sidearms, batons, handcuffs, chemical spray, or weapons of any type. The officer should not hand deliver official medical or administrative documents (e.g., hospital records, departmental complaints, court records) to the examiner, to reduce the chances of examinee tampering. Any such communication or documentation should be transmitted to the examiner separately (U.S. mail, courier, etc.) as allowed for by departmental regulation or contract with an external provider. Electronic means of transmission (e-mail, fax, etc.) is not reliable or secure at present and should be avoided for the transfer of important or sensitive materials. The officer should be reminded to expect to respond to numerous written and verbal questions of many types. An FFDE will almost always consist of a face-to-face, structured interview and formal, professional psychological testing and questionnaires. A general history will be taken from the officer, touching upon significant medical, behavioral, historical, legal, conduct, military, and mental health issues that are important considerations in an evaluation. The officer should be asked to bring certain important information, such as the names and addresses of current or recent treating physicians, and medications that he or she takes on a regular basis (in their pharmacy bottles if possible). The officer should be asked to bring military discharge papers (DD 214) if the officer has been in the service in the previous ten years or for whatever number of years since discharge as required by departmental regulation. Contradictions between claims of military service and conditions of discharge that are obtained by contrasting the DD 214 with the officer's verbal reports may be an important source of information.

THIRD-PARTY OBSERVATIONS

The officer should be told not to report for the FFDE accompanied by his attorney, family members, or friends, except for transportation purposes. Most police psychologists will refuse to conduct an FFDE if such parties insist on participating in or observing the evaluation. This is because the presence of such parties may distort or alter the requisite interactions needed by the psychologist to provide meaningful consultations and recommendations to the referring police executive. Special circumstances may exist in which others (fellow officers, supervisors, or relatives) may have a formal role in the procedure by providing detailed information, but the basic FFDE usually requires the conditions of privacy and unimpeded professional opportunity to obtain the officer's written and verbal responses.

Exceptions to the **examinee-only rule** may be made based upon extreme circumstances. For example, the court allowed an attorney to be present in at least one case in which disability was disputed (*Gensbauer v. the May Department Stores*, 1999). In general, the officer has no absolute right to have an attorney present at a psychological evaluation. For example, the Massachusetts Superior Court upheld an order for a psychological examination of a problem officer. The court further held that the officer to be evaluated had no right to have an attorney present at the time of the evaluation (*Nolan v. Police Commissioner of Boston*, 1981).

A special issue exists regarding the right (in labor law) to have a co-worker (usually the union steward) present during investigative interviews that might result in disciplinary action by the employer. In 1975, the Supreme Court ruled that private sector employees covered by the **National Labor Relations Act (NLRA)** may have union representatives present during a medical examination *(NLRB v. Weingarten, Inc.)*. Many states have adapted public sector employee laws that mirror the **Weingarten rule.** In one recent decision (*Epilepsy Fdn. of Northeast Ohio v. NLRB*, 2001), this right was certified for nonunion workers. Clearly, the *Weingarten* rule was meant for disciplinary hearings and not FFDEs, but since there is a possibility that a preliminary disciplinary outcome may result for an FFDE, the FFDE provider may be faced with such a demand and must decide whether to allow the third party into the examination or withdraw from the FFDE process because of this unanticipated contamination.

ELECTRONIC RECORDINGS

An ever-present problem in FFDEs is the denial on the part of some officers that certain information that the provider has reported was actually obtained from the officer. For example, the officer may recount to the examiner that he had been "out of control" in a particular situation, but the officer later claims that he did not report this information and the provider either lied or misunderstood him. In another case, the officer admitted to the used of an illicit drug during the interview, but later denied such an admission when it became part of the treatment recommendations section of the FFDE report. This problem may be mitigated partly by having as much of the information as possible collected from the officer in *written* form. Unfortunately, not all officers are equally proficient at written self-expression, and some background issues can be fully explored only by the spoken word for reasons of efficiency or to observe the accompanying emotional responses. For this reason, audio or video recordings of the entire FFDE interview may be desirable. The provider should be able to demonstrate clearly that the officer was aware of and agreed to the recording of the interview. The agreement should be in writing and should also be part of the recording itself, with the provider asking the officer to verbally acknowledge, while being recorded, that he or she understands that such a recording is being made and that he or she agrees to the procedure. Such electronic records should be treated with the same care and storage security as all written FFDE records.

COPY OF THE REPORT

Individuals who undergo law enforcement psychological evaluations have not been entitled to receive a copy of their reports. The Fair Credit Reporting Act (FCRA; see Chapter 15) and the Health Insurance Portability and Accountability Act (see Chapter 13) may have an influence upon this practice in the future, although the impact of such laws has not been decisive in settling issues regarding FFDEs and individual officers. As a general rule, the FFDE provider should convey no final FFDE report to law enforcement executives that would be inappropriate as an official public document. That is, any reasonable educated person, including examinees and their representatives, should be able to understand the reasons of evaluation, the general findings, and conclusions (without diagnosis and unneeded details) in departments that use such examinations. In that manner, as rules evolve, the essential and appropriate information regarding risk and liability may be transmitted without violation of confidentiality, privacy, or other implied rights.

The underlying examination upon which the FFDE report is based must be sound and defensible, regardless of what is included in the transmitted document to the law enforcement executive. Thus, the FFDE provider has a need to gather personal and technical information that is kept separate from the official FFDE report and is available only for legal and administrative purposes at a later time. In contrast with many non–law enforcement employees, the evaluations of law enforcement officers involves a public interest in safe and effective hiring, promoting, and monitoring, which usually outweighs the individual's interest in obtaining results of evaluations. The Illinois Appellate Court acknowledged that information from a psychologist's report would allow a prospective applicant to determine what pattern of responses the psychologist found indicative of fitness for police work. The issue of test security takes on a special meaning when the examinee is an armed agent with the power to take life or suspend an arrestee's civil rights. An aspiring (or serving) police officer, armed with insight into issues related to risk determination, could attempt to tailor his responses accordingly in future assessments and subsequently defeat the procedure (*Roullette v. Department of Central Management*, 1986). This principle of the need for test and methodology security is even more cogent regarding a serving officer than it is for an ordinary employee.

Under certain circumstances the release of the FFDE report may either be required or recommended on a case-by-case basis. For example, when there is a direct judicial appeal of the findings or recommendations of the evaluation (not just an action threatened by the officer or his or her attorney) or if there is a right to an appeal in a particular case (*Cremer v. City of Macomb Bd. of Fire and Police Com'rs*, 1994), records may be released. An appropriate release of records may occur when the officer is recommended for a psychologically based disability benefit and the disability board, or a review agency requires a copy of the report to determine appropriate action. The Fair Credit Reporting Act may require the release of an unedited consumer credit report to an employee, although it is clear from the legislative history of the FCRA that FFDE police psychological reports were not intended to be included in this requirement. Where an FFDE report has recommended counseling, it may be appropriate to release the report to a treating therapist only, as a means of assisting in and directing therapy to the relevant public safety issues. In all cases, the officer's written consent for release of confidential information to a specific party for a specific purpose must first be obtained. There may also be circumstances in which the officer may ask that the FFDE report be sent to a medical specialist (cardiologist, internist, neurologist, etc.) because the FFDE indicated a need to treat an medical condition (i.e., seizures secondary to a gunshot wound to the head).

DEFAMATION

In general, the courts have held that psychological reports may not be attacked legally from the perspective of defamation. In 1996 the appellate court in New York rejected a defamation suit brought by a rejected police applicant. The plaintiff and his wife sued upon learning that the plaintiff was not selected for the North Castle, New York, police department following a preemployment psychological evaluation. The plaintiff alleged that the psychologist had written defamatory statements about him to the department, resulting in the loss of his employment opportunity. The court held that statements contained in a preemployment psychological report are protected by a qualified privilege. To overcome this privilege, the plaintiff would have to "make an evidentiary showing" of actual **malice,** which he clearly failed to do (*Bopp v. Institute for Forensic Psychology*, 1996). The FFDE provider must reasonably be able show that he or she acted in way that was not in reckless disregard of whether it (FFDE information and conclusions) was false or not.

MISREPRESENTATION ON FFDES

The U.S. Supreme Court has held that lying to an investigator (anyone with the authority to conduct a lawful inquiry) is "good grounds" for terminating an employee (*LaChance v. Erickson*, 1998). In this case, federal employees were charged with misconduct and lying to investigators when questioned about job-related misconduct. The Court concluded that a citizen may decline to answer a government question, or answer it honestly, but cannot with impunity knowingly and willfully answer it with a falsehood. This ruling would appear to support directly any adverse action that was taken against either an incumbent officer or a recruit for lying during a background investigation and psychological exam in preemployment screening and FFDEs.

RÉSUMÉ FRAUD AND FREE SPEECH

Officer Draphy Durgins filed an administrative complaint, contending that the discipline of fellow officers involved in a horseplay incident had been insufficient for the infraction. The subsequent investigation into her complaint revealed that she had concealed her own criminal record regarding her application to the department. She was suspended and then fired, with the discharge later upheld by the Board of Police and Fire Commissioners and an Illinois state court. Officer Durgins then filed a federal court suit, contending that her right of free speech had been abridged. A jury awarded her $175,000 plus attorneys' fees, and the city was required to reinstate her. When the city appealed, the Seventh Circuit Court of Appeals ruled that a jury improperly awarded the officer $175,000 on her claim that she was fired in retaliation for exercising her free speech rights. She had in fact been fired for résumé fraud only and her First Amendment claim should not have gone to the jury. The appeals court noted that employee communications about personnel matters are not covered by the First Amendment and the subsequent discovery that she should not have been hired in the first place justified her termination (*Durgins v. City of East St. Louis*, 2001).

FFDE CONFIDENTIALITY IN COURT ACTIONS

In general, the question of the confidentiality of FFDE records in regard to third-party lawsuits does not appear to have been settled. In *Scott v. Edinburg* (2000), Officer Edinburg shot and killed Phillip Scott, whose estate brought a wrongful death action against the officer. Mr. Scott's heirs sought to obtain documents concerning a psychological evaluation that Officer Edinburg underwent at the order of the police chief after the shooting. In this case, the district court held that the confidentiality did not apply to statements in official documents (such as the FFDE report) and that official documents were discoverable material.

On the other hand, in *Caver v. City of Trenton* (2000), a group of African-American officers brought a civil rights action against their department. The plaintiffs filed a motion to compel the production of psychological records and reports of a white officer and four nonwhite officers that they felt were important to their case. The district court held that the confidentiality-protected psychological reports and records of the defendant police officer and four nonparty officers and their privacy interest outweighed the plaintiffs' need for the information, warranting the issuance of a protective order. Future court rulings will doubtlessly clarify the standing of FFDEs as applies to confidential and compelled orders of report release in court proceedings.

ADMINISTRATIVE FORMS OF FFDEs: INTERNAL AND EXTERNAL PROVIDERS

As introduced previously, fitness-for-duty evaluations have been conducted traditionally by either providers who are employees of the pertinent LE agency (internal providers) or by independent providers who may have contractual arrangements with many LE agencies (external providers) or departments for such services. Both arrangements require that the police psychologist or other FFDE provider be well qualified to deliver such services on a professional and educational basis (see Chapter 3). However, some real differences between these two administrative forms or business arrangements have importance for both the police psychologist and the LE administrator.

Internal FFDE Providers

Employees of any law enforcement agency, such as police psychologists, must owe their allegiance to their employer and may reasonably be considered to be part of the administrative hierarchy of the organization. In almost all cases, internal providers report to the chief or superintendent and may also report to middle-level executives, such as a section chief or commander. Internal providers must operate within the job description set by their agency, the civil service regulation for their position, or at the pleasure of the chief. If the provider does not conform to any element of the job's requirements, he or she may be may be discharged for insubordination, as may any employee of a law enforcement agency. The FFDE provider may be subject to direct orders of senior personnel or to departmental policy directives, even if such orders or directives contradict the provider's professional role obligations. Historically, military needs, such as for discipline, cohesion, and readiness (seen as essential in protecting the lives of large numbers of persons in military situations), have been viewed by the general command structure as more important than the civilian ethical standards of confidentiality and privacy as they would apply to individual personnel. Even in paramilitary settings, a law enforcement executive's belief that an armed, subordinate officer is mentally unbalanced may have a powerful effect upon the police psychologist's ultimate findings and opinions (because of the extraordinary harm that may result), especially if the executive is also the police psychologist's administrative superior. It is the rare psychologist who would wish to be responsible for civilian injuries and subsequent lawsuits that may follow the release of an impaired officer to duty that the chief believed was impaired.

Once challenged as an administrative or legal procedure, the internal FFDE provider's opinions can be viewed as an extension of the opinion of his or her organizational commanders. Even if untrue, the dependence of the internal provider upon his or her employer might open questions regarding the independence and scientific fairness of the examination and, by extension, the conclusion of the FFDE. To avoid an administrative conflict of interest, the burden falls on internal providers and their departmental structure to develop and maintain independent checks on the meaningfulness and accuracy of the FFDEs that are generated.

External FFDE Providers

Police psychological and FFDE providers may offer services to public and private LE or security agencies on an independent and contractual basis, that is, outside of the status of employees. Since such external providers are not employees of the LE agency, they do not answer directly to the chief or commanders but rather have a contractual connection to the department. Although they can be dismissed, as any contract can be voided, they are seldom exclusively dependent on a single person or agency for their livelihood or reputation. While both internal and external providers contribute to law enforcement agencies, their ultimate orientation and role identification is somewhat different. Internal providers may be viewed as an essential part of a functioning law enforcement unit, and may be in a good position to respond quickly to the many needs of the agency (e.g., counseling, debriefing, selection, fitness, profiling). External providers may be seen as independent professionals, sharing experience and practices across agencies and offering a broad range of consultations in an independent manner.

Since external providers may not automatically share the LE agency's executive immunity to ordinary lawsuits and may have special burdens in federal law (see Chapter 15), they may find it critical to be ready to defend their independent decisions at any time against a legal or administrative challenge by any party. Such limitations make it imperative for the external provider to maintain strict, professionally defendable methods and procedures in arriving at decisions and recommendations, or they may face expensive legal consequences. For these reasons, the external provider acts as a consultant only, maintaining some distance from the referring authority. The external provider may also need to consider issues of malpractice insurance coverage or contractual indemnity agreements (agreements by a department to refund provider costs associated with defending against a lawsuit if the provider is found not to be culpable) to maintain financial stability as a provider of services. Ironically, such pressures may make the internal provider's demonstration of objectivity in the FFDE process more easily defendable against a charge of administrative conflict of interest than may be the case for the internal provider.

ARE FFDEs MANDATORY?

The concept of FFDEs in law enforcement settings developed out of military medical examinations that date back to the nineteenth century. In cases where military personnel have been physically injured or become ill, their readiness to continue active duty (medically or psychologically fit) had to be verified by commanders for the military unit to retain the adequate fighting strength required by their mission. Refusal to submit to medical examination or failure of the medical examination by the soldier has long been seen as a valid reason for discharge or retirement in military settings. In general, law enforcement work has been considered a form of paramilitary activity. Officers with serious medical conditions that adversely affect job performance could not be allowed to remain in a position in which the safety and life of others depend upon the officers' capabilities. By extension, refusal of medical or psychological examinations in military or public safety situations has not been permissible because the presence of an impairment may result in serious harm to both the injured officers and to those who count upon the officers to afford protection.

Each department must make the decision whether to treat the FFDE as a mandatory or as an optional administrative procedure. In mandatory situations, the officer is ordered by a law enforcement executive to report for and submit to a psychological evaluation for liability assessment purposes. The department specifies the provider and methodology (by an employee regulation or by contract with an external provider) and the officer is ordered to cooperate in the process as a condition of employment. The department often pays for all expenses in connection with the FFDE, including transportation and lost work time. Evidence of failure to cooperate, such as may be demonstrated by refusal, evasiveness, dishonesty, and evidence of invalid psychometric test production, is considered insubordination. Unfortunately, some problems exist with the mandatory method. The compelled nature of ordered, mandatory testing may result in less than open responding as a matter of course, reducing the utility and clarity of the FFDE findings. Since the ultimate objective of the FFDE is to indicate the nature of the difficulty and recommend remediation of the problem where possible, failure to cooperate defeats the process at its origin.

An alternative to the mandatory approach is the optional method. The officer is given a choice between submitting to an FFDE as a professional inquiry for the purpose of detecting psychological problems that may explain behaviors that would otherwise result in discipline or discharge. The selection of full and effective participation is shifted from the LE executives to the officers, who now, it is hoped, understand that they may request assistance through the FFDE process or reject the offer of assistance a priori and defend against accusation of inappropriate behaviors that are described in the complaint. This is analogous to a DWI suspect pleading not guilty and going to trial, as compared to pleading an extenuating circumstance (e.g., substance abuse disorder) and asking the court to consider alternative solutions (therapy, medication, AA, probation).

LYBARGER ADMONISHMENT

To make matters more complex, all information that is obtained from procedures that are ordered (interrogations, FFDE examinations) by the police commanders may be legally considered to be coerced and not usable of criminal prosecutions (*Garrity v. State of New Jersey,* 1967). Sometimes called the **Lybarger admonishment,** a statement may be made prior to the interview in which the officer is informed that his or her required responses to questions cannot be used against him or her in criminal actions. In some ways, this is the diametric opposite of the Miranda warnings ("Anything you say can be used against you . . .") that suspects are given upon their arrest. Since it is likely that the officer will see the FFDE, especially by an internal provider, as a confirmation of his or her belief that the department is "biased" against the officer, he or she is likely to **stonewall** the examiner (deny any possibly abnormal behavior). This strategy may produce an invalid outcome. Such conduct may result in a finding of insubordination, which defeats the intent of the FFDE and yields little psychologically significant information. Neither the officers (who may have benefitted from treatment) nor the departments (who now may lose the officers) have benefitted by the refusal to cooperate. The Lybarger admonishment may serve the public policy intent of encouraging the officer to cooperate with the FFDE in an unguarded manner by reducing potential, criminal repercussions that may stem from such cooperation.

INSUBORDINATION

Where there is a well-prepared set of mandatory rules for an FFDE, an officer can be fired for refusing to participate in an ordered psychological examination. In one case, a Chicago police officer had been accused of sexual misconduct and was ordered to submit to an FFDE. He refused, apparently believing the order to be unlawful. The appellate court ruled that an

> officer does not have the prerogative of actively disobeying an order from a superior while the officer subjectively determines whether the order is lawful . . . such a practice would thwart the authority and respect which is the foundation of the effective and efficient operation of a police force and destroy the discipline necessary in a paramilitary organization. (*Haynes v. Police Bd. of the City of Chicago*, 1997)

In most jurisdictions, failure to submit to a psychological evaluation, when reasonably ordered to do so, amounts to insubordination, justifying discipline or removal.

> The fitness-for-duty examination is a useful procedure to determine an employee's competency to perform his duties . . . [and] failure to submit to such an examination, when there are good reasons for directing an employee to submit to it, is insubordina-

tion and can justify discharge. (*Risner v. U.S. Dept of Transp.*, 1982)

In *Smith v. U.S. Air Force* (1978), the court found substantial grounds for the termination of an Air Force civil service employee who failed to report for an ordered psychiatric evaluation. Even in nonsecurity situations, as in *Schwartz v. Hicksville Union Free School Dist.* (1996), a New York appellate court sustained a two-year disciplinary suspension of a teacher who refused to undergo psychological testing. The principle of court recognition of FFDEs as a valid and appropriate method of inquiry into the competence and capability of officers, as a matter of public policy, appears to have been well established.

As with all areas of public life, constitutional challenges are to be expected regarding FFDE procedures. FFDEs of public safety officers have been challenged on several constitutional grounds, including invasion of privacy and violations of the First and Fourteenth Amendments (including religious, political, social, familial, and sexual rights). A federal court has held that psychological evaluations conducted for the Jersey City Fire Department did not violate any of the plaintiffs' constitutional rights. It held that where there was an intrusion upon constitutional rights; this intrusion was justified by the state's compelling need for the psychological evaluations (*McKenna v. Fargo,* 1979).

Fitness-for-duty evaluations can clearly be a defendable, useful, and even powerful instrument in assisting LE executives in their administrative and ethical duties to both the public and their subordinate law enforcement personnel. There are, however, many complex pitfalls and difficulties in the intelligent management of FFDE procedure. In the subsequent chapters, the issues of scientific methods and procedure are examined as a means of providing the LE executive with a practical knowledge of the application of psychological theory and assessment, so as to place that executive in a knowledgeable position to understand the methods and concepts of the policy psychologist.

Chapter 8

Assessment: Methods and Procedures

University degrees are a bit like adultery: you may not want to get involved with that sort of thing, but you don't want to be thought incapable.

Sir Peter Imbert
British police commissioner

Organization is the key to most complex human behavior. The FFDE provider must have solid training in psychological assessment, interviewing techniques, psychopathology (abnormal behavior), psychometrics (psychological testing), as well as police culture and forensic psychology. The provider must also possess a detailed awareness of the needs of the department for whom the service is being provided. This chapter is intended to offer (1) some practical guidance for the law enforcement executive regarding procedures in processing the officer through the FFDE; (2) a framework to understand the differences among distinct goals in evaluation preparation; (3) a brief discussion of the sort of instruments often employed in FFDEs; and (4) a brief groundwork to comprehend some of the technical and statistical issues in the FFDE process.

PROCESSING THE OFFICER INTO THE FFDE SETTING

Once the FFDE procedures have been authorized and established within the LE department, the officer may be referred to the location of examination. Upon arrival, evidence of the officer's identity should be examined and photocopied for the provider's records. The FFDE provider should explain the evaluation's function to the officer and offer to answer questions before any psychological examination (in contrast to the collection of simple identifying data) is conducted. In spite of adequate prereferral arrangement (see Chapter 7), many officers will arrive at the testing site with minimal understanding of the FFDE process. Unnecessary delays before examination should be avoided, since excessive waiting time will often evoke excessive emotionality in an anxious officer. An attempt will normally be made to establish a degree of rapport between the officer and the FFDE provider. All methodological questions should be answered directly and honestly, such as those involving the nature of the examination and the relationship between the FFDE provider and the referring agency. The collection of general material (the face information sheet, rules of examination and confirmation of the identity of the officer) should proceed without delay. During the initial phase of the FFDE, some officers will refuse to sign needed documentation or submit to interview and testing. Both the LE executive and the FFDE provider should anticipate this likelihood before the first officer arrives, and have an established procedure in place to deal with this possibility. In some cases, the officer may sign a refusal notice and return to the department for further disciplinary procedures. In other cases, the department may prefer that the officer call his or her contact person (supervisor, chief, IA coordinator, etc.) within his or her department to discuss the matter before the officer departs. Although it is technically possible for the FFDE provider to proceed without consent in some settings (e.g., where the FFDE psychologist is an internal provider and the officer is covered under a mandatory program), the outcome is likely to be less than maximally helpful.

Once the officer has agreed to proceed, the FFDE provider will inform the officer of the general reasons for performing the FFDE in a manner that has been agreed between the department and the FFDE provider. For example, the FFDE provider may state, "I have received information [from the chief] that you have pointed a weapon at a fellow officer in the past week in violation of departmental regulations, and I have been asked to discuss that event and events that led up to it with you." At this point in the interaction, the other required tasks (the sorts of testing to be done) may be introduced and described. Once in agreement to proceed, the officer may be asked to describe the reasons that he or she understands have resulted in the referral for an FFDE. If the officer protests that he or she does not know the reason, the FFDE provider may provide an opportunity for discussion in which the officer is encouraged to describe suspected reasons, with the examiner cueing the officer as to events that may be likely to have led to the referral. For example, the FFDE provider may state, "I understand you have had some difficulty with your supervisor." This may give the officer an opening to discuss his or her problems with, or treatment by, the department. In no case should the FFDE provider show or surrender reports or documents to the officer that were transmitted by the department unless specifically authorized to do so by policy or contract. It is strongly advised that some method be used to have the officer report his or her view of the reason for FFDE in written format. When most of the officer's responses are verbal, the FFDE examiner should record a summary of the interview at the time it occurs and arrange for audio and video recording.

The FFDE provider should make it clear that no medical or psychological treatment of the officer (e.g., no doctor-patient relationship) or labeling of the officer (e.g., diagnosis) will take place as part of the FFDE. In no case should the FFDE provider continue an examination with any person with whom some earlier social or clinical connection exists (see Chapter 6). Such an officer must be referred to another qualified party without prejudice.

If the FFDE provider is an employee of the department or governmental agency (internal provider), the order from the commanding LE executive that the officer be examined should be shown to the officer and discussed verbally. The officer should be given appropriate warnings and **caveats** about all predetermined subjects (confidentiality, self-incrimination, and freedom to decline to answer questions), both verbally and in writing (see Appendix F). The FFDE provider should read aloud all consent-related documents to the officer while the officer reads along on an identical document so that the FFDE provider can be assured that the officer understands his or her rights. In some cases, officers may later claim that they did not comprehend the documents, were too apprehensive to appreciate their meaning, or misread them. Have the officer sign all individual written documents outlining the rules of the FFDE and verifying that the officer understands and accepts all the information contained in the written documents. Some FFDE providers may wish to separate the documentary components of the agreement (e.g., statement of purpose, confidentiality agreement, request for ADA [Americans with Disabilities Act] accommodation) into separate written documents for signatures to indicate an understanding of each section, whereas others may combine all such information into a few documents.

It is recommended that a standard release of information be obtained, although sometimes unnecessary under the departmental rules, to allow the provider to communicate with the LE executives and important others connected with the FFDE procedure. In cases in which outside clinical providers have treated the officer in a hospital or institution in the past, it is recommended that the examiner obtain independent releases of information for each party. The release of information for the treating hospital (usually a corporation) may or may not be valid releases of information for the individual treaters in that setting. The interview or direct data collection (such as testing) should not begin before all agreements have been signed. In the final analysis, the FFDE provider may offer to discontinue the entire FFDE if the officer cannot or will not cooperate fully and openly in all verbal and written agreements and tasks. The outcome or consequence of a refusal to continue must be made clear by both the FFDE provider and the referring departmental authority, and a citation of the appropriate rules should be made available (e.g., civil service regulation, departmental code of conduct) to the officer.

EXPLAINING THE NATURE OF ALL SELF-REPORT MATERIALS

The FFDE provider will most likely have a structured questionnaire or interview guide available for completion by the officer. Since the FFDE is an examination that is focused upon a distinct complaint or set of complaints, the interview guide should elicit responses to questions related to those complaints that brought the officer to the FFDE procedure, in addition to more general information. The contrast between the reports obtained individually from supervisors, civilians, family, and fellow officers and that of the officer under evaluation is an important part of the information that the FFDE provider must consider, and touches upon the officer's truthfulness, cooperation, sincerity, and attitudes. Since it is likely that the officer will be very concerned with being viewed as "not crazy" (a matter of worry for officers who are concerned about losing their gun and badge because of unfitness), the officer can be expected to avoid embarrassing or uninviting issues. Knowing the issues that are likely to be discussed can be critical to the FFDE provider in cases where the officer is in denial or is stonewalling during the examination.

The FFDE provider should review the structured questionnaire with the officer, asking for information to complete the social/behavioral picture offered by the officer, correct misunderstandings, and add information that has not been covered in sufficient detail by the questionnaires. For example, the officer may deny the use of alcohol in response to questions in the biographical document or questionnaire, only to state during examination that he or she meant not "on the job," or "since Saturday," or "more than a six-pack a week." Prompting may be useful in such cases (e.g., "Most people do a little drinking. I'm a little surprised to see you never have"). An officer may report that he or she does not recall any complaints about his or her work on a questionnaire, only to detail complex confrontations with a superior when reminded of an incident that he or she did not consider to be a "complaint." Wherever information is altered, revised, or modified by the officer between questionnaires and later oral examinations, the examiner should note changes in responses for later consideration. In some cases, the officer may omit information, such as by not responding to a written inquiry about a medical condition. The FFDE provider should be prepared to discuss the concept that underlies the missing response to be assured of the officer's understanding.

All officers must agree to proceed in a truthful, cooperative, and direct manner and avoid omissions, distortions and manipulations, or the procedure will surely be invalid. If the officer has been referred for FFDE under the optional model, and indicates that he or she considers the evaluation to be punishing or coercive in any way, the officer should be offered an immediate opportunity to discontinue the examination. The officer may be reminded that if he or she cannot or will not fully comply, the officer may refuse the evaluation and face administrative consequences at the officer's workplace. It may be useful for the FFDE provider to remind the officer that submitting directly to the FFDE process may have certain advantages. An analogy may be made with accepting a medical problem (e.g., high blood pressure) and correcting the difficulty (e.g., medication) before it leads to more serious problems (e.g., stroke).

If the officer has been referred under the mandatory model, the evaluation cannot be simply discontinued. However, the FFDE provider may remind the officer that refusal of complete participation may be viewed as insubordination to a lawful order, and is likely to result in further departmental charges. The officer should be instructed that full and unguarded disclosure is required and that the unwillingness or inability to cooperate in that manner will invalidate the evaluation. The officer should be asked to acknowledge verbally and in writing that the external provider is a consultant to his or her department and does not make police policy or decisions about his or her retention or discipline or treatment independently of his or her department. Refusal to accept or acknowledge this status is considered a form of noncooperation and raises the question of the procedure's validity. If allowed by contractual agreement, the FFDE provider may remind the officer that the opportunity to be examined by a disinterested professional party is a privilege that may be rejected in favor of administrative remedies. Review Chapters 14 and 15 for an analysis of the rights that the officer may retain under the Americans with Disabilities Act or the Family Medical Leave Act (FMLA).

ENDING THE FFDE CONTACT WITH THE OFFICER

Following formal testing, the FFDE provider should ask the examined officer whether he or she wishes to offer any final information for clarification or reconsider any of his or her responses. Frequently asked questions may be anticipated by the examiner and the LE executive, such as the following:

1. When will the officer "hear" about the results of the FFDE?
2. How will he or she hear of the results?
3. To what degree and in what way will he or she will get to review the findings?
4. Can the examiner tell him or her immediately what the report will find?

There are no fixed or universal responses to such questions. The LE executive and the FFDE provider may wish to prepare answers to these questions well in advance of the first FFDE referral.

IMMEDIATE LE EXECUTIVE FEEDBACK

In some cases, a general impression regarding the question of fitness may be conveyed verbally by the FFDE provider to the referring LE executive, pending a formal written report. Unfortunately, immediate feedback without the benefit of a careful review of all data, including psychometric testing, must be considered tentative and may do more harm than good in many situations. For example, if the candidate appears to have few problems, but further examination of testing results raises serious concerns, the department may have already taken action (placed the officer back on duty) following the initial impression, creating an unnecessary dilemma. Therefore, it is recommended that the FFDE provider wait until all materials have been examined before any recommendation is conveyed to the LE executive. In special or emergency situations, it may be possible to accept tentative findings of overall fitness/unfitness so that a plan may be made to replace the officer or reinstate the officer in order to have immediate patrol coverage. If this occurs, all parties must be prepared to defend such a decision with clear evidence and data that are likely to survive subsequent scrutiny.

THE MINIMUM NECESSARY RULE

It is important to acknowledge that the police psychologist must convey only *necessary* information to the referring LE executive within the FFDE report, in order to preserve the officer's privacy and maintain an employment-relevant tone to the report. This is because of the **minimum necessary rule.** The LE executive must not expect a complex examination of the officer's life outside of the events connected to the reason for referral, although the FFDE provider may have such information in his or her confidential files. The written FFDE report should be in the form of a consultation to the LE executive or agency, without including diagnosis or embarrassing detail.

The FFDE provider serves as the custodian of all technical and detailed information that may be in excess of that which is required to produce a meaningful report. In general, the department will be given only the information that it must have to meet its public safety and business necessity obligations in the employment context. The FFDE provider should examine all available documentation (such as information from medical and psychological providers), but such confidential information should not be conveyed directly to the LE executive. The FFDE provider should report only that information had been received from medical or mental health sources and the contents of this data had been integrated into the final recommendations, all without revealing protected health information.

INDEPENDENT TREATMENT REVIEW SERVICE

At the request of the law enforcement agency, the FFDE provider may offer an **independent treatment review service.** The purpose of the service is to allow for an unconstrained consultation between the FFDE provider and the law enforcement agency regarding the appropriateness and effectiveness of the purported treatment employed to address problems noted in the FFDE. Some departments, recognizing the variability in the treatment providers' understanding of the needs of law enforcement agencies within a given community, may wish an independent verification that the officer is undergoing effective treatment in preparation for a return to duty. The FFDE provider must secure a **release of information** from both the law enforcement agency and the examined officer before making inquiries or requesting records from clinical professionals or institutions that may have treated the officer. It is recommended that FFDE providers include in this document a statement to the clinical professional that the HIPAA (see Chapter 13) does not apply to administrative actions, and that the clinical professional should have the officer acknowledge and sign a full release of his or her records for FFDE purposes. All interested parties should be aware that the officer's treatment process may not be accessible to outside inquiry in many cases (see Chapters 13, 14, and 15), even with the explicit and informed consent of the officer.

PSYCHOLOGY AND LAW ENFORCEMENT PERSONNEL METHODS

There are many general methods by which the data collection and analysis regarding an FFDE may be conducted professionally. The following is a model outline of one recommended approach to FFDE data collection. Standard published psychological testing (psycho-metrics) has been a normal part of both FFDEs and clinical examinations for many decades. These instruments have the advantage of allowing the psychologist to compare the responses of one officer with the combined responses of many persons that are in one way or another similar to the examinee. This form of examination is similar to the way a physician uses blood testing to supplement general history taking and physical examination in medical assessments. A number of technical problems in psychometric test use should be understood by the police executive in the FFDE process. Many concerns are beyond the scope of this book, but a general introduction of psycho-metrics may be useful for LE executives and other nonpsychologists who are responsible for officer supervision and referral to FFDE procedures. Psychometric instruments should never be employed by unqualified persons, for FFDEs or otherwise.

Objective Psychological Personality Testing

Objective personality testing refers to psychometric tests or instruments that are interpreted by comparing an examinee's responses (usually in the form of scores) to a summary of standardized responses obtained from a large sample of persons in earlier testing. In contrast, subjectively scored tests require special tester judgment in observing or scoring responses (such as an inkblot test) and the meaning of the score or response may vary from test examiner to test examiner. Objective tests often involve the presentation of a large set of statements to which the person responds by "endorsing" (indicating by making a mark on the scoring sheet) a multiple-choice or true-false option. For example, the statement, "I cannot sleep," may be followed by an opportunity to agree or disagree or to respond on a scale from "very true" to "very false." The method allows for complex statistical comparisons of the subjects' responses or patterns of responses with persons who have known difficulties. For a simple example, persons suffering from depression are much more likely to endorse statements about being sad, not having an interest in life events, and thinking of suicide than are others, even if they are reluctant to speak about their depression in conversation. The degree of depression may be ascertained if scientific studies have established that persons who are more depressed report a larger number of such complaints than others without serious depression. In addition, studies using certain tests may have demonstrated patterns of responses that reveal attempts to maximize or minimize a person's willingness to be open and honest, indicating a degree or bias or distortion in his or her responses (which may be summarized as validity scales). Although many forms of psychological testing **(cognitive testing)** have been used in FFDEs, objective personality testing is the most commonly used and practical procedure. Following is a brief discussion of some of the most commonly used objective personality tests.

The Minnesota Multiphasic Personality Inventory, Second Edition (MMPI-2)

The MMPI-2 (Butcher et al., 1989) and its predecessor have been called the workhorses of police psychology. Although developed initially for mental illness diagnostic purposes, this test is actually mandated for officer candidates' selection by law or custom in some venues. It is composed of 567 statements that sample a variety of emotional and mental issues, which the officer indicates to be true or false as they apply to him or her. It is useful in comparing a given person's responses against those of clinically described subgroups on a statistical basis (Graham, 2000). Some disagreement exists about its use with nonclinical groups (such as police officers) given its clinical norming, a problem that has been recently addressed with the inclusion of law enforcement norms to supplement the standard scoring system (e.g., placing officers on a distribution of responses against other officers).

Although developed in the 1940s, the uses of the MMPI have been supported by numerous **concurrent** and **predictive validity** studies since that time. The MMPI and its revisions (MMPI-2) provide a graphic profile (chart) of the basic thirteen scales in which high scores generally indicate statistically significance relevant to possible mental problems (Graham, 2000). The validity scales provide information about the degree to which the person's self-reports may be considered trustworthy.

In *Soroka v. Dayton Hudson Corp.* (1989), a class action was filed against Target for using the original MMPI as a job-screening tool. The district court found that the test items as then existed to be intrusive and offensive. Such concerns contributed to the development of the MMPI-2, in which offending questions were removed. In 1989, the test publisher, University of Minnesota Press, introduced the revised MMPI-2. This revision updated the wording of test items, introduced new scales, and provided norms that better reflected the current population. However, this change caused some loss of the usability of decades of research that had been an outgrowth of studies using the original MMPI. For example, the predictive power of earlier MMPI studies with police officers did not retain its strength with the MMPI-2 (Brewster and Stoloff, 1999). Many subsequent studies within police academies and selection procedures for municipal and state police officers (Rostow et al., 1999; Davis et al., 1999) have supported the current continued use of the MMPI-2 in police populations, although in ways that may differ from the original test. The MMPI remains a clinical test that is useful in, although never specifically designed for, law enforcement FFDEs.

Personality Assessment Inventory

The **Personality Assessment Inventory** (PAI) is a relatively recent objective test in which social and personality statements can be endorsed with a "false" to "very true" four-option format (Morey, 1991). The PAI is composed of statements that are less complex than those in the MMPI-2, reportedly requiring a minimal reading level in order to complete the test. This instrument has a number of psychometric advantages over earlier tests, including the use of dual norms, which allows the officer to be compared with both normal and abnormal standardization groups. Because the test comprises 344 statements only, the test-taking time is reduced substantially when compared with the MMPI-2, although some psychologists believe that important information may be lost because of the smaller statement pool. A supplemental norm set (PAI-SP) was developed for law enforcement use, based upon two cohorts of 2,088 state and county police and 1,419 municipal officers. In spite of such norms and promising psychometric features, little validity information exists regarding the predictive uses of this test with law enforcement populations.

Inwald Personality Inventory

One of the earliest and best-recognized police tests, the **Inwald Personality Inventory** (Inwald, 1980, 1984), was normed on a sample of 1,512 male and 873 female public safety applicants. It is a 310-item true-false response instrument that was designed to assess psychological functioning in law enforcement settings (Inwald and Shusman, 1984). Scales include Alcohol, Drugs, Driving Violations, Job Difficulties, Trouble with the Law and Society, and Absence Abuse. Attitudes and temperament are also measured.

Other Personality Inventories

Other available instruments include the Law Enforcement Assessment and Development Report (LEADR), the Millon Clinical Multiaxial Inventory-III (MCMI-III) (Millon, Davis, and Millon, 1997), the California Psychological Inventory (CPI) (Gough, 1996), and the Sixteen Personality Factor Questionnaire (Cattell, Cattell, and Cattell, 1993). In addition, a large number of specialty tests may be used to address specific questions raised by a particular assessment question ("Does the officer suffer from post-traumatic stress disorder?"), such as the Posttraumatic Stress Diagnostic Scale (Foa, 1995), none of which have law enforcement–specific norms or validity studies. The LE executive should be comfortable in the knowledge that police psychologists are familiar with the application and limitations of whatever tests they choose for FFDE use.

COGNITIVE TESTING AND FFDEs

Cognitive (intellectual) or **neuropsychological testing** (brain functioning) may also be employed in FFDEs if called for by the circumstances of the referral or the reported symptoms or behaviors of the officer. For example, an officer may have suffered a head injury in some manner, and current neuropsychological ability may be questioned. Such testing tends to be time-consuming and expensive, requires specialized examiner training, and, therefore, is seldom employed in FFDEs. The infrequency of the use of such testing in the FFDE setting means that its use for police employment purposes may depend upon its extrapolation from clinical (general population) situations. In general, the LE executive must verify that the FFDE provider possesses the specialized training and experience needed in work with armed, commissioned law enforcement officers within important questions of public safety.

INTRODUCTION TO STATISTICAL CONSIDERATIONS FOR POLICE EXECUTIVES

The LE executive may have noted references to terms such as *norms* and *standardization,* the basic machinery of statistical interpretation and decision making. Norms are statistical distributions of responses to test questions in which the response patterns of persons who have taken a test under standard conditions can be compared meaningfully. Standardization refers to the conditions under which the norms were collected, including the characteristics (age, race, occupation, education, etc.) of the group from which they were collected. Consider the following example:

The Case of Student Jim

Jim answers a set of math problems on given test and obtains a score of 15 (i.e., 15 correct answers out of 30 items). There is no meaning to this number until the distribution of scores from a relevant reference group (e.g., his math class) is considered. The score of 15 may be very low for college students or CPAs, or very high for grade school children or persons suffering from Alzheimer's disease. Norms can express where the test taker stands in terms of others taking that test, once the comparison group is clearly described. Only then can the instructor decide whether Jim is doing well or needs remediation. The person using such test data may also wish to know whether the test was taken in a busy office under time pressure or a quiet classroom with unlimited time. This is the test's standardization, or standard manner of administration, a bit of information that is useful in understanding the meaning and uses of the test score.

Most norms are obtained as a result of some research study or set of studies performed in one or more places with specific populations by the test author or persons who have similar research interests. Most tests used in police work have norms that were established originally with the general population (nonpolice) or by testing certain clinical groups (such as persons suffering from PTSD), to determine the typical distribution of responses by those certain persons compared with others.

When it comes to establishing police officer norms, some studies use large numbers of subjects in their sample; others have small numbers. Some studies have been conducted in small departments and other in large agencies. Some include sizable women and minority representation in their studies, and others have little such diversity. The psychologist must always be alert to the particular manner in which a given test was normed and standardized. Among the issues that police psychologists assess when looking at the utility of a test is the inclusion of police officer norms and the degree to which the standardization group was similar of the current department. Therefore, tests must be used with care in making important decisions since the original **normative group** or standardization method may be totally dissimilar to the currently examined group. It should be noted that the court are concerned about psychological test decisions regarding the similarity of the standardization sample to the parties to whom it should generalize (see *U.S. v. White Horse* in Chapter 10). This is another reason why the use of "computerized" testing without a competent psychologist overseeing and interpreting the test profile outcome is dangerous and inappropriate in an FFDE situation.

PREDICTIVE VALIDITY

Psychological testing includes many forms of validity, but the one of greatest concern in police psychology should be that of predictive validity. Even if the normative sample is an exact model (in membership and method of data collection) of the current department from which the referred officer has been drawn, the results of such an FFDE may still have little meaning without demonstrated predictive validity. *Predictive validity* is used to describe the relationship between test scores and a **criterion measure** (some important outcome or result) that has been shown to have existed in past research. In other words, does the test score predict some later event or set of events (such as the officer's excessive use of force) that is clearly important for the LE executive?

Student Jim and Predictive Validity

Jim's math score of 15 put him at the ninetieth percentile (he did better than 90 percent of other members of the class that took the test). Does this mean that he can make change and keep simple accounts in a retail store? The relationship between a score of 15 and the some practical measure of actual retail store "work" is one example of predictive validity. Here the psychologist is trying to predict successful performance in certain situations that may be somewhat different from the testing circumstance, information that would be very useful if is trustworthy. Without this information, knowing where a student stands on the math test is of little use for the forecasting of his or her actual work performance. In addition, the demands of math-related work may vary from store to store. Some stores require employees to actually make change for customers "in their heads" in real time, whereas other stores have computerized cash registers that do this for them. Even if the test can forecast some "real-life" capabilities, an alteration in the specific demands of a given employer can easily upset this prediction.

Consider a proposed score on an LE officer self-rating test (a test in which officers report how well they think they perform a set of police-related jobs). The test scores may be compared against systematic reports by supervisors in a way that is common and meaningful in police work (e.g., if officers say that they perform well, do the supervisors agree?). The relationship between the officers' self-ratings and the supervisors' reports contributed to the psychologist's understanding of the meaning of that test's score. Only studies with meaningful outcome criteria can reveal the practical significance of a given score on a given test. The provider should attempt to connect the data derived from testing and interviewing with officers to recommendations based upon research-based considerations.

CLINICAL, FORENSIC, AND FITNESS-FOR-DUTY EVALUATIONS

It is clear that the FFDE provider should be able to answer certain questions regarding the technical features of the procedure that had been selected in the assessment methodology. One way to understand the special difficulties of the psychological FFDE is for the LE executive to understand differences among traditional forms of evaluation, such as the clinical evaluation, the forensic evaluation, and the FFDE.

The **clinical evaluation** is a psychometric and interview-based procedure conducted with a person who has submitted for examination voluntarily, often at some personal cost, because of some mental, emotional, or medical difficulty within their lives. A confidential, patient-doctor relationship is often established as part of this process, and it is generally understood that the client "owns" the evaluation and controls its use and disposition. The provider cannot release any report or speak/transmit information (whole or part) without explicit permission from the patient (see Chapter 13). The goal of the evaluation is to diagnose one or more problems and offer possible therapy recommendations for treatable conditions. The patient may self-refer for the evaluation or be referred by a specialist (e.g., family practitioner, psychiatrist) or significant other (e.g., family member). Treatment may begin simultaneously with the evaluation. Referral to others (e.g., neurologists and substance abuse programs) may be recommended with or without concurrent treatment by the evaluator.

The **forensic evaluation** is a psychometric and interview-based procedure conducted with a person who may or may not have submitted voluntarily for examination but who was referred by a court or attorney as a condition of making some claim of injury or disability in an administrative/civil court (worker compensation or personal injury claim) or criminal court (insanity). A confidential, patient-doctor relationship is usually absent, and there is usually an agreement that the referring source pays for and controls the disposition of the report. The provider can release the report or speak/transmit information (whole or part) without explicit permission from the patient in most cases. The goal of the evaluation is to diagnose one or more problems and to reflect upon possible therapy modalities for treatable conditions. The patient does not usually self-refer for the evaluation but is referred by a specialist or administrative/legal entity (e.g., WC, courts, or attorney). Treatment does not usually begin simultaneously with the evaluation, and the evaluator may or may not continue to provide services to the patient. Referral to others may or may not be recommended.

The fitness-for-duty evaluation (FFDE) is a psychometric and interview-based procedure conducted with a person who usually does not request examination. It is at no cost to the employee and is always requested by an employer who has reason to believe that the employee represents some difficulty (safety or business necessity) regarding the workplace as a result of some mental problem. A confidential, patient-doctor relationship is always absent, and it is generally understood that the referring source (employer) controls its use and disposition of the report. The provider must be able to release the report or speak/transmit information (whole or part) to the employer without explicit permission from the patient once proper consent is obtained prior to evaluation. The goal of the evaluation is less to diagnose problems than it is to determine the likelihood that the person presents a mentally or emotionally based danger to the employer or other persons by active misconduct (positive risk) or the inability to perform the job (negative risk). In some cases, the goal of the evaluation is to determine whether the employee is impaired in a manner that precludes being able to perform the core tasks of the job. Treatment by the FFDE provider does not occur as a matter of clinical conflict of interest. Referral to others may or may not be recommended.

The LE executive and the police psychologist must have a clear vision of the uses and goals of the FFDE and the role played by various data sources in the understanding of the referral problem and the recommendations that may follow. Each step in the practical application of the FFDE methodology should reflect concern with scientific and rational application of psychometric and clinical techniques in the examination and data collection phases of the process. To turn such matters over to the FFDE provider without a clear understanding of that individual's approach to assessment and evaluation may result in serious consequences for the LE executive (see *Robles v. Hoyos,* 1998). Lacking such an understanding, the LE executive may not be in a position to differentiate between useful and inappropriate provider opinions. It is important to understand that the LE executive is ultimately responsible for designating the internal or external FFDE provider, and should be able to make an educated judgment about the adequacy of any given procedure before the matter becomes an issue in a legal tribunal or civil service hearing.

Chapter 9

Fitness-for-Duty Report Recommendations

Although I can accept talking scarecrows, lions and great wizards of emerald cities, I find it hard to believe there is no paperwork involved when your house lands on a witch.

Dave James

As noted previously, the FFDE provider should avoid generating reports that contain intrusive clinical or personal information, which, in any case, are seldom needed by police managers. Observations and discussions about early physical or sexual abuse, or details of old, limited substance abuse should usually not be included in the report. Detailed neutral commentary, such as a discussion of educational history or early adult living circumstances, may be unnecessary and distracting. Of course, relevant (violence, threats, recent or intense substance dependency, etc.) behaviors must be included because they are generally considered to be critical law enforcement liability issues

SPECIAL RECORDS SECTION

Once the FFDE provider renders the report, it must be stored in a specially protected file, regardless of whether it was produced by an internal or external provider. If placed in the general personnel file, the information is likely to be discovered by clerical and other administrative persons—a matter of grave concern if the officer's confidentiality is breached and the report contents become a matter of common conversation. This breach of privacy is not only damaging to the personal reputation of the officer and his or her family, but it also defeats the future policy of the department to employ high standards of responsible supervision. In addition, such an eventuality may result in legal action against the department and its leadership (see Chapter 13), reduced morale within the department, and discourage both supervisors and officers who may wish to may elect the FFDE procedure from doing so rather than moving directly to disciplinary or discharge procedures. The presence of an FFDE report in a general personnel file may result in the report being inadvertently exposed to non–law enforcement persons who may access the file for reasons unconnected to the FFDE report (e.g., health insurance providers, retirement division personnel).

One answer to the problem would be to create a **special records center,** inaccessible to immediate supervisors, clerical workers, and employment specialists (insurance, administrative), but secured by the chief and highly placed senior commanders. In addition to FFDE reports, medical records and other specially protected documents may be kept at this location. It is recommended that such "health records" files be kept apart from internal affairs files. IA files may be defined as records that pertain to investigations of officers by departmental personnel for criminal breaches of the official rules of the department. Although IA may recommend the referral of the officer for an FFDE, the product of such a FFDE should not be stored in an IA file because of the need for the review of such files by those parties (e.g., outside auditors, litigants) who may violate the officer's privacy inadvertently. An examination of the FFDE report by IA personnel may be necessary in the course of investigation (so that guidance may be obtained in how to proceed with a given case), but the report itself should be removed to a protected location thereafter.

The actual tests and interview notes obtained or created by the FFDE provider should remain within the protected control of the FFDE provider. In the case of internal providers, the psychology services division may provide a protected **psychology records repository** in which both the test protocols, interview records, and the final report may be secured. When an external provider conducts the FFDE, the test protocols and report may be secured within the control of the contractual provider, as is common with most medical and psychological practices. The external provider becomes the custodian of these records, protecting the officer and the department by preventing unnecessary exposure of sensitive and easily misunderstood materials to personnel who should not possess this information. Outside parties may request (or subpoena) a release of such information by contacting the department (owners of the records) who may then direct the custodian to release that required information. One important reason for the use of outside providers for FFDE purposes is because of the greater assurances against misuse of psychological records that may be difficult to avoid within a bureaucratic system.

POSTEVALUATION OUTCOME ASSESSMENT AND DISTORTION

Officers who are referred for FFDEs may show a strong desire to contest the notion that they are mentally impaired out of a variety of social or personal motivations. Officers have been known to state that they would rather be found to be corrupt or criminally culpable than labeled as "crazy," because of the response of fellow officers (see Chapter 2). Even substantial evidence of emotional dyscontrol or verified reports of bizarre behaviors are unlikely to convince the officer to acknowledge his or her own mental illness during the FFDE procedure. Resistances to the assessment procedure, lack of effort in assessment participation or distortion of the responses to direct questions are commonly found in both interviews and psychometric test responses. For such reasons, it is important that the FFDE report indicates whether the officer had been cooperative in the examination (both interview as well as formal testing) or has attempted to defeat the examination in some way. Such response patterns result in an invalid assessment (sometimes called "fake good" outcome) and are a form of insubordination and noncompliance within the requirements of the FFDE. During the interview, the officer may have avoided answering questions directly, appeared to add impossible story elements to his or her description of the complaint, or showed hesitation, inconsistencies, or contradictions. His or her report of the event that led to the referral may be at extreme divergence from the witness reports of the same events. In such divergent report circumstances, it may be advisable for the FFDE provider to report both the officer's and department's versions, with contrasting commentary, and allow the responsible police executives determine the degree to which the officer had been evasive.

POSTASSESSMENT TREATMENT RECOMMENDATIONS

A consideration of the FFDE process concerns the issue of post-evaluation treatment if a mental or emotional problem is found. Often, law enforcement agency health insurance coverage for mental health problems is inadequate or the health insurance carriers may not authorize coverage for the FFDE treatment recommendations. In some cases, the insurance contract may allow for a few "counseling meetings" or a referral for medication management when, in the opinion of the FFDE provider, the officer requires a great deal more assistance. An attempt should be made to anticipate this difficulty and resolve the lack of treatment resources in one of a number of ways that may include setting aside a special fund for such treatment or establishing a special program with the departmental health insurance provider to offer services to those who may benefit from treatment.

On many occasions, the outcome of the FFDE may not be a recommendation for standard mental health treatment, but rather it may suggest a need for special training or supervision (*City of Canton, Ohio v. Harris,* 1989). Plans for such recommendations should be made long before the need is forced upon the agency, so as to avoid an urgent "scramble" to find appropriate services under time pressure. The agency and the FFDE provider should develop practical arrangements to make use of such training or supervision programs under circumstances in which treatment does not appear to address the needs that the FFDE has identified. Contacts with professional law enforcement training corporations may allow the LE executive to identify useful and relevant programs to train officers in racial/cultural fairness, management of mentally impaired suspects and witnesses, and sexual harassment.

On rare but important occasions, the FFDE provider may have an obligation to report that the officer suffers from a condition that presents a clear danger to the community (i.e., sexual predator). The FFDE provider should be prepared to alert LE executives to the need for independent investigation as a public protective measure, since the FFDE itself will likely not be usable in criminal prosecution.

FFDE PROVIDER RECOMMENDATIONS

The defensibility and usefulness of FFDEs may rest ultimately on the recommendations offered by the provider to the law enforcement executive responsible for the officer. As noted previously, the FFDE is neither a general discussion of the officer's life nor an attempt to convey detailed technical and diagnostic materials to the LE executive. The FFDE provider should be able to offer written conclusions that have been built around one of four major outcome recommendations (unfit, unfit but treatable, no discernable mental health problems, and invalid presentation). Although the outline of the referral complaints against the officer and the officer's responses to those complaints may be covered in the written report, the details concerning collected data (including psychometric testing) are given as a brief description only. The interpretation of the data is presented indirectly in the outcome recommendations. The FFDE provider should make a conscientious effort to avoid clinical language, unnecessary personal detail and explicit treatment recommendations in any report to a law enforcement executive **(minimum necessary rule).** Similarly, issues that may personally embarrass the officer should be avoided in any discussions with LE executives, as they had been in the body of the written report. A number of specific and detailed recommendations within the basic report are possible, such as adding a finding of work-related injury (a possible workers compensation issue) when an officer's psychological or physical impairment is related to a clear employment incident or event (e.g., gunshot injury). As a general rule, remaining within the limits of the following series of options is an effective guide in both maintaining the privacy of the officer and providing the department with needed information.

Officer Is Unfit

The officer is unfit and unlikely to become fit in any foreseeable short-term treatment sequence. Examples may include a significant injury to the brain or the emergence of a psychosis (severe loss of contact with reality). If an unanticipated resolution to the reported problem occurs, the officer may reapply for active service at a later date.

In one such case, a veteran officer had inadvertently shot himself through the head in a staged suicide attempt meant as a bid for sympathy from his family. He had a history of mishandling firearms and had earlier made threats of self-destruction to obtain concessions from his family. A history of such conduct, even without his current traumatic brain injury, would not be a positive indicator of desirable future officer conduct. There were ample signs of cognitive and motor/sensory deficits secondary to the injury as was revealed by the psychological and neuropsychological evaluation. The officer's verbal ability was compromised by the injury and the officer had a severe visual decrement. Recovery to the level that would allow the officer to work safely in a standard law enforcement setting was judged by the police psychologist to be unlikely, and a medical retirement was suggested.

Officer Is Unfit but Treatable

The officer is currently unfit, but there is a fair possibility of problem resolution with treatment within a reasonable time frame. In some cases, the officer may be given medical leave for the duration of acute treatment, either because the nature of the treatment requires activities that interfere with business necessity (e.g., hospitalization) or for reasons of public safety. In some cases, the officer may only require modification of duties (e.g., desk job) during the treatment period or until the officer has been restored to acceptable levels of functioning. Examples may include stress disorders, transient depressive and anxiety disorders, and alcohol abuse difficulties. It is important to recognize that the possibility of recovery is not a guarantee of restoration, and that many factors may interfere with the officer's response to treatment.

A ten-year veteran patrol officer had been exhibiting depression over a period of weeks, characterized by low self-esteem, insomnia, and thoughts of hopelessness. He had been hiding from his superiors and avoiding areas of likely traffic violations or accidents which might have created a demand for him to perform his duties. Other officers had complained that he had not been responding to radio calls and that his absence had placed them in some danger because of insufficient manpower to cover their responsibilities. He was aware that he was in need of assistance and responded to treatment following a major depressive episode several years earlier. After reporting his difficulties to his superiors, the officer was referred for an FFDE. In some settings, a referral to an EAP may have been an option as well, but the department sought assurance that the officer did not represent a threat to departmental efficiency. An EAP referral will usually result in having at least some part of the officer's communications held in confidence by the EAP provider (see Chapter 2) and not accessible to the department. If the LE executive has reason to believe that the officer's behavior may pose a threat to the public or to the safe and effective operation of the department, an FFDE referral may be preferable, since it should more directly inform responsible LE executives of the liability risk posed by an officer.

The FFDE revealed a renewed depressive episode, and the officer was given medical leave to be treated intensively in a hospital-based, day treatment program involving medication management and both individual and group cognitive therapy. The officer had recovered well when placed in this same program some years earlier. The officer was comfortable with this solution, since it did not require that he embrace a new treatment approach or unfamiliar therapists. His family was supportive and participated in phases of the treatment. Following a **posttreatment reevaluation** (that included a review of treatment records and comparison psychometric testing), he as returned to full duty in four weeks and has remained on duty for many years.

This example is a particularly good instance of how an FFDE procedure involving the officer, his or her department, and the police psychologist can yield maximal benefit to all concerned. Unfortunately (see Chapter 16), a number of FFDE-related difficulties appear to be developing that may sadly result in the treatment recommendation being employed less frequently in the future. Among these are the difficulty of finding and engaging police-knowledgeable treatment providers, securing payment for treatment, obtaining clinical records upon which to base a reasonable return-to-duty review, and accepting release-to-duty letters as reliable and founded in an understanding of the risk to public safety that such a release implies.

In many cases, counseling (also called **psychotherapy** or cognitive therapy) can be ordered lawfully as an alternative to disciplinary sanction. FFDEs often result in a recommendation of mandatory counseling or other psychological or psychiatric treatment. In one example, an officer was ordered into counseling after engaging in a graphic discussion regarding his earlier sexual encounters in the presence of two female employees of the police department. A Missouri court held that a department's order that the officer submit to counseling was lawful, and sustained his termination for refusal to seek treatment. That same officer was known to use loud and abusive language with co-workers and profanity (not just with fellow officers) while performing official police duties (*Curtis v. Bd. of Police Com'rs of Kansas City,* 1992). In some states, such as Wisconsin, LE administrators are permitted to require counseling prior to allowing an officer to return to duty (*Brown County Sheriff's Dept. v. Brown County Sheriff's Dept. Non-Supervisory Employees Association,* 1995).

Officer Showed No Burden of Mental Illness

The officer shows no discernable mental health or suspected medical problem either on detailed examination or by self-report. The difficulties or conflicts that motivated the referral for an FFDE may be best accounted for by personality, attitude, or social relationship difficulties for the officer and, if the behavior associated with such difficulties is prohibited by departmental or other regulation, the officer should be referred for disciplinary, training, or administrative action.

After complaining about supposed preferential treatment given to racial and cultural minority officers in his department, an officer was confronted by his sergeant, who was a member of one such minority group. The officer insisted that he had a right to interpret life events through his "personal experiences," which he claimed were based in "traditional values," and which were characterized by the use of racially derogatory names and concepts. Shortly thereafter, the officer made a set of insubordinate administrative decisions that were in direct defiance of orders given by that same sergeant. The superior officer interpreted these events as an example of insubordinate behavior, which stemmed from the officer's racial attitude, and referred him for an FFDE, a step that was approved by the departmental commander.

During the FFDE, the officer appeared rigid and self-important, but he did not appear to be suffering mental illness or psychopathology by any current definition. He enumerated specific instances of preferential treatment that he claimed had been given to minority officers, and which were denied majority officers. His psychological evaluation was unremarkable and revealed no psychopathological symptoms or impairments. In an open interview, the officer denied a claim of illness and expressly rejected the possibility that his behavior was in any manner defective, emotionally driven, or inappropriate. The officer did not request assistance in any way and requested an opportunity to "clear his name" through some form of departmental review or hearing.

He indeed held nonviolent views regarding race that were deemed by the examiner to be archaic and repugnant, but which were not uncommon in parts of his local community. The sociological origin of his views could be readily identified. It was suggested that disciplinary action go forward without regard to considerations of possible mental impairment. A recommendation was made to his department that consideration be given to offering the officer an opportunity to attend racial fairness training and other forms of diversity-based educational experiences. There was no evidence of immediate danger or threat posed by the officer's conduct. Referral for counseling was not seen as a promising alternative given the stigma that the officer believed was associated with such a referral.

Officer Produced an Invalid Presentation

The lack of cooperation, honesty, effort, or openness by the officer has resulted in a failure to allow for an examination by which the examiner would be able to reach reasonable psychological conclusions.

Following an incident in which an officer, assigned to a position as a firearms instructor, killed a trainee in a training accident, the officer appeared to sink into confusion and depression. His wife told the officer's commander that the officer had stopped his normal sleeping routine, and fellow officers noted that his description of the accident (which was witnessed by many persons) had begun to change in self-justifying ways. He now reported that the use of a loaded weapon (which had been prohibited in the training area) had been part of the "planned" training exercise that resulted in the fatality. In the FFDE, the officer reported that he suffered "no effect" of the incident upon his psychological life, appeared to blame the trainee for the accident and denied reports of distress mentioned by others. On psychometric testing, validity scales were elevated (indicating that he may be underestimating the degree of his emotional difficulty) and no useful self-report information could be obtained. The officer informed the examiner that he was to be returned to a firearms training position soon, but communications with the department indicated that the officer was clearly informed that he could never perform that function in the future. The departmental and officer reports did not correspond with each other. He seemed to have lost the esteem of his colleagues and his cherished position as a firearms instructor, and clearly had suffered a significant setback in his career. Yet his psychometric and interview presentation was superficially that of an ideally happy person, almost to a delusional degree. In the face of such a stonewalled response to the FFDE, the examiner concluded that the officer had declined the opportunity to cooperate with the FFDE and that no reasonable picture of the officer's mental functioning could be given relative to his vocational functioning. In a manner of speaking, this outcome was no different than the officer refusing to submit to psychological evaluation.

RELEASE OF RECORDS TO THIRD PARTIES

As a general rule, it is not advisable to share FFDE reports with anyone outside of the limited circle of decision makers within the LE agency (chief, IA commander, departmental attorney, civil service board, etc), except under special conditions. In general, the FFDE is not a simple clinical examination (see Chapter 7), and is not meant to be a guide for treatment, although a qualified treatment provider may find it useful. As noted previously, the courts have held that exposure to the content of such reports to examined officers may allow them to manipulate subsequent impressions given in succeeding FFDEs and defeat the purpose of the examination. In the same manner, technical psychological documents (test material, questions, scoring, etc.) are withheld from nonpsychologists, including the LE executive, to prevent subsequent misuse and a destruction of the utility of testing. Deparmental personnel who are not involved directly in the issues surrounding the FFDE should not be informed about the FFDE (the reasons why it is needed) and should have no access to oral or written information in connection with the FFDE.

In cases in which feedback of FFDE results to the referred officer is required, it may be satisfied in one of three ways: (1) in a meeting format, often with an open discussion involving the LE executives and legal counsel; (2) in an brief written report; or (3) as a closed communication to treatment providers at the appropriate professional level. Note that the Fair Credit Reporting Act (see Chapter 15) may require a release of the unedited report to the officer, making the need to simplify and provide only minimal materials very important.

On occasion, third parties may wish to secure the FFDE report for some unintended purpose, such as an effort to amplify the weaknesses of an officer in support of a lawsuit against him or her and the department. For the most part, a third party should find it extremely difficult to obtain an officer's psychological report, even if subpoenaed in a civil rights suit against the officer and the department. In *Mason v. Stock* (1994), a citizen filed a federal civil rights suit against a department and individual officers for "roughing him up" and wrongly accusing him of DUI. In the course of the litigation, the plaintiff subpoenaed copies of the officers' entire personnel files and internal affairs records. The federal district court held that all records were to be released, except the psychological reports. These were viewed as being of too highly sensitive and personal nature as to justify a privilege.

On the other hand, the need of the courts for evidence may be balanced with the need for officer privacy. New Jersey Superior Court (trial level) held that a "balancing test" must be applied to determine whether an officer's psychological report may be released in a suit against the officer and the department. The city of Newark was sued for **negligent retention** of an officer accused of assaulting a citizen. The plaintiff sought copies of the officer's prehire psychological records and a subsequent fitness-for-duty psychological report. The court held that these records are ordinarily confidential, but a balancing test must apply where due process rights are clearly at stake. It held that the reports have clear relevance to the claim against the city of its alleged breach of its duty to properly psychologically and psychiatrically evaluate the officer. The court wrote that the release of the reports were required, since "the existence and nature of the examinations performed on the City's behalf are crucial to the proof of the plaintiff's case" and are "similarly crucial to the City's defenses" in order to "refute plaintiff's allegations of negligence and gross negligence" (*Valentin v. Bootes,* 1998).

Once an FFDE report is produced by the internal or external provider, the LE executive should be able to understand and apply its contents with discernment and intelligence. The FFDE report itself must be treated with confidentiality and respect (for example, kept in a special protected file) above other forms of personnel documentation. Exposure of information contained in such reports may be damaging to all parties concerned, and may result in adverse and embarrassing legal repercussions. As explained previously, the report should contain minimal personal information only to ensure privacy and discourage misuse. Since the body of the FFDE report does not contain detailed personal information or diagnostic suggestions for the department's consumption, the LE executive should place the greatest emphasis upon the recommendation section. It has been suggested that the available recommendations be understood and approved by general stakeholders (civil service board, personnel section, human relations, internal affairs, police union, command staff, etc.) as it pertains to the particular department before the first FFDE is attempted. Nonapproved recommendations should be avoided because of the risk of overstepping the department's authority in addressing personal matters. Although somewhat limiting to the report writing options of the FFDE provider, the advantages of a uniform and consistent use of FFDE recommendations cannot be overestimated. Fluctuating and inconstant recommendations not only invite lawsuits, but also open the FFDE method to contempt and derision of many stakeholders, since the differential or controversial treatment of referred officers creates the appearance of a subjective and cryptic FFDE procedure.

SECTION III:
FORENSIC ISSUES IN
FITNESS-FOR-DUTY EVALUATIONS

Chapter 10

Expert Witnesses and the Defense of Selection/Fitness Decisions

The criminal trial today is . . . a kind of show-jumping contest in which the rider for the prosecution must clear every obstacle to succeed.

Robert Mark
Commissioner, London Metropolitan Police

THE CASE OF DETECTIVE REED

Detective Reed has made a remarkable number of undercover narcotic arrests for the Anytown Police Department. His supervisor, however, has noted that Reed seemed to be physically involved in the subduing and handcuffing of every arrested suspect, regardless of whether he was serving duty as decoy or backup. After noting that many suspects who were arrested by Detective Reed required hospitalization before incarceration, Detective Reed was referred for an FFDE. The FFDE found Detective Reed fit for duty, although several recommendations were made to improve the detective's training and supervision. The department followed these recommendations, and efforts were made to improve both the officer's training opportunities and the directness of his supervision. Sometime thereafter, a lawsuit was filed against Detective Reed and departmental policymakers in connection with an accusation of civil rights violations (43 USC 1983) suffered by a number of suspects. The police psychologist was able to testify as an expert that the department had engaged in appropriate methods to explore the possible mental impairment that might impinge upon law enforcement duties in a relevant and scientifically defendable manner. The municipal liability aspect of the complaint ended in a summary judgment for the defense.

There is no point in conducting an FFDE if expert testimony regarding such a procedure is not admissible in court as part of the defense of the department. In the usual circumstance, the department may be sued for failure to responsibly select, examine, and supervise an officer who is said to have done something unlawful (e.g., violate constitutional rights). For example, an officer shoots a person in a situation in which the legitimacy of that action is questioned. The injured party files a lawsuit, during which time it becomes clear that the officer had a history of personal and law enforcement-related behavioral difficulties (see Chapter 11). The plaintiff's attorney deposes the responsible law enforcement executive and asks what had been done to deal with the questionable officer at the time that such conduct had been reported. The fitness-for-duty methodology designed by the departmental police psychologist may be offered in response (along with selection, training, and supervisory methods). The attorney for the department may attempt to introduce the police psychologist as an expert to defend the scientific and professional adequacy of the department's FFDE procedures.

In another case, an incumbent officer may be dismissed following an FFDE that indicated that the officer was unfit to continue with law enforcement duties. The department and its policymakers may be accused by the officer's attorneys with unlawfully discharging the officer, whom they claim to be "completely unimpaired." They sue the FFDE provider and LE executive for malpractice (or conspiracy or defamation) or related torts. When challenged, the chief must turn to the psychological professionals (providers) who have designed and executed the FFDE method. The FFDE provider should be able to produce the technical and scientific information that underlies any recommendation that an officer be suspended or discharged. An unsupported or clearly speculative recommendation in regard to such a serious matter must be considered unacceptable. The chief will expect the departmental (internal) or contracting (external) FFDE provider to be able to withstand the rigors of qualifying to appear in court as an expert and defend his or her methodology. These scenarios make it clear that it is important for the LE executive to examine how experts are qualified for court testimony.

FEDERAL RULES OF EVIDENCE 702

An **expert witness** is any person who is a specialist in a subject, often scientific or technical, who may aid the court by presenting his or her expert opinion to the judge or jury without having been a witness to any occurrence **(eyewitness)** relating to the reasons for the criminal or civil events of the case. It is an exception to the frequently expressed rule against a witness coming to conclusions in trial or deposition, provided that the expert is qualified by training and special knowledge. If the expertise of the expert witness is challenged, the attorney for the party calling the witness must make a showing of the necessary background to qualify his or her witness as an expert, through questioning in court (a procedure called voir dire). Traditionally, the trial judge has the discretion to rule that the witness is or is not an expert, or is an expert only in regard to limited subjects. Experts are usually paid for their services. Experts may enjoy certain special privileges in many jurisdictions, such as immunity from **sequestration** (being asked to leave the court so as not to be affected by other witnesses' testimony) and the rule of **hearsay** (they may testify to information obtained from other experts).

Federal legal procedures have been widely used guidelines for a number of state legal procedures, including the rules regarding expert testimony. Congress adopted the first modern and comprehensive federal standard for court procedures on August 1, 1975. Made effective July 1, 1975, the **Federal Rules of Evidence (FRE),** a systematic code of federal procedural regulation, has also been adopted by most states to one degree or another. Over the years, the tendency toward a preference for uniform (standard) codes of legal procedure has had a strong influence on the American judicial process, although some states prefer local judicial traditions regarding procedure. As the federal government has become more influential, and the national (as compared to local or regional) character of most educational and business methods have become standardized, the state courts have found uniform standards of procedure helpful.

The most important rule that applies to expert witnesses is referred to as Federal Rules of Evidence, Section 702 or FRE 702. FRE 702 has, to a large degree, replaced the earlier federal procedure rule, which was known as the *Frye* **standard.** The *Frye* standard arose from a case that revolved around a defendant who had been accused of a felony within a federal jurisdiction. James Frye had attempted to qualify an expert in order to offer testimony on his behalf in a novel, psychologically based examination method called the **systolic blood pressure test (SBPT)**. The SBT was an early lie-detector method that Frye attempted to introduce to prove he had been truthful in his description of the events concerning the alleged crime. The court rejected his attempt, and Frye appealed to the Supreme Court. The Supreme Court ruled the following:

> Just when a scientific principle or discovery crosses the line between the experimental and demonstrable stages is difficult to define. Somewhere in this twilight zone the evidential force of the principle must be recognized, and while courts will go a long way in admitting expert testimony deduced from a well-recognized scientific principle or discovery, the thing from which the deduction is made must be sufficiently established to have gained general acceptance in the particular field in which it belongs. (*Frye v. U.S.,* 1923)

The *Frye* standard had been the basis of the procedures regarding the admission of expert witness testimony, particularly in federal courts, since the 1920s. By this standard, the court would accept an expert who had standard qualifications in the relevant scientific or professional specialty and general acceptance by his colleagues in the appropriate professional community. The *Frye* standard for admitting most conventionally trained persons (such as admitting a witness regarding a surgical procedure question who is a board-certified surgeon) as "experts" was accepted in all federal and most state courts. It had worked well in many ways, and had screened out overreaching and unfounded testimony for the most part (such as attempts to introduce **astrology** into court proceedings). But as science moved ahead, legal experts became more concerned that the method upon which the experts based their testimony should be objective and scientific, even at the expense of professional membership. In some cases, the available science seemed to move ahead of professional acceptance, and at other times, established professional opinion seemed to jurists to be little more that conventional speculation.

FRE 702 was very simple and read as follows:

> If scientific, technical or other specialized knowledge will assist the trier of fact to understand the evidence or to determine a fact in issue, a witness qualified as an expert by knowledge, skill, experience, training or education may testify thereto in the form of opinion or otherwise.

Little happened until 1993 when the Supreme Court ruled in *Daubert v. Merrell Dow Pharmaceuticals, Inc.* The case involved the Supreme Court's review of testimony by a series of experts who were said to have special knowledge pertaining to **Bendectin,** an antinausea drug that was prescribed for women during pregnancy. By the late 1980s, several class-action suits were brought, either by persons who had suffered birth defects that they blamed on the drug or by their families. The defense had produced experts who were able to show that, in thirty studies with more than 130,000 subjects, the rate of birth defects associated with women who took the medication was no higher than for the general population who had not been exposed to the drug. Then the plaintiffs called eight expert witnesses. Their testimony involved animal analog studies (the use of lower animals) that purported to show that animals given large quantities of the drug showed higher rates of abnormal births than did those without the drug. Other experts claimed that Bendectin had a similar biochemical structure to known cancer-producing chemicals and therefore may be expected to produce a similar effect. The final group of plaintiff experts testified to an unpublished reanalysis of the original Merrell Dow birth-defect data, using somewhat different statistical techniques, that they claimed revealed a low-level teratogenic (defect-causing) effect.

After examining the expert testimony, the Supreme Court held that experts under FRE 702 must reach their conclusions through the use of standard scientific methods that are uniform and consistent with the questions presented in the lawsuit. The court also ruled that permissible testimony must be based on results that have undergone **peer review** and publication. They ruled that the proposed experts must work regularly in the specific area about which the testimony is given (not just touch on the area for the particular case), and they must be able to specify probability and error rates (the exact likelihood of being correct or incorrect over many decisions) connected with their conclusions. The Supreme Court did not mention the *Frye* standard explicitly, but they added that acceptance by the general scientific community to which the expert belonged was also important.

Daubert created a rapid succession of events that put forth a gauntlet of challenges to the usual and customary ways that most courts looked at expert testimony. A critical elaboration of the *Daubert* standard soon emerged in two cases (which, along with *Daubert,* are called the **Daubert triad**).

GE v. Joiner *and* Kumho v. Carmichael

In *General Electric Co. v. Joiner* (1997), a worker developed cancer and claimed that the illness was caused by **PCBs (polychlorinated biphenyls)** that leaked from GE manufactured machinery in his workplace. The court accepted as fact that PCBs cause cancer and that the plaintiff suffered from a cancerous condition. However, the court ruled that there was no evidence that a specific exposure to PCBs had occurred in that particular case. The judge ruled that the trial court may conclude that there is simply too great of an analytic gap between the data and the opinion proffered, and the expert opinion (that this case was due to PCBs exposure) was rejected under the *Daubert* principle.

In 1999, *Kumho Tire v. Carmichael* came before the Supreme Court. Patrick Carmichael, the plaintiff, claimed that the tires manufactured by the defendant failed because they were defective, causing damage and injury in a particular accident. The plaintiffs put forth an expert, Dennis Carlson, who was offered as a tire engineer. Carlson, who had worked for many years in the tire industry, had examined the tire visually and by touch and had determined that wear and treatment did not account for the tire failure (in spite of three improper puncture repairs) but rather that the tire's design had been faulty. The court essentially rejected the expert's opinion based on the *Daubert* standard. The court ruled that Carlson had no standard method of determining the relative contribution of wear versus structural defects to the tire failure, could not specify probability and error rates, and had not had his methodology reviewed by other professional engineers (peers) in the tire construction industry. The plaintiff's objections to applying the *Daubert* standard to a professional practice, as compared with experimental scientific evidence, were brushed aside by the court. In other words, the court ruled that the *Daubert* standard applies not only to abstract scientific conclusions from structured research, but also to professional practice standards. This finding is likely to bring important changes to the nature of expert testimony for the psychological professions, including police psychology.

Psychology Testing and White Horse

The potential importance of the *Daubert* standard may be illustrated in a case that touched upon actual psychological testimony. In *U.S. v. White Horse* (2001), a federal court produced a significant ruling regarding expert testimony as it affects professional (including police) psychology and psychometric testing related to FRE 702 and its progeny. Guy Randy White Horse, a Native American, was charged with sexually abusing his son on the Pine Ridge Indian Reservation in South Dakota. White Horse's attorney hired a psychologist to conduct a psychosexual evaluation of White Horse. This evaluation included a clinical interview and the **Abel Assessment for Sexual Interest,** a psychometric test. The psychologist concluded that White Horse did not have a sexual interest in underage boys, and White Horse intended to offer this testimony during the guilt phase of this case.

Part I of the Abel Assessment measured the amount of time a subject viewed slides of clothed and partially clothed people. The premise was that a consistent correlation exists between sexual response and the length of time spent viewing sexual stimuli ("viewing time"). Part I also incorporated a questionnaire that delineated such variables as sexual behaviors, cognitive distortions, and information related to social desirability (the degree to which the examinee was prone to report statements that he thinks others want him to report). The completed questionnaire was scored and then combined with "viewing time" for Part II of the test, which used three predictive logistic regression equations. The equations produced a probability score that purportedly predicted the subject's interest in girls under the age of fourteen, boys under the age of fourteen, and liar-deniers (invalid responses).

One *Daubert* element required evidence that the Abel Assessment has been tested. Dr. Abel's publications and at least four independent studies of the Abel Assessment have found Part I to be generally valid for the mainstream population. There was no evidence, however, that the Abel Assessment has been tested using a statistically significant sample of Native American subjects, leading the court to conclude that the instrument not been sufficiently tested with regard to Native Americans.

A second *Daubert* element required peer review of the Abel Assessment. Multiple independent reviews of the Abel Assessment methodology had been conducted, and, although the reviews had not been uniformly positive, the court found sufficient evidence to substantiate peer review requirement. The third *Daubert* element is the known or potential rate of error. The court found that Dr. Abel's own study of the Abel Assessment concluded that almost one-quarter of admitted pedophiles were inaccurately classified as nonpedophiles. The court found that a *24-percent rate of false negative* (i.e., the examinee was a pedophile but the test said that he or she was not) results did not assist the jury in understanding the evidence or determining a fact in issue.

The fourth *Daubert* element was the acceptance of the Abel Assessment within the scientific community. The **Association for the Treatment of Sexual Abusers (ATSA)** was identified as the relevant scientific community for this area of research. The ATSA opined that **penile plethysmograph (PPG) testing** is usually preferred over "viewing time" measures in the assessment of deviant sexual interests. However the court found that even the PPG was not generally acceptable as a reliable or valid diagnostic tool. The court found that the Abel Assessment had not achieved widespread acceptance within the scientific community.

After balancing these four factors, the court found that Part I of the Abel Assessment did not satisfy the admissibility requirements of *Daubert*. Furthermore, the Part II results of the Abel Assessment test were also not admissible because White Horse was accused of an incest-only offense. According to Abel's 2001 published article, incest-only cases were excluded from his validation study because incest offenders often act for reasons other than sexual interest (Abel et al., 2001). In addition, no peer review of *Part II* had been conducted, and no evidence existed that it was widely accepted in the scientific community. Part II of the Abel Assessment was, therefore, not admissible because it did not meet *Daubert* standards.

An analogy can be made between the attempt to admit testimony based upon the Abel Assessment and any attempt to admit expert testimony to support a psychological recommendation regarding an incumbent officer. Although it is not clear that any particular expert preparation would result in acceptance (the Abel Assessment had been accepted as admissible in other courts), the greater the weight of scientific evidence when used as a basis for expert testimony, the greater the likelihood of acceptance by the court. This is a matter that can have a profound impact upon the credibility and reputation of the police department and the careers of the LE executives who are ultimately responsible for FFDE decisions.

EXAMINING THE EXPERT'S METHODS

In previous chapters, the scientific and methodological preparation of the internal and external FFDE provider was addressed in traditional professional and technical terms. In the current chapter, the logical conclusion of the process of the separation of speculation and opinion from substantial science is put to the next logical test, that of the judicial system that must examine claims or equity and liability. Every law enforcement organization has a stake in how the recommendations of its consultants may guide its decisions, which in turn may have far-reaching consequences. The supervisory failure to examine an officer in the face of reasons to suspect personal impairment and then have that officer cause an injury or loss to persons in the community which that officer is sworn to protect by irrational action or inaction will likely result in a lawsuit. However, to examine an officer and then use the recommendations of that examination to deprive the officer of his or her career and livelihood without proper support may also result in a lawsuit. The arbiter of the reasonableness of the recommendation and the administrative decisions that follow is likely to be a federal or state judge. In this chapter, it was noted that the issues that concern adequate psychological science appear, to an ever-increasing degree, to be the same factors that are considered by the courts in arriving at legal decisions. Membership in professional societies or organizations (the *Frye* standard) is now on a part of the collection issues under scrutiny by the courts before the department's consultant can assist in defending the department's decisions as an expert. The *Daubert* standard also calls for an analysis of the probability that the expert's testimony was derived rationally, the error rates in the decision are acceptable to the court, and the appropriateness of the supporting research has been demonstrated. The reach of this sort of analysis has touched expert testimony that has classically been considered "professional" and not subject to usual research considerations (see *Kumho v. Carmichael*). The age of the chief of police assigning a friend with nonspecific experience or credentials in police psychology and FFDE methodology to perform important selection and fitness tasks is giving way to the use of expert consultants who will be able to support the department when challenged in court.

Chapter 11

Reasons for Fitness-for-Duty Evaluations

Perhaps it had nothing to do with sin and everything to do with sociopathy, that most incurable of human disorders because all so afflicted consider themselves *blessed* rather than cursed.

Joseph Wambaugh

The purpose of an FFDE is to professionally inform the police executive and his department of information that touches upon behavioral, mental illness or personality issues that may impact an officer's performance of his or her official role. Referral questions may involve issues of positive and negative risks of harm said to be associated with officer behaviors from a psychological perspective. The intent of the report from the FFDE provider to the law enforcement executive is to inform regarding risk or liability and to assist the latter in consultation regarding possible solutions. The FFDE provider does not make the final decisions about departmental actions that are recommended for the examined officer, and provides only one input into the potentially complex task of determining the desired course of action open to the chief or responsible LE executive. The FFDE report should be written with the LE executive in mind, and should offer recommendations and options (if appropriate) that are both understandable to LE executives and which contain information that allows the executive some freedom of action to resolve the difficulty that brought about the FFDE.

THE KEY ISSUES

The key to a fitness-for-duty evaluation is the reason for referral. It is critical to envision that the FFDE is not a standard clinical mental health report. In an FFDE, the nature of the complaint or sets of complaints about the officer circumscribes the entire purpose of the procedure. Tangential or collateral issues often may not be considered, even if potentially significant regarding some issue that stands apart from law enforcement. This is important because the FFDE findings should focus on the question of occupational or vocational functioning (such as public safety or the ability to perform critical police functions capably), and because, unlike usual clinical work, the subject of the examination is unlikely to be open about problems of living. In addition to concerns of unemployment and financial loss, the officer may be consumed by the idea that he or she will be labeled as mentally impaired. To many officers, losing their gun and badge is a terrifying experience, regardless of the rational justification for the FFDE.

The focus on job performance, as noted throughout this book, should not imply official blindness concerning activities that are reasonably connected to likely law enforcement officer problems. Misconduct, irrational behavior and unacceptable actions (spousal abuse, sexual misconduct, and violence in the general community) may be warning signals that an officer may be unfit. Only the most reckless LE executive and police psychologist may ignore extreme officer behaviors in normal social life.

REASONS FOR REFERRAL

The Case of Officer Sam

Officer Sam, an Anytown Police Department officer, was dismissed following a departmental hearing in which it was conclusively shown that he had violated the civil rights of four female drivers. One female plaintiff testified that Officer Sam had stopped her and, after telling her she had failed a sobriety test, made her strip to her underpants and high heels and walk four blocks. A second woman who had reportedly been accused of DWI by Officer Sam was made to strip and stand outside in the cold. A third testified that she had been handcuffed, driven to a remote area, and released only after showing Officer Sam her breasts. Yet another female motorist testified that she had been manually "examined" in a sexually explicit manner by the officer after having been handcuffed. If any of these cases goes to civil trial, attorneys would be able to introduce evidence that several departmental supervisors knew that Officer Sam behaved inappropriately toward women on and off the job.

The implication that LE executive knew of such misconduct begs the question of why the department did not have an FFDE procedure in place to psychologically examine this grossly disturbed officer. The answer, in part, is that many LE executives do have a clear vision of the appropriate reasons why such an evaluation should take place. The following represents a set of common, appropriate reasons for a fitness-for-duty evaluation referral by a police executive to a police psychologist or FFDE provider:

1. *The officer appears to exhibit behavioral problems that, although not individually catastrophic, suggest a collapse of integrity, motivation, effectiveness, or judgment.* For example, an officer may show excessive and unexplained absenteeism and moodiness, which is frequently known to be connected with a substance abuse problem or clinical depression. The observation that such an officer often smells slightly of alcohol and appears to have become indifferent about his or her appearance may be further reasons for an FFDE referral. Whether abusable substances are at the root of the crisis is less important than the need to detect an apparent impairment in the functional ability of this officer.

2. *When an officer has a good history of conduct and behavioral control, the sudden onset of forgetfulness, hostility, depression, withdrawal, or irrational speech points to the need for an FFDE.* Some officers become evasive and hide from confrontation, whereas others may become resistant to supervision and verbalize that a conspiracy exists against them. Accusations of sexual misconduct, particularly of recent origin, are nearly always a reason for an FFDE (*Haynes v. Police Bd. of the City of Chicago,* 1997). The LE executive must be aware of two variables: the time sequences or rates at which undesirable or inappropriate behaviors appeared and the type of behavior that is almost always indicative of serious future difficulty.

Regarding **rate of appearance,** a sudden or dense series of reports of inappropriate or undesirable behavior should be considered more alarming than a slow or gradual accumulation of similar complaints. For example, in a department where each officer averages less than one complaint a year regarding overly familiar conduct with motorists, an officer who suddenly is the recipient of a half-dozen sexually related complains in a two-month period may require both an IA inquiry and an FFDE. Regarding type of behavior, reports of an officer's common rudeness (no violence or threats of unlawful arrest) is less likely to justify an FFDE referral than similar behaviors accompanied by threats of any sort of unlawful or harmful officer conduct. The determination of the need for an FFDE referral has a rational component that is an important element in appropriate LE supervision.

3. *The emergence of prejudicial, bigoted, or overbearing written or spoken conduct or behavior, especially when it is connected with threats of the violation of the rights of citizens.* For example, offensive comments about woman or racial or cultural minorities cannot be tolerated in a modern department and must lead to some administrative response. No department can tolerate officers who express verbal threats to harm or discriminate against some community group or culturally identifiable population. This is especially true when evidence of actual hurtful behavior exists, such as may be seen with officers who appear to become involved in frequent or unfounded violent confrontations with persons of certain races or who appear to frequently refuse to make arrests of men in domestic violence situations. The need for disciplinary action is appropriate when the action seems independent of the personal burden of mental illness, but the FFDE may be useful when the bigoted conduct appears to be an outgrowth of a psychological disorder, such as paranoia.

4. *Allegations of the excessive, inappropriate, and unexplained use of force is an automatic reason to refer an officer for an FFDE* (Conte v. Horcher, *1977*). A premium is placed upon any means of preventing an abusive or brutal officer from injuring anyone and, perhaps more important, undermining the confidence that the entire society places in law enforcement officers for protection and security. When such officers appear to be attracted to the masculine and physically confrontational aspect of police work to an excessive or unusual degree, an FFDE may be appropriate. Such officers may come to the attention of police executives because of frequent citizen complaints about arm twisting, punching, and the use of electrical stun devices, tight handcuffs, and the like. Care should be taken to document and investigate all such instances prior to the FFDE referral, since devia-

tions from standard procedure may be vital to the question of the possibly excessive nature of the referred officer's conduct.

5. *Threats or insinuations of violence ("I can understand how some cops can 'go postal' after the way the department has treated me"), particularly when associated with aggressive displays toward colleagues, superiors, or the public, such as making threats of uncontrollable desires to act out.* A federal appeals court upheld a warden's order for a corrections officer to submit to a psychiatric examination after he was accused by several co-workers of making threats of physical harm (*Flynn v. Sandahl,* 1995). Officers who appear to be speaking indirectly about issues of harm ("I just don't know what I might do!") may be in special need of the FFDE procedure because direct disciplinary action may not be justified by such oblique statements, and yet the LE executive has the responsibility of ensuring the safety of his or her department and the public. Officers who point or gesture inappropriately with their weapons when seeming to be irritated or distressed with others may also be included in this category. Special attention may be given to officers who appear to overreact with violence or unlawful threats of arrest to unpleasant, but lawful, civilian behaviors, such as the use of vulgar language. For example, shouting abusive comments at officers and answering them with sarcasm, may be seen as "no more than criticism of the police" so long as it does not incite others to imminent unlawful violence (*Resek v. City of Huntington Beach,* 2002). In general, the courts have held that any display of seemingly defective behavior is a suitable reason to refer for an FFDE. In *Sullivan v. River Valley School Dist.* (1999), the court affirmed summary judgment of the employee's lawsuit where the employer dismissed an employee who refused to submit to mental and physical fitness-for-duty exams. The employee exhibited odd and threatening behavior in the workplace, and the psychiatrist who examined the employee concluded that the employee had a possible psychiatric disorder.

6. *"Mystery" medical conditions characterized by reports of debilitating physical complaints that are not detected in repeated, standard medical examinations and are associated with excessive sick leave and absenteeism.* Often this type of problem may appear in the guise of multiple requests for medical leave to treat or diagnose some set of apparently physical problems that do not appear to resolve nor

do such exams produce understandable diagnoses. Requests of medical fitness examinations may fail to reveal a reason for the problem, which continues to require repeated sick leave and requests for special accommodation without clear justification. On occasion, the examining physician may posit that the officer's complaints have a psychological component, a finding that should led to an FFDE if the problem impacts on work-related performance. In one case, a chief was found to be justified in ordering an FFDE for a paramedic officer who demonstrated excessive absenteeism, tardiness, high use of sick leave, and rapid variations in mood (*Wertz v. Wilson,* 1996). It should be remembered that according to EEOC regulations, any examination ordered by an employer must be restricted to discovering whether the employee can continue to fulfill the essential functions of the job (29 C.F.R. Part 1630, App. at 1630.14 [c]).

7. *Complaints by family, relatives, friends, or associates of threatening or bizarre off-duty behavior, frequently in the form of spousal abuse, can be a significant reason to refer for an FFDE.* Care should be taken to separate angry, but nonspecific accusations by a distressed spouse from those complaints that seem to touch upon violence and reports of suicidal/homicidal ideation or substance abuse. Spousal abuse reports have taken on a greater importance in police administrative work in recent years. If the agency ignores such reports or observation, there may be subsequent liability for deliberant indifference in connection with any injuries caused by that officer if such injuries touch upon some aspect of the official law enforcement role of the officer (*McKenna v. Fargo,* 1978). In certain localities, when officers are charged domestic violence, even if the charges are dropped, the officers must have their weapons removed and may not return to duty until they are cleared psychologically by the department-appointed psychologist (State of New Jersey, 2000). An additional complication regards the **Lautenberg Amendment** to the Gun Control Act of 1968, which took effect on September 30, 1996, and which makes it a felony for any person convicted of a misdemeanor crime of domestic violence to ship, transport, possess, or receive firearms or ammunition. A "misdemeanor crime of domestic violence" is generally defined as any offense, whether or not explicitly described in a statute as a crime of domestic violence, which has, as its factual basis, the use or attempted use of physical force, or the threat-

ened use of a deadly weapon, committed by the victim's current or former spouse or domestic partner, parent, or guardian. There is no exemption for peace officers under this act. It is a federal felony to violate this part of the law and the punishment may be substantial. If found guilty, an individual could face up to ten years imprisonment and a fine of up to $250,000. The Bureau of Alcohol, Tobacco, Firearms and Explosives (ATF) and the Justice Department have issued guidelines to local law enforcement agencies regarding this law. These guidelines put the primary responsibility for compliance on the individual officer, but the ATF has also advised federal, state, and local agencies to devise procedures to ensure compliance with the new law. In cases where individuals refuse to relinquish their firearms, however, ATF recommends that LE agencies contact their local ATF office. If the public employer is not proactive, or if the public employer does not actively attempt to identify officers who may be in violation of the law and take appropriate remedial or disciplinary action, then significant liability could result.

8. *When the officer proceeds with a lawsuit alleging mental injury by either his department or others, he should be referred for an FFDE.* The very claim of mental illness or psychological injury as part of a lawsuit, particularly in combination with the legal assertion that the officer is unable to perform the duties of his or her position, is sufficient reason to require the officer to undergo an FFDE. For example, an academic employee who was suing the employing institution for severe emotional distress and sexual harassment initially refused an FFDE. The court confirmed that he could be compelled to undergo medical and psychological examinations on the strength that his lawsuit attested to his own belief that he was unable to function in his job (*Vinson v. Superior Court,* 1987). In an unrelated case, a federal judge in Chicago ordered an employee who alleged an ongoing mental injury, to submit to a psychological evaluation by his employer as a reasonable step in ensuring the safety and proper operation of that company (*Jansen v. Packaging Corporation,* 1997).

9. *If any signs of emotional instability are present following a shooting incident or any traumatic, job-related incident, even if the officer was in no way at fault in the event, an FFDE is justified.* It is accepted in common culture that anyone who is exposed to a traumatic event, such as the killing or the seriously injuring of a person, is

likely to require some form of emotional assistance. This principle may also be extended to any party who experiences a horrible, frightening, or disgusting event (e.g., seeing a mutilated body, watching a person being burned) and any such officers may be ordered to submit to an FFDE to verify their capability to continue in their particular LE position. This right to order an FFDE is particularly important when the officer exhibits significant, subsequent behavioral change to supervisors or significant others. For example, a Massachusetts appellate court upheld the right of the police chief to disarm an officer who was involved in a shooting incident and about which the department had reasonable conduct/behavioral concerns based upon reports from supervisors and fellow officers (*City of Boston v. Boston Police Patrolmen's Assn., Inc.*, 1979).

10. *Sexual inappropriateness or acting out, especially in regard to unwanted sexual advances or implications of the misuse of police authority to further a sexual action or interest by the officer.* Sexual misconduct appears to constitute a reason for action against a police department if evidence exists that the supervisors knew of the inappropriate sexual conduct and failed to act. The courts have held that sexual intrusion or distasteful conduct is indefensible in LE work. In *Fontana v. Haskin* (2001) a plaintiff claimed that following her arrest for DWI, and on the way to the station, she was sexually harassed. She reported specifically that the officer who sat next to her in the backseat of the police vehicle commented on her "nice legs," reportedly proposed that he become her "older man," and massaged her shoulders. At the station, he reportedly offered to "help her" in the rest room, and then commented with personal interest upon her light eyes, blonde hair, "perfect body," and nice legs. He reportedly asked her if she had a boyfriend and tried to determine where she lived. The court denied the officer's motion for summary judgment, noting that the Fourth Amendment prohibits unreasonable intrusion on one's bodily integrity. The court ruled that the constitutionality of police action during a seizure involves the balancing of the nature and quality of the intrusion on the individual's Fourth Amendment interests against the countervailing governmental interest at stake. The court noted that there can be no countervailing governmental interest to justify sexual misconduct at any time. The court wrote that there is no situation that would justify any amount of purposeful sexual verbal and physical

predation against a handcuffed arrestee. Officers who are reported to exhibit any similar misconduct should be referred for an FFDE.

11. *Any form of behavior prohibited or circumscribed by civil service or personnel rules.* Every department should have a code of conduct or borrow such a code from the prevailing state administrative body. Any violation of such established regulations or official policies, when combined with a suspicion of mental or emotional impairment or substance abuse impairment, may create an appropriate reason to refer for an FFDE.

In spite of the general notion that FFDEs are meant to inform commanders and law enforcement executives of the psychological problems of serving officers, the actual employment of FFDEs is complex. Reports of simple criminal conduct are not reasons to refer for an FFDE. Those complaints should be investigated by internal affairs of the appropriate criminal investigating section of the department. A commander's passing curiosity about the personal life of a given officer is also not a valid reason for referral. In general, good reasons may be identified as related to the relatively recent emergence of or increase in behaviors that most police supervisors would understand to be likely to interfere with the judgment or capability of officers. The greater the irrationality or absurdity of the appearance of the observed or reported behavior, the more appropriate an FFDE referral is likely to be. The sudden onset of such behaviors is usually more noteworthy than those behaviors that appear to be a variant of long-standing, irritating officer conduct. Those behaviors that involve violence, the threat of personal harm or property damage, sexual inappropriateness, racially explosive conduct, and behaviors that imply poor work performance (e.g., neglect of duty, insubordination, or sleeping at work) are more important reasons for FFDE referrals that less intense problems (e.g., disagreement over a work schedule). The LE executive should also pay special attention to issues of potential substance abuse (because of the devastating and general effects of this problem) and to domestic violence (because of the Lautenberg Amendment), even though non-work-related conduct is normally not the focus of fitness-for-duty evaluations. In the end, the most appropriate referrals should be work related and reasonably connected to a suspicion of mental or emotional illness or defect.

Chapter 12

Misuse of Fitness-for-Duty Evaluations

You know your children are growing up when they stop asking you where they came from and refuse to tell you where they're going.

P. J. O'Rourke

THE CASE OF OFFICER TIM

Officer Tim has been a problem for his department for more than twenty years. He has the reputation of carrying a book of regulations with him while on duty, often quoting its contents to justify his refusal to comply with the orders of his superiors. He has often refused orders by referring to the "chapter and verse" which, in his particular interpretation, placed the supervisor outside of proper procedure. Officer Tim has called in sick at times that seem suspicious, such as during holidays when he had been assigned to difficult duty. He has filed long lists of complaints against both his senior and younger fellow officers for supposed infractions, which he claimed were his "duty" to report, although none of the complaints had been sustained following investigation. When Officer Tim lost control of his vehicle and suffered an MVA (motor vehicle accident), he immediately filed both a workers compensation claim and a union grievance (because he claimed the accident had been caused by poor auto maintenance by his department). When referred for an FFDE, his commander indicated to the FFDE provider that Officer Tim "must be crazy" because he was such a difficult officer.

Officer Tim is not a generally good candidate for an FFDE referral when actual behaviors resulting in the complaint of misconduct are examined. The complaints are not of recent origin, nor have they recently intensified. Officer Tim is a pest and his conduct is transparently self-serving and a nuisance rather than bizarre or dangerous. If there was no reason to consider him to be an intolerable problem twenty years ago and there is no special reason to consider that matters have changed for the worse, why is an FFDE needed now? Officer Tim may be a disciplinary problem ("a slacker," "stationhouse lawyer," and an insubordinate officer) that has been long ignored. The FFDE was never meant to substitute for proper administrative solutions to problems that should have been employed years ago.

A number of circumstances exist in which an LE executive and a police psychologist may not wish to conduct a fitness-for-duty evaluation. FFDEs are much like any tool available to deal with a difficulty. It can be very helpful at restoring a good officer to duty, but can needlessly complicate the issues at hand when applied improperly. The following is not an exhaustive list of misguided FFDE referrals, but may be useful in revealing the general principles of determining when the FFDE is unlikely to be fruitful.

1. *In a situation in which the officer has engaged in the clear violation of the criminal justice code, it is best to decline to order an FFDE and instead consider an arrest and arraignment.* For example, an officer committed a bank robbery and then claimed that he was impaired because he was under the influence of cocaine at the time. An FFDE for this officer may only complicate the role of the department in making the criminal apprehension and, in any case, the officer is unlikely to ever be returned to duty following a felony. If that officer's defense attorney wishes to argue some form of insanity mitigation, then he or she must employ his or her own experts in addressing that question and not rely upon the departmental FFDE provider as an information resource. In another case, the FFDE referral may stem from the department's health and safety division (HSD), although there are suspicions that criminal activity (possible prescription theft) may have been involved. The internal affairs section should be consulted prior to any referral so as to avoid the possibility that HSD is acting at cross-purposes with an independent IA criminal investigation. Of course, mentally ill people commit crimes as well as nonimpaired persons, and therefore, impairment and criminality may coexist. The policy of the department, however, should be unambiguous regarding the intentions of the FFDE methodology. FFDEs are primarily for the purpose of salvaging good officers who need assistance, not in protecting or rehabilitating criminally inclined officers. Where little is to be gained from the viewpoint of potential officer rehabilitation, the FFDE is usually questionable.

2. *When a desire exists to dispose of a marginal or annoying officer whose behavior has not changed substantially in recent times, an FFDE is usually inappropriate.* Fitness examinations should not be a cheap method of compensating for inadequate supervision or personnel policies (as in the case of Officer Tim). For example, an officer who has always been sloppy in appearance should not be referred for an FFDE only for that reason. If the officer has performed adequately (if only marginally) for many years with similar traits and behavior, why is a question of impairment being raised now? FFDEs are most useful in the examination of officers who are showing new uninviting or inappropriate behavior or a notable worsening of previous conduct. For example, an FFDE is appropriate for an officer who has always been aggressive, but now is violent and has begun to show a dangerous tendency to ignore firearms regulations (carrying an AK-47 in his official vehicle against departmental policy). In such an example, acceptable sets of behaviors (such as an aggressive law enforcement style) may appear now to have contributed to potentially hazardous conduct and, therefore, an FFDE referral is desirable.

3. *The use of obscene language by an officer, which is limited to fellow officers who are willing to accept such language, appears to be a case in which it is advisable to avoid FFDEs in favor of other remedies.* Although general agreement exists among LE executives and psychologists that obscene or vulgar verbal conduct is distasteful and may presage more destructive emotional and character difficulties, the courts have taken a very broad First Amendment interpretation of objectionable language, per se. The use of obscenities with superior officers is usually seen as insubordinate and a matter that brings disrepute upon a department. When unremitting, especially in the face of repeated warnings or disciplinary procedures, continued use of vulgarities with superiors may be a good reason to order an FFDE. This, however, does not appear to be the case when such language is used *with fellow officers only*. In at least one case, the use of obscene language to another police employee did not justify an order that the crude officer submit to a psychological exam (*Maplewood v. Law Enforcement Labor Service,* 1996). On the other hand, the use of vulgarity (beyond that which may be customary in a given assignment) with civilians or with subordinates is often a valid reason for FFDE referral, since it may suggest potential danger to the public or job-related abuse of authority. The interaction of FFDEs and the First Amend-

ment is a very complex issue and requires an analysis that is too ambitious for this current review. In general, matters that are issues of public concern (such as whether suspects are being treated properly or that the department's budget is being abused) are covered by the First Amendment. Officers may not be disciplined or referred to an FFDE for expressing opinions (oral or written) about such topics. Personal gripes and attempts to undermine confidence in the agency (such as publicly claiming that the chief is incompetent or by promoting a Nazi Party rally) are usually not covered and may result in justifiable adverse action or referral for an FFDE. The need for the public to learn of problems within a governmental agency must be balanced against the need for discipline, confidentiality, and a practical working relationship in the department.

4. *Great care and reflection must be used when referring an officer for an FFDE in circumstances in which that officer has an unresolved lawsuit or grievance against the department.* In no case should there be a reasonable appearance that the FFDE procedure is being used as an instrument to defame or discredit an officer who has brought a valid complaint to the attention of proper legal or administrative authority. This policy may be viewed as a version of "retaliation" against a "whistle-blower" or a means of labeling an employee as "mentally unfit" to undermine a legitimate civil action (H.D. 4311, PL 101-12, Title 5, Sec. 1221). There must be no reasonable basis for suspicion that an FFDE is politically motivated. If an officer has a legitimate complaint or grievance against a department or any member of that department by any objective standard of appropriateness, then the use of FFDEs that are connected with the complaint becomes questionable, at least until the complaint is cleared. Mentally ill officers can file authentic complaints. The naive manufacturing of complaints should not block the referral of an impaired officer. Once the grievance has been examined thoroughly and can be shown clearly to be independent of the reason for the FFDE, it may proceed with the full awareness of the FFDE provider and significant LE executives regarding the relevant issues. For example, an officer who sued his department with the claim that he suffered a mental injury could be examined with an FFDE since the suit itself attested to his mental impairment (*Vinson v. Superior Court,* 1987).

5. *It is inappropriate to use an FFDE as a means of punishing one or more officers for certain behaviors, when other contemporary offi-*

cers or employees are not required to meet the same standard. Official standards of conduct within a department or agency should be clear and uniform. The reasons for referral must be nondiscriminatory and symmetrical regarding all departmental members, especially regarding such variables as age, gender, race, ethnicity, and religion. For example, a female officer who had been sexually active with a number of male officers was referred for an FFDE for her violation of departmental sexual misconduct regulations. However, upon closer inspection, it was revealed that no action had been taken against the male officers who had been willing and active partners in this violation, creating the appearance of a selective, discriminatory FFDE referral against the female officer. Correction of misconduct of this variety should involve general reforms in the administrative code followed by universal regulatory enforcement, and not by the use of an FFDE to remove a specific officer. In another case, the membership of an African-American officer in a race-centered political or social organization cannot itself be the reason for an FFDE referral, unless concurrent prohibitions exist for all such memberships (regardless of race), or the activities of the organization can be shown to interfere with the proper and essential operation of the agency.

6. *FFDEs should not be used to supplement the collection of information within a criminal investigation of officer misconduct.* Information collected in an FFDE under order from the LE department should be viewed as *compelled* and is not useful in criminal or even civil proceedings that may follow (Lybarger Admonishment). In general, officers cannot be deprived of Fifth Amendment rights simply because the department demands incriminatory information as a condition of employment. Information that is obtained from the officer that would not otherwise have become known (the **fruit-of-the-poisoned-tree doctrine**) is likewise contaminated for persecutory use if obtained without proper *Miranda* protection. However, a behavioral dysfunction that is also a criminal action that is revealed within the FFDE (the finding of pedophilia in an officer assigned to juvenile work) must be conveyed to police executives in order to guide independent decision making regarding the dangers that a particular officer poses. Subsequently, IA officers may then investigate that officer's official conduct to detect criminal violations. In general, the FFDE provider may recommend that the officer is unfit for reasons

connected with criminal conduct, and events may follow that lead to criminal inquiries outside of the FFDE method.

7. *On occasion, an FFDE may be ordered when it is learned that an officer has been receiving mental health treatment for reasons that may or may not be connected with law enforcement duties.* Although it may be appropriate to request an FFDE under circumstances in which it becomes known to the police managers that an officer suffers from a serious disorder (*Bone v. City of Louisville,* 2000), FFDEs should never be conducted out of simple curiosity. The discovery that an officer is using psychotropic medications (drugs used to treat depressive or anxiety disorders, for example) is sufficient to refer that officer for an FFDE if such a regulation has been included in the departmental code of conduct or personnel rules. The question of an effect of the medication or of the underlying disorder upon the efficiency and capabilities of a serving law enforcement officer is a valid public safety issue and job necessity inquiry. On the other hand, the simple discovery of an officer seeking marital counseling (in which no suspicion of violence exists) or career assessment services is not sufficient to require an FFDE. Admittedly, the line is not always clear, and the customs and standards of both the department and community in which it is a part may play a part in the identification of whether an FFDE is appropriate.

IMPROPER FFDE REFERRALS

Corporal Charles of the Anytown Police Department reported to his supervisor that he (Charles) was being "watched" at his desk assignment by nonspecific others in a "threatening manner." The departmental psychiatrist examined Corporal Charles and reported that he was "fit for duty" (i.e., not disabled by mental illness), but included a list of abstract concerns about Charles' "emotional stability" in the official report. Corporal Charles was allowed to return to work under the conditions that he submit to "counseling" and that the mental health provider submit a monthly report on his progress. Corporal Charles refused to pay for counseling and pointed out that the departmental report had found him "fit for duty" and, therefore, presumably not in need of treatment. He was suspended and eventually discharged for refusing a direct order.

Corporal Charles then filed a complaint with the Equal Opportunity Employment Commission, which has the responsibility to enforce a number of federal civil rights laws, including the Rehabilitation Act of 1973 and the Americans with Disabilities Act. Since Corporal Charles had been declared "fit for duty" by the departmental FFDE provider, he challenged the "business necessity" (see Chapter 14) of required treatment and the embarrassing monthly mental heath reports to the department. The EEOC demanded that the department justify the order for treatment with proof of risk to the public, or other foreseeable liability, which was thought to stem from Corporal Charles' medical condition.

Failing to receive such evidence, the EEOC ruled that the department had exceeded its authority by requiring post-FFDE treatments and examinations, since no connection appeared evident between the fitness-for-duty report and the order to report to a treatment provider. Since employees may not be disciplined for refusing improper requests for medical examinations or treatment, Corporal Charles was restored to his police position and received back pay and benefits. To make matters more embarrassing and expensive, the Anytown PD was ordered to conduct a "supplemental investigation" to determine whether compensatory damages should be awarded to Corporal Charles. The department was also told to arrange for sixteen hours of staff training in the legal rights of employees who are believed to suffer medical or psychological disability within a public agency.

This case is an example of the difficulties that departments must anticipate before a FFDE procedure is introduced into the personnel management system. The failure to demonstrate the risk that Corporal Charles posed to the well-being of others or to the effective functioning of the department led ultimately to the EEOC's rejection of the recommended plan. Confusion about the goals and proper methods of conducting an FFDE was compounded by a lack of awareness of legal requirements regarding the procedure on the part of both the department and the FFDE provider. In the following section, a brief review of federal laws that impinge upon the use of FFDEs is offered so that the LE executive involved in such a procedure may interact in an informed manner with those who propose to offer FFDE services.

SECTION IV:
FEDERAL LAW
AND FITNESS-FOR-DUTY
EVALUATIONS

Chapter 13

Confidentiality of Psychological Information and the HIPAA in Police Psychology

Experience should teach us to be most on our guard to protect liberty when the Government's purposes are beneficent. Men born to freedom are naturally alert to repel invasion of their liberty by evil-minded rulers. The greatest dangers to liberty lurk in insidious encroachment by men of zeal, well-meaning but without understanding.

Supreme Court Justice
Louis D. Brandeis

In a well-known ruling, the Supreme Court affirmed the importance of confidentiality in the provision of mental health services (*Jaffee v. Redmond,* 1996). In a decision creating a psychotherapist privilege in the federal system, the Court appeared to provide extensive legal protection for the principle of confidentiality. There is no reason to believe that such a privilege stops when the parties involved are in some way connected with law enforcement. The Court wrote:

Effective psychotherapy . . . depends upon an atmosphere of confidence and trust in which the patient is willing to make a frank and complete disclosure of facts, emotions, memories, and fears. Because of the sensitive nature of the problems for which individuals consult psychotherapists, disclosure of confidential communications made during counseling sessions may cause embarrassment or disgrace. For this reason, the mere possibility of disclosure may impede development of the confidential relationship necessary for successful treatment.

Many state and federal laws have, in modern times, protected the confidentiality of health care information, including information related to mental health and substance abuse treatment. Unfortunately, a notable loss of confidential protections has been brought about by the introduction of managed care or **health maintenance organizations (HMOs),** which may be defined as health insurance programs that require an approval process which may pay for medical services from among a limited panel of providers. In general, the rules that govern the approval process require a disclosure of the patients' detailed health problems to administrative agents who must authorize treatment in order for it to be paid. This disclosure is usually in the form of a required detailed written report of the mental health problems of the potential patient. The patient (officer) in need of assistance may or may not have a difficulty that is deemed worthy of the HMO's treatment coverage under his or her policy, no matter how important the issue is for the patient or the employer. As described previously, the problems of confidentiality are even more important in work with law enforcement officers than for typical clinical patients. Not only is there reason to believe that officers avoid assessment and treatment because they believe it stigmatizes them with their departments, but a special public safety concern exists regarding the conduct of commissioned officers that is seldom true for civilians.

ETHICAL ISSUES ABOUT CONFIDENTIALITY

Confidentiality is the maintenance of written or verbal information in a manner from which some persons or institutions are excluded. It assures patients that materials obtained in a personal manner by a professional therapist will not be disclosed publicly, an assurance made necessary because of the sensitive and embarrassing nature of psychological information. Confidentiality always has limits, such as when the patient poses a clear danger to others, or in some states, has been abusing children or elderly persons. On the other hand, specific information that is needed for a provider to be able to treat a patient has usually been considered confidential, such as details of personal habits or fears. Many states have established specific statutes that guarantee the privacy of medical and psychiatric records. Drug and alcohol abuse records are protected under a separate federal regulation.

Police psychology is a branch of professional psychology (clinical, counseling, etc.) that involves all psychological issues that touch upon law enforcement. As described previously, psychological employment screening and FFDEs may fall under special guidelines and are not considered to be typical or usual clinical services. However, counseling and psychotherapy (psychosocial treatments) are considered clinical or mental health services, whether they are conducted with a police officer or with any other party. As with other mental health services, confidentiality among psychologists is a pivotal ethical principle. The right to confidentiality belongs to the person receiving services (Campbell, 2000), but in the case of an FFDE, this right is held jointly between the officer and the department to whom he or she responds. The right to waive confidentiality to third parties also belongs to the officer and to his or her department jointly, since both are stakeholders in the FFDE process.

The ethical codes of the various professions, and most confidentiality laws, obligate professionals to take steps to protect confidentiality. For example, the **Ethical Principles of Psychologists** (American Psychological Association, 2002, p. 7) state:

> Psychologists have a primary obligation and take reasonable precautions to protect confidential information obtained through or stored in any medium, recognizing that the extent and limits of confidentiality may be regulated by law or established by institutional rules or professional or scientific relationship.

The principle of confidentiality is meant to advance prosocial values. Counseling or psychotherapy is unlikely to be useful if the patient is unwilling to share potentially disturbing and distasteful information. Confidentiality may reduce the stigma associated with seeking and receiving mental health treatment and may foster openness in the therapeutic relationship. These goals may not fit comfortably with the goals of protecting the public, ensuring reasonable conduct from armed, commissioned officers, and allowing the agency to operate with efficiency. For that reason, the police psychologist must act with extreme care and discretion in balancing the values that underpin this work. For example, addicts are thought to be more likely to accept treatment, and the rest of society will benefit, if treatment is confidential. At the same time there are socially important reasons why the behavior of the patient while in substance abuse treatment (such as may occur when a person is fulfilling a condition of parole) may be revealed. In one instance, the court rejected a claim of damages when details of treatment about the substance treatment of a plaintiff was revealed to an interested party, noting that only the fact of being in treatment (already known in this case) was protected (*Chapa v. Adams,* 1997).

Every officer knows that the term *mental illness* may be used as a code word to warn other officers of the potential for violence (e.g., "Be careful! He is mental!"). Improved educational requirements for law enforcement officers have worked to reduce the idea that mental illness is a universal marker of danger and unpredictability, but police training continues to encourage officers to be alert to "the unstable" suspect. Confidentiality laws seek to protect both the fact that an individual has sought mental health treatment as well as some of the disclosures that are made during treatment.

In general, confidentiality is considered to be a cornerstone of a doctor-patient relationship, because many therapists assume that mental health treatment will be more successful if the client has a trustworthy relationship with the provider. In the FFDE situation, no doctor-patient relationship is said to exist, and the "client" is often defined contractually or administratively as the referring department, not the officer. The duty to protect the client is then owed to the agency and society, not to the officer.

CONFIDENTIALITY AND MENTAL HEALTH TREATMENT

The values that underlie confidentiality assume that people will be less likely to seek needed help (Corcoran and Winsalde, 1994) and less likely to disclose sensitive information if they believe that the information may be disseminated outside the treatment relationship. Persons who were told that confidentiality is absolute are more willing to disclose information than are individuals who were told that confidentiality is limited (Nowell and Spruill, 1993). Taube and Elwork (1990) found that patient self-disclosure was influenced in large measure by how important the legal limits on confidentiality were to the patient in his or her particular circumstances. The officer's caregiver is obligated ethically to disclose to the client the limits on confidentiality. This conflict between the role of the police psychologist as the protector of the public interest (in prevention of the possible loss of liberty and security of the citizen) and the potential needs of the clinically impaired officer is difficult to resolve. This is the cardinal reason why it is recommended that the FFDE provider never be the same person as the treatment provider in police psychology. In essence, the police psychologist practices within two diverse professional roles. The FFDE provider has the ethical responsibility to serve the public interest and evaluate the officer from the viewpoint of professional LE standards of conduct. The treating psychologist must have a working knowledge of police psychology, but is also a clinical provider who has a functioning doctor-patient relationship with the officer. He or she is required to observe all the attendant legal and ethical obligations that are common to all treatment, and which may not reflect adequately the ethical issues of security in law enforcement work.

CONFIDENTIALITY LAW

The laws governing the confidentiality of health care information have been described as a crazy quilt of Federal and state constitutional, statutory, regulatory and case law that erodes personal privacy and forms a serious barrier to administrative simplification (Waller, 1995). Persons who hold this view have been the driving force behind the movement for a national standard for the confidentiality of health care information in general, epitomized by the enactment of the HIPAA. Earlier, a national standard governing the confidentiality of substance abuse treatment information had been codified independently. As one reflects upon the confidentiality issue, keep in mind that there may be very good reasons for information to be exchanged among providers or agencies, particularly in law enforcement settings where public safety is a key issue.

Consent by the Person in Treatment

The most common exception to the rule of confidentiality is when the patient consents to a waiver of confidentiality. For example, the provider may ask that the person sign a consent form authorizing the release of confidential information to another treatment provider or insurance company. This reflects the fact that the right to confidentiality presumptively belongs to the patient, who may relinquish it for his or her own reasons. In ordinary clinical work, the patient may also wish to avoid release of certain information and direct that the provider not include sensitive personal information when releasing a clinical file, for example, regarding an embarrassing sexual difficulty. This means that the FFDE provider must expect that materials obtained by voluntary release from clinical providers may not be complete records and potentially important officer information may have been omitted.

Procedures for the release of personal health information typically include requirements that (1) the **consent** be in writing, (2) the name of the individual or entity to which disclosure of information is to be indicated clearly, (3) the purpose or need for disclosure and the type of information to be disclosed be indicated, and (4) a statement of the period for which the consent is effective is included (such as an expiration date). The dated signature of the patient and one or two witnesses to the signing is also a common requirement.

Disclosure to the Client

Many state laws provide that individuals (such as officers in treatment) have a right of access to health care records containing information about them. Some provide that a clinician may restrict access to the record, if in the clinician's judgment, access would cause harm to the client. Some statutes also provide that a clinician may restrict access to particular parts of the record if access might harm the client or if third parties (such as a spouse) provided information with the expectation that it would be held in confidence. Some experts have suggested that limiting client access undercuts the principle that information contained in the record belongs to the client (Campbell, 2000). This access applies only to cases in which a confidential relationship has been established, which should never apply to an FFDE procedure.

Disclosure to Law Enforcement Agencies

Many state laws limit access to information regarding civilians with mental illness by police agencies to situations in which an individual has eloped from an involuntary hospitalization or to situations in which a crime has been committed or threatened. A handful of state laws provide access for the purpose of investigating health care fraud. It is important to make the distinction between law enforcement agency access to records of suspects with a mental illness history and to records of law enforcement officers who are employed or are seeking employment as armed agents. The issue of suspect records may be important for the police psychologist acting in the role of hostage negotiator or criminal profiler, but this issue has limited applicability for issues of FFDEs. On the other hand, access to records may be vital in making the judgment to reinstate an armed officer to duty following mental health treatment. An edited record, with distressing details omitted, may be of limited use in the FFDE decision process.

Disclosure to Protect Third Parties

In 1976, the California Supreme Court ruled that a mental health professional has an obligation to take steps to protect identified third parties that the professional reasonably believes might be endangered by a client (*Tarasoff v. Regents of the University of California,* 1976). This ruling grew out of the supposed failure of a therapist to warn a person whom a patient threatened to kill, resulting in the death of the threatened party. This decision was controversial at the time on the grounds that it required mental health professionals to perform a task for which they were ill suited (that is, assess future risk) and that it would compromise confidentiality. Since the court's decision, many states have addressed this topic. The majority now provide that a mental health professional who concludes that his or her client represents an imminent danger to an identified third party may take steps, including notifying the individual and law enforcement officials, to protect the third party without becoming liable for a breach of confidentiality (the Tarasoff rule). In addition, most states permit or mandate disclosure in other situations where certain third parties might be at risk for harm, such as might be the case in child abuse and elder abuse circumstances.

Alcohol and Drug Abuse Confidentiality Laws

In an effort to create incentives for people with substance use and alcohol problems to seek treatment, federal law governs the confidentiality of information, obtained by federally assisted, specialized substance abuse treatment programs (42 U.S.C. 290dd-2; 42 C.F.R. 2.1, et seq.). Disclosure of patient-identifying information by federally assisted programs is permitted only in explicitly delineated circumstances. The person receiving services can waive confidentiality, but written consent must state the purpose of the disclosure and be signed by the client. Disclosures may be made without consent to other service providers if providers have entered into a "qualified service agreement" with the treating program. This is to permit the treating program to obtain collateral services, such as blood work, that are not performed by the program itself.

Disclosure also is permitted to law enforcement officials when there was a crime committed on the premises or against the personnel of the treatment program. Even in this case, information provided is to be limited initially to the name, address, and last known whereabouts of the individual who committed the crime. Other circumstances in which disclosures are permitted without consent include medical emergencies, child abuse reports, court orders, and criminal investigations of "extremely serious crimes" as defined in the regulation.

Other federal statutes have limited applicability to the confidentiality of health care information. The **Privacy Act of 1974** prohibits disclosure of an individual's record without prior written consent and provides patient access to review, copy, and correct records. However, the act applies only to federally operated hospitals and to research or health care institutions with federal contracts, so it does not cover the vast majority of organizations and entities collecting health care information.

Confidentiality is a matter of both ethical and legal concern. As noted earlier, each of the major health care professions endorses confidentiality as a core matter. However, it is generally the law that establishes the basic rules that govern confidentiality in practice. The judicial system can expand confidentiality, as the U.S. Supreme Court did when it ruled that a **psychotherapeutic privilege** would apply in federal court. The court rulings may decide that the principle of confidentiality must yield to other values, as the California Supreme Court did when it decided that mental health professionals had an obligation to protect third parties whom the professional reasonably concluded could be endangered by a client in treatment. In some cases, as with the Privacy Act of 1974, Congress may create laws that impact upon professional practice in many ways. One such act was the **Health Insurance Portability and Accountability Act of 1996 (HIPAA).**

THE HEALTH INSURANCE PORTABILITY AND ACCOUNTABILITY ACT OF 1996

In the absence of confidentiality protections, some individuals with mental illness may decide that the benefit of treatment is outweighed by the risk of public disclosure. This may be harmful to the individual and to a public that has a stake in the mental health of its members. The U.S. Supreme Court summarized this public interest succinctly in the decision quoted at the beginning of this section:

> The psychotherapist privilege serves the public interest by facilitating the provision of appropriate treatment for individuals suffering the effects of a mental or emotional problem. The mental health of our citizenry, no less than its physical health, is a public good of transcendent importance. (*Jaffee v. Redmond*, 1996)

The Health Insurance Portability and Accountability Act of 1996, Public Law 104-191, which amended the Internal Revenue Code of 1986 (also known as the Kennedy-Kassebaum Act) was meant to improve efficiency in health care delivery by standardizing electronic data interchange, and protection of confidentiality and security of health data through the setting and enforcing of enforceable standards. It requires the standardization of electronic patient health, administrative and financial data, unique health identifiers for individuals, employers, health plans, and health care providers and security standards protecting the confidentiality and integrity of individually identifiable health information, in the past, present, or future. It was meant to apply to all health care organizations. This includes all health care providers, even single provider offices, health plans, employers, public health authorities, life insurers, clearinghouses, billing agencies, information systems vendors, service organizations, and universities.

In general, this act provides for standard, especially electronic, enrollments of patients in any treatment program or facility and the adoption of standard code sets to be used in all health transactions. For example, coding systems that describe diseases, injuries, and other health problems, as well as their causes, symptoms, and actions taken, must be uniform. The HIPAA Security Rule also focuses both on external and internal security threats and vulnerabilities. It demands that all clinical or health-related material be secured from misuse or theft in any stored format. Organizations must protect against careless staff or others who are unaware of security issues and from curious or malicious outsiders and insiders who deliberately take advantage of system vulnerabilities to access and misuse personal health information.

For LE executives and police psychologists, the HIPAA appears to impact in two major ways, although a working knowledge of the act may be useful in dealing with a variety of health care situations that are commonly encountered in police work. The HIPAA appears to impact police psychology in (1) collection of information about the mental health treatment of officers before and following an FFDE and (2) the need to clarify the FFDE provider's position as other than a covered entity.

Protected Health Information

The HIPAA is intended to set a minimum level of security regarding **protected health information (PHI),** such as that regarding the treatment of mental illness. **Covered entities** are organizations that are affected by the HIPAA, and include health plans, health care providers, and health care clearinghouses. All are required to assess potential risks and protect against threats to information security and unauthorized use and disclosure. All CEs must implement and maintain security measures that are appropriate to their needs, capabilities, and circumstances. Finally, the CEs must ensure compliance by training and disciplining all staff that has patient contact or information.

The safeguards that comprise HIPAA-mandated security focus on protecting data integrity, confidentiality and availability of individually identifiable health information by (1) administrative procedures that manage the execution of security measures, (2) physical safeguards for computers and written material, (3) security services to protect information access, and (4) technical security mechanisms to prevent unauthorized access to data that are transmitted over a network.

Privacy and Confidentiality

Security should not be confused with privacy or confidentiality. **Privacy** refers to the right of an individual to control personal information and to not have it divulged or used by others without permission. Confidentiality becomes an issue only when an individual's personal information has been received (usually from the patient) by another entity (say a doctor) and is therefore already divulged. Confidentiality is a means of protecting that information, usually by asserting additional rights regarding disclosure. **Security** applies to the spectrum of physical, technical, and administrative safeguards that are put in place to protect the integrity, availability, and confidentiality of information.

Five Basic Principles

The HIPAA reflects five basic principles:

- *Consumer control:* The regulation provides consumers with certain new rights to control the release of their medical information.
- *Boundaries:* With few exceptions, an individual's health care information should be used for health purposes only, including

treatment and payment. The use of liability information derived in part from psychological instruments was not addressed, and the role of clinical information that may be important in public safety areas was similarly not mentioned directly.

- *Accountability:* Under HIPAA, for the first time, specific federal penalties may be levied if a patient's right to privacy is violated. HIPAA calls for severe civil and criminal penalties for noncompliance, including fines up to $25,000 for multiple violations of the same standard in a calendar year and fines up to $250,000 and/or imprisonment up to ten years for knowing misuse of individually identifiable health information. Civil penalties are permitted for health plans, providers, and clearinghouses that violate these standards. Civil money penalties are $100 per incident, up to $25,000 per person, per year, per standard.

- *Public responsibility:* The new standards reflect the need to balance privacy protections with the public responsibility to support such national priorities as protecting public health, conducting medical research, improving the quality of care, and fighting health care fraud and abuse. Protection of the public safety was not addressed by the act, but it would seem to be reasonably related to those named elements in the balance of national priorities.

- *Security:* It is the responsibility of organizations that are entrusted with health information to protect it against deliberate or inadvertent misuse or disclosure of protected information. From the prospective of the police psychologist, diagnostic and treatment information from a treatment provider or agency will be much more difficult to obtain in the future because of the severe penalties of any HIPAA rule violation.

Health Records Require Special Consent
for Nonhealth Purposes

With few exceptions, an individual's health information can be used for health purposes only.

- Health information cannot be used for purposes unrelated to health care, such as use by employers to make personnel decisions, without explicit authorization from the individual. Thus the need to fully inform and obtain consent for FFDE purposes becomes vital.

- Disclosures of information must be limited to the minimum amount necessary for the purpose of the disclosure. This regulation places a special burden upon the FFDE provider to avoid disclosure of confidential, personal, or unneeded information obtained either from the officer orfrom records in the FFDE report (see Chapter 8).
- Nonroutine disclosures with patient authorization must meet standards that ensure the authorization is truly informed and voluntary. Thus, special efforts should be extended to ensure that the officer in an FFDE understands fully the limitations, purpose, and methodology involved in the FFDE procedure before information is collected.

Consent and Authorization

Consent should not be confused with **authorization.** Consent allows for use and disclosure of PHI for treatment, payment, and health care operations only. Authorization allows for use and disclosure of PHI for other purposes. An authorization must be in writing and be specific. Authorization is needed to disclose PHI contained in treatment or session notes, such as may be needed by a police psychologist inquiring into the stability, safety, or similar concerns on behalf of the public or a law enforcement agency.

A provider who wishes to employ a third party in treatment must obtain the written consent of the patient before sharing PHI. In police psychology, this regulation is most important when the officer wishes for FFDE information to be released to a potential treatment provider. Both the officer and his department (the client in the FFDE) procedure should give consent for the release of any information.

The consent form itself must be written in plain language, inform the individual how the information may be used, state the patient's right to review the provider's privacy notice as well as request restrictions and revoke consent, and be dated and signed by the individual. The HIPAA requires only that consent be given. It does not set a time limit on how long a signature is effective (note that many state privacy laws do set an expiration date for signatures).

Research

It is permissible to use PHI without the consent of the patient so long as the identity of the patient has been removed from the information. The CE may still disclose the information for research, even without consent, as long as a privacy board (human research board) has approved the release, the PHI is necessary to develop a protocol, and the research will not involve removing PHI from the CE. The information may also be used if the individual is deceased, and the decedent's PHI is used solely for research.

Public Responsibilities and Privacy

Social values that are involved, other than privacy, are acknowledged but not usually specified, in the HIPAA operating rules. They involve unsettled exceptions to PHI uses that will be addressed by the courts and regulators in the future:

- Oversight of the health care system, including quality assurance activities
- Public health questions, such as contagious disease containment
- Research, generally limited to when a waiver of authorization is independently approved by a privacy board or institutional review board
- Judicial and administrative proceedings
- Limited law enforcement activities
- Emergency circumstances
- Identification of the body of a deceased person or the cause of death
- Registration in facility patient directories
- Activities related to national defense and security

Patient consent or authorization must be obtained before information is released, such as from clinical providers to the FFDE examiner. Patients have the right to request restrictions on the uses and disclosures of their information. The restriction or deletion of certain information from medical or psychological records clearly presents certain problems to police psychologists who are participating in a process that is meant to protect the public from conduct that is unacceptable in armed, minimally supervised law enforcement officers. Detailed personal information may be vital to making an intelligent decision regarding fitness issues in officers, a problem that was not contemplated by the HIPAA authors, who had focused almost exclusively upon methods to protect individual persons from medical privacy infringement. Compulsions or urges concerning violations of persons' civil rights (murder, rape, sadistic treatment, etc.), for example, or hidden substance abuse problems that may impair the ability of the officer to coherently enforce the law, are not private matters. To allow an officer to redact or edit his or her medical record to evade detection of such problems is a public safety issue and should not be permissible in the strict context of an FFDE. Unfortunately, once CEs establish procedures to comply with ordinary HIPAA requirements, explaining the employment and administrative issues that should exclude FFDE medical inquiries from HIPAA restrictions may become a difficult and time-consuming matter.

No Right to Information in FFDEs

Patients normally have access to their medical records. However, in the case of most FFDEs, HIPAA regulations provide that "patients do not have the right of access to information compiled in reasonable anticipation of, or for use in, a civil, criminal, or administrative action or procedure" (45 CFR 45 164.508 and 164.524[a][1]). The evolutions of applications of this rule are central to future FFDE utility.

Psychotherapy Notes

Psychotherapy notes (which are used only by a psychotherapist) are held to a higher standard of protection because they are not part of the medical record. Special authorizations will be required to obtain such notes, although the definition of psychotherapy notes appears to be very narrow. If a broad definition of psychotherapy notes emerges, restriction on access will make obtaining psychiatric records very difficult when the FFDE provider has reason to believe that important public safety information may be contained in past treatment records.

Minimum Necessary Rule

The minimum necessary rule states that the PHI sent to a recipient should contain the least information needed by that party. The minimum necessary rule is meant to force CEs to evaluate and improve their practices to avoid inappropriate and unnecessary access to PHI. This rule should not be considered as automatically overriding professional judgment or standards regarding necessary information.

Hybrid Entities

Hybrid entities were defined as only those entities whose **primary activities** are not covered under HIPAA. For example, law enforcement agencies that operate on-site EAPs, counseling, or health clinics may fall into this category. Hybrid entities had the right to designate those components that engage in covered functions (referred to as "health care components") and are therefore subject to regulation under HIPAA. This right permits hybrid entities to limit their HIPAA compliance to only those components that engage in covered activities. Many police psychology operations may be defined as hybrid entities. For example, it is reasonable to consider that an independent contractor that provides an EAP service must operate under HIPAA. Some external police psychology corporations may provide certain discrete services that are health care related (e.g., an independent counseling clinic), but other service divisions may provide only screening or hostage negotiation services, that may not be directly covered by HIPAA.

SUGGESTIONS FOR THE LAW ENFORCEMENT EXECUTIVE AND POLICE PSYCHOLOGIST

HIPAA is a heath systems reform act that affects police psychologists who are providing health care services, particularly regarding the electronic transmission of information. It will doubtlessly spill over into all forms of information transmission, especially as they involve issues of privacy and confidentiality. Those police psychologists that are providing direct services (such as in an EAP) will feel a more direct impact from the HIPAA than those who specialize in liability, administrative, and training services. However, as with nearly all federal government intrusions into the practical areas of human conduct, there will be more gray areas than straightforward applications of regulation.

The following are recommended as good general guides until the courts make the HIPAA clearer in practice through emerging case law:

1. Develop fixed policy and procedures that are likely to conform to the spirit of HIPAA, particularly in EAP or public or private clinical service programs. This may be achieved most practically by the purchasing of preplanned computer software, forms, releases, insurance coverage, and operation manuals from commercial sources. Be prepared to document your compliance policy and retain important documentation related to the policy for six years from the date of creation.
2. The general principles of locking up all records, not leaving documents where others can see them, and coding materials in computer files are commonsense rules that should become second nature.
3. Personnel policy for staff should include documented training and supervision of staff procedure, as well as documented sanctions for the violations of privacy rules in the office.
4. Create and make available a standard and simple complaint process and keep a file of complaints. Identify a compliance officer from among staff members (regardless of whether the services are provided by internal or external professionals) and assign the responsibility of overseeing the complaint system to that party.
5. Prepare to document **duty-to-mitigate** errors. If a mistake occurs (e.g., the police psychologist staff sends clinical information to the wrong departmental division), document how an attempt at recovery and correction took place.
6. Be prepared to follow the case law as it develops in regard to HIPAA and be prepared to make needed adjustments in procedure and policy as the courts clarify the issues of application.

Chapter 14

The Americans with Disabilities Act and Fitness-for-Duty Evaluations

Bureaucrats write memoranda both because they appear to be busy when they are writing and because the memos, once written, immediately become proof that they were busy.

Charles Peters

In many states, no doctor-patient relationship is said to exist when the doctor (such as the FFDE provider) is paid by the employer to examine the employee. Nevertheless, it may be helpful for the police psychologist to review the law in the particular state and to make the employee aware (as in a formal document) that the FFDE provider answers exclusively to the law enforcement agency and not to the examined officer. Nevertheless, FFDEs must touch upon elements of medical and psychiatric functioning, and that brings the FFDE provider into contact with federal laws that concern the relationship between labor and civil rights regulations and medical conditions. To make matters more complex, a law that was written to reduce confusion over creditworthiness investigations may have inadvertently complicated the FFDE process as an administrative enterprise. This chapter is an introduction to such issues.

THE AMERICANS WITH DISABILITIES ACT

The **Americans with Disabilities Act of 1990 (ADA)** offers civil rights protections to individuals with disabilities similar to the way such protections are provided to individuals on the basis of race, sex, national origin, age, and religion. It guarantees equal opportunity for individuals with disabilities in public accommodations, employment, transportation, state and local government services, and telecommunications. Title I of the ADA contains employment provisions that apply to private employers, state and local governments, employment agencies, and labor unions. The ADA prohibits discrimination in all employment practices, including job application procedures, hiring, firing, advancement, compensation, training, and conditions and privileges of employment. It applies to recruitment, advertising, tenure, layoff, leave, fringe benefits, and all other employment-related activities.

The ADA prohibits employment discrimination against applicants and employees who are qualified individuals with disabilities. An individual is considered to have a **disability** if he or she has a physical or mental impairment that substantially limits one or more major life activities or has a record of such impairment. The ADA applies to persons who have impairments that substantially limit major life activities such as seeing, hearing, speaking, walking, breathing, performing manual tasks, learning, caring for oneself, and working. An individual with epilepsy, paralysis, AIDS, a substantial hearing or visual impairment, mental retardation, or a specific learning disability is covered, but an individual with a minor condition of short duration, such as a broken limb, is not.

An ADA-qualified individual is one who meets legitimate skill, experience, education, or other requirements of an employment position that he or she holds or seeks and who can perform the essential functions of the position with or without reasonable accommodation. Requiring the ability to perform essential functions ensures that an individual with a disability will not be considered unqualified simply because of inability to perform marginal or incidental job functions, such has requiring a police dispatcher to lift heavy weights. An employer is otherwise free to select the most qualified applicant available and make decisions based on reasons *unrelated* to a disability. In other words, an employer can hire the fastest stenographer of the two applicants, even if the slower applicant has a disability.

Post–Initial Offer Examination

An employer *may not* ask or require a job applicant to take a medical examination before making a job offer. An employer cannot make any inquiry about the nature or severity of a disability that proceeds a conditional employment offer. An employer may make a job offer dependant on the satisfactory result of a medical or psychological examination or inquiry if this is required of all entering employees in the same job category. Not all elements of a postoffer examination or inquiry have to be job related and consistent with business necessity. However, if an individual is not hired because a postoffer examination or inquiry reveals a disability, the reason(s) for not hiring must be job related and consistent with **business necessity,** meaning that the impairment or disability makes the practical performance of the job unattainable (e.g., a blind pilot). The employer also must show that no reasonable **accommodation** (such a providing an amplification device to a hearing-impaired receptionist) was available that would enable the individual to perform essential job functions, or that accommodation would impose an **undue hardship** (e.g., unreasonable expense) on the employer. A postoffer medical or psychological examination may also disqualify an individual from employment if the employer can demonstrate that the individual would pose a **direct threat** in the workplace (e.g., a significant risk of substantial harm to the health or safety of the individual or others). A postoffer medical examination may not disqualify an individual with a disability that is currently able to perform essential job functions because of a **speculation** (a supposition without clear evidence) or a **myth** that the disability may cause a risk of future problems.

As an incumbent employee, a medical examination or inquiry must be job related and consistent with business necessity. Employers may conduct employee medical examinations where there is evidence of a job-performance or safety problem. For example, evidence that a truck driver has had a seizure while driving a truck is a valid reason to conduct a medical fitness-for-duty examination. Voluntary examinations that are part of employee health programs are also permissible. Information from all medical and psychological examinations and inquiries must be kept *apart* from general personnel files as a separate, confidential medical record, available only under limited conditions.

Substance Abuse

Tests for current use of illicit drugs are *not* medical examinations under the ADA, and employers are not subject to any drug-testing restrictions. Questions regarding current drug use are not excluded from the pre–initial offer application. Individuals who currently engage in the illegal use of drugs are excluded specifically from the definition of a "qualified individual with a disability" protected by the ADA when the employer takes action on the basis of their drug use. Past drug use is a covered ADA condition, but evidence of the use of drugs or alcohol that affects current employment ability (such as intoxication at work) is not considered an ADA issue. An employer can discipline, discharge, or deny employment to an alcoholic or drug abuser whose use of alcohol or drugs adversely affects job performance or conduct. An employer also may prohibit the use of abusables in any workplace and can require that employees not be under the influence of abusables at work, regardless of whether they were consumed off premises or before work began. The ADA does not override health and safety requirements established under other federal or state laws, even if a standard adversely affects the employment of an individual with a disability.

Reasonable Accommodation

Reasonable accommodation is any modification or adjustment to a job or the work environment that will enable a qualified applicant or employee with a disability to participate in the application process or perform essential job functions. Examples of reasonable accommodation include making existing facilities used by employees readily accessible to and usable by an individual with a disability; restructuring a job; modifying work schedules; or appropriately modifying examinations, training, or other programs. Reasonable accommodation also may include reassigning a current employee to a vacant position for which the individual is qualified, if the person is unable to do the original job because of a disability, even with an accommodation. However, employers are under no obligation to find a position for an applicant who is not qualified for the position requested.

An employer is required only to accommodate a known disability of a qualified applicant or employee. In general, the requirement will be triggered by a request from an individual with a disability, who may suggest an appropriate accommodation. Accommodations must be made on an individual basis, because the nature and extent of a disabling condition and the requirements of a job will vary in each case. If the individual does not request an accommodation, the employer is not obligated to provide one, except where an individual's known disability impairs his or her ability to know of, or effectively communicate a need for, an accommodation that is obvious to the employer. In addition, an employer is not required to make an accommodation if it would impose an undue hardship on the operation of the employer's business. Undue hardship is defined as an action requiring significant difficulty or expense when considered in light of a number of factors, such as the size, resources, nature, and structure of the employer's operation. In general, a larger employer with greater resources would be expected to make accommodations requiring greater effort or expense than would be required of a smaller employer with fewer resources. An employer is not required to reallocate essential functions of a job as a reasonable accommodation.

An employer can hold employees with disabilities to the same standards of production/performance as other similarly situated employees without disabilities for performing essential job functions. An employer can establish attendance and leave policies that are uniformly applied to all employees, regardless of disability, but an employer also may be required to make adjustments in leave policy as a reasonable accommodation.

False Information

An employer may refuse to hire or may fire any person who knowingly provides a false answer to a lawful postoffer inquiry about his or her medical or psychiatric condition or worker's compensation history, even if the individual is disabled under ADA.

State and Local Governments

Local government entities must eliminate any eligibility criteria for participation in programs, activities, and services that screen, or that tend to screen, persons with disabilities, unless it can establish that the requirements are necessary for the provision of the service, program, or activity. As noted previously, the local government may adopt legitimate safety requirements necessary for safe operation if they are based on real risks, not on stereotypes or generalizations about individuals with disabilities.

Although state governments are mentioned as covered organizations under the ADA, it appears that the Third, Fifth, and Eighth Circuit federal courts have ruled that the application of the ADA to state institutions is unconstitutional (*Board of Trustees of University of Alabama v. Garrett,* 2001). The federal government may not infringe upon states' rights in matters of employment policy. This exemption from the ADA, however, does not apply to governmental units below the state level.

ADA DISABILITY DEFINITION AND THE SUPREME COURT

The Supreme Court began the process of defining the meaning of the term *disabled* shortly after the law was passed. It focused upon issues of what was meant by limitations in daily activities, the degree to which each case should be taken on its own merit, and the role of correction by medications or appliances in the claimed **disability.** This resulted in four landmark cases that have worked to set important standards regarding ADA discrimination claims. It is worthwhile for the LE executive and police psychologist to consider theses four cases in detail so as to anticipate the court's thinking regarding the ADA and generalize that understanding to law enforcement employment problems.

Kimberly Hilton and Karen Sutton sued United Airlines (*Sutton v. United Airlines,* 1997), claiming that their ADA rights had been violated when United Airlines (UA) denied them the opportunity to become pilots due to their need for corrective lenses because of myopia. The twin sisters had uncorrected visual acuity of 20/200 or worse, but with corrective measures both functioned as individuals without visual impairments. The sisters applied to UA, a major commercial airline carrier, for employment as commercial airline pilots, but were rejected because they did not meet UA's minimum requirement of uncorrected visual acuity. Consequently, the sisters filed suit under ADA. Among other things, the ADA defines an employee as disabled if he or she has "a physical or mental impairment that substantially limits one or more major life activities," or if the employee has "been regarded as having such an impairment" (the **"regarded as" standard**) §(42 U.S.C.12102[2][e]). The district court dismissed the complaint and held that the sisters were not actually disabled because they could fully correct their visual impairments with lenses.

The Tenth Circuit affirmed this decision. The court ruled that disability existed only where an impairment "substantially limits" a major life activity, not where it "might," "could," or "would" be substantially limited if corrective measures were not taken. The original EEOC guidelines that directed persons to be judged in their uncorrected or unmitigated state were found to run counter to this mandated, individualized inquiry. The congressional finding that 43 million Americans have one or more physical or mental disabilities, required the conclusion that Congress did not intend to bring all such persons under the ADA's protection when the condition was corrected. Because the petitioners alleged that their corrected vision was 20/20 or better, they are not disabled under ADA.

To further their claims, *Sutton et al.* alleged that UA had an impermissible vision requirement that was based on "myth and stereotype" (prohibited by ADA) and that UA mistakenly believed that, due to their poor vision, petitioners are unable to work as global airline pilots and are thus limited substantially in the major life activity of working. The court ruled that setting physical criteria for a job does not violate the ADA. The ADA allowed employers to prefer some physical attributes to others, so long as those attributes do not rise to the level of a substantially limiting impairment. An employer is free to decide that physical characteristics (that are not impairments) are preferable to others. In addition, the court ruled, the ADA requires, at least, that one's ability to work be significantly reduced. The court found that the position of global airline pilot was not the only pilot work available. Indeed, a number of other positions using similar skills, such as regional pilot and pilot instructor, were available.

In *Kirkingburg v. Albertson's, Inc.* (1998), a truck driver named Hallie Kirkingburg was examined in 1990 before he began his job with Albertson's, Inc., a grocery retailer, to determine whether he met the Department of Transportation's (DOT) basic vision standards for commercial truck drivers. This standard required corrected distant visual acuity of at least 20/40 in each eye and distant binocular acuity of at least 20/40. Although he had amblyopia, an uncorrectable condition that left him with 20/200 vision, the doctor had erroneously certified that he met the DOT standards. When Kirkingburg's vision was correctly assessed in a 1992 physical, he was told that he could get a waiver of the DOT standards under a waiver program. Albertson's, however, fired him for failing to meet the basic DOT vision standards and refused to rehire him after he received a waiver. Kirkingburg sued Albertson's, claiming that firing him violated the ADA. In granting summary judgment for Albertson's, the district court found that Kirkingburg was not qualified for the job because he could not meet the basic DOT standards and that the waiver program did not alter DOT standards. The Ninth Circuit reversed, finding that Kirkingburg had established a disability under ADA.

The Supreme Court reversed again, ruling that the ADA required that monocular individuals must prove a disability by offering evidence that the extent of the limitation on a major life activity caused by their impairment is substantial. They ruled that Kirkingburg's amblyopia was not a physical or mental impairment that "substantially limits" a major life activity. Monocularity embraced a group whose members vary in the ultimate scope of the restrictions on their visual abilities. An employer who requires a job qualification that is a federal safety regulation does not have to justify enforcing the regulation solely because it may be waived experimentally.

In *Murphy v. United Parcel Service* (1998), the United Parcel Service (UPS) hired Vaugn Murphy as a mechanic, a position that required him to drive commercial vehicles. In order to drive, he had to satisfy certain DOT health certification requirements, including having no current clinical diagnosis of high blood pressure likely to interfere with his or her ability to operate a commercial vehicle safely. Despite Murphy's high blood pressure, he was granted certification erroneously and commenced work. After the error was discovered, UPS fired him because his blood pressure exceeded the DOT's requirements. Murphy brought suit under Title I of the ADA. The district court granted UPS summary judgment, and the Tenth Circuit affirmed. The court of appeals held that the petitioner's hypertension was not a disability because when medicated his high blood pressure does not substantially limit him in any major life activity. UPS argued that it did not regard the petitioner as substantially limited in the major life activity of working, but, rather, regarded him only as unqualified to work as an UPS mechanic because he was unable to obtain DOT health certification. It was undisputed that he was generally employable as a mechanic. As a matter of law, Murphy was not limited substantially in the major life activity of working.

In *Toyota Motor Mfg. Kentucky, Inc. v. Williams* (2002), the Supreme Court unanimously set the standard for determining when an individual who claimed to be limited in the ability to perform a specific task met the disability definition and would be protected under the ADA. The employee in this case claimed that her employer failed to accommodate her with a job assignment that would not aggravate the carpal tunnel syndrome (CTS) that she reportedly developed while working on the employer's assembly line. Williams argued that she was entitled to an ADA disability accommodation because her CTS substantially limited the major life function of performing manual duties. The Sixth Circuit Court of Appeals ruled that she was disabled and entitled to an accommodation.

The Supreme Court disagreed and overturned the decision because it found that the appeals court applied the wrong standard to determine whether the employee was disabled. It held that the Sixth Circuit overvalued the evidence showing that the employee's CTS prevented her from performing a class of work-related manual tasks. Instead, it should have taken into account broader evidence showing clearly that she could perform a variety of fundamental, non-work-related activities. It ruled that in order for a person to be substantially limited in the "major life activity" of performing manual tasks, the person must have had an impairment that prevented or severely restricted the individual from doing activities that are of central importance to most people's daily lives. To meet this standard, the impairment's impact must be permanent or long term and cover many non-work-related functions, such as driving and cooking.

Punitive Damages Against Public Entities

In *Barnes v. Gorman* (2002), the Supreme Court, ruled that although suits for compensatory damages against municipalities are permitted under the ADA, Title II did not authorize suits against municipalities for punitive damages. The plaintiff, a wheelchair user, was arrested after an altercation with a nightclub bouncer in Kansas City, Missouri. He was transported in a police van that had no wheelchair locks. Over his objection, the police removed him from his wheelchair and attempted to secure him with his belt to the back of the van. During the ride to the police station he fell and ruptured his urine bag, which he had not been allowed to empty before being transported. Injuries to his neck and shoulder caused by the fall left him unable to work full-time. He sued the Kansas City police and received a jury award under the ADA of more than $1 million in compensatory damages and $1.2 million in punitive damages. The Department of Justice argued successfully in an amicus brief that the U.S. court of appeals had made an error in upholding the award of punitive damages against Kansas City because Congress did not indicate clearly that such damages were available under the ADA.

Public Safety

The Americans with Disabilities Act (ADA) allows employers to refuse to hire or retain a disabled person who poses a direct threat to the health or safety of others in the workplace. Direct threat means a significant risk to the health or safety of the employee or others that cannot be eliminated by reasonable accommodation (42 U.S.C. §12113). An employee who poses a direct threat is not a qualified individual with a disability (*Daugherty v. City of El Paso,* 1995). The determination that an individual poses a direct threat must be based on an **individualized assessment** of the individual's present ability to perform the essential functions of the job safely. The assessment must be based on a reasonable medical or psychological judgment that relies on the most current scientific or professional knowledge and/or on the best available objective evidence

For example, an employer can refuse to hire a disabled person who suffers from uncontrollable seizures for a position that requires working with dangerous chemicals or vehicle driving. In law enforcement work, the ability to operate vehicles, devices (such as weapons), and engage in physical confrontations may be critical in protecting the well-being of the public. The inability to perform such functions may be described as posing a direct threat in the workplace.

The U.S. Supreme Court decided that this rule extended to situations in which the applicant's or employee's own life or health would be endangered by the job. In *Chevron U.S.A., Inc. v. Echazabal* (2002), the Court ruled that employers can refuse to hire applicants for positions that would pose a direct threat to their own health or safety. The Court found that Chevron was within its rights when it refused to hire Mario Echazabal to work in an oil refinery because Echazabal had been diagnosed with Hepatitis C and doctors found that his condition could be aggravated by exposure to toxins at the refinery.

Employees and their advocates have criticized this decision, arguing that disabled employees should be entitled to decide for themselves whether a job creates an unacceptable risk of harm. Employers countered that they have legitimate reasons for not hiring employees who would endanger themselves on the job, such as avoiding excessive turnover and sick leave, personal injury lawsuits, and claimed violations of health and safety laws

This general pre-ADA principle was anticipated in regard to law enforcement in a 1986 state court ruling. In Indiana, an appellate court was faced with a case in which an officer with a long history of emotional illness asked the court to compel his department to reinstate him despite his difficulties. The court ruled that a policeman frequently works alone, wields great authority, and carries lethal weapons. Law enforcement therefore, is not an occupation for a person with questionable emotional stability (*City of Greenwood v. Dowler*, 1986).

The "Regarded As" Standard and FFDEs

The ADA, in an apparent attempt to protect persons who may be perceived as handicapped, but who have not been formally determined to be disabled, included a section that addresses the issue of persons who are "regarded as" disabled by the employer (42 U.S.C. §12102[2]). It provides that persons will be treated as having a disability if he or she: (1) has an impairment that is not substantially limiting but that the employer perceives as constituting a substantially limiting impairment; (2) has an impairment that is substantially limiting only because of the attitudes of others toward such an impairment; or (3) has no impairment at all but is regarded by the employer

as having a substantially limiting impairment (29 C.F.R. §1630.2[l]).
Thus, some courts have held that the mere inquiry into an employee's
potential disability (such as an FFDE) can establish a "regarded as"
claim. Such a finding is possible when the employer does not have
objective evidence on which to base its request for an FFDE. When
rational or material grounds exist for an FFDE request, a court is less
likely to validate a "regarded as" claim—a special reason to clarify
the reasons for referral.

Medical Information

The Americans with Disability Act may place some limits on an
employer's right to secure common medical information, particularly
if it is not job related. As discussed previously, the ADA is meant to
prevent employers from discriminating against medically or psychologically ill employees or employment applicants in the same manner
that other civil rights legislation is intended to prevent gender, age, or
racial discrimination. However, it allows that some forms of illness
may interfere with the business necessity of the job. Personality or social interaction problems are not usually covered under the ADA (in
contrast with mental illness), implying that simply being a difficult or
unpleasant person alone is not protected behavior. Indeed, in *Duncan
v. Wis. Dept. of Health* (1999) a three-judge federal appellate panel
ruled that "personality disorder" is not covered by the ADA, whereas
mental illness is covered. This dependence of the ADA on explicit diagnosis in mental health areas makes the use of qualified, independent
evaluators extremely important since the exact nature of the purported difficulty may become the central legal question. Understanding the complexities of the ADA regarding behavioral problems is an
important dual function of the departmental attorney and the FFDE
provider. FFDEs may be invaluable in two ways. First, if the officer
has a remediable illness, the department can comply with the spirit of
the ADA by assisting the officer in rehabilitation or, perhaps, by offering accommodations while the rehabilitation proceeds. Second,
the FFDE may delineate clearly the illness or the absence of illness,
an important question because not every social or behavioral problem
is an illness.

Justification and Need

The special care that must be taken when the ADA case involves particularly intrusive procedures can be seen in *Krocka v. Bransfield* (1997). An officer who claimed to suffer depression for which he was required to take medication sued the city and the police surgeon under the ADA and Civil Rights Act of 1991. Both plaintiff and defendant moved for summary judgment. The court held the automatic placement of the officer into a medication-level blood test monitoring program because he was taking particular psychotropic medication was an adverse employment action and was not justified by safety concerns. The plaintiff received a five-day suspension, because he appeared as an attorney at an arbitration, which is prohibited by departmental rules and regulations. The court ruled that the officer failed to establish a retaliation claim based upon justified disciplinary action. The court ruled the blood test served no public interest and violated the Fourth Amendment and the ADA, and the departmental surgeon who ordered the test was not entitled to qualified immunity from civil rights claims arising from unlawful testing.

The court ruled that intrusive tests or examinations (such as requiring the drawing of blood on a regular basis) are permissible only when the department can articulate an important governmental or public interest in order to overcome the requirements of constitutional and ADA protections. In this case, no analysis of the officer's behavior had raised any suspicion that a blood analysis was likely to address, but the department only indicated that the procedure was automatic. The ruling reinforced the idea that a scientific, demonstrable approach must lay the foundation for any requirement that supposedly addresses a concern with public safety or business necessity in a law enforcement agency, if that procedure impacts upon the officer's work status.

Regulations Reserving Light-Duty Positions

In 2002, the U.S. Department of Justice, Civil Rights Division, entered into a settlement agreement with the city of Inkster, Michigan, resolving a complaint of employment discrimination referred to the department by the **Equal Employment Opportunity Commission.**

The city of Inkster refused to provide a police sergeant with an accommodation under its policy prohibiting reassignment of employees to an existing light-duty position if the employees have non-duty-related injuries. The city of Inkster agreed to remove this restriction on reassignment to light-duty positions, restore the sergeant's sick leave hours to his leave bank, and provide ADA training to employees responsible for responding to requests for reasonable accommodation (U.S. Department of Justice, 2003).

In *DeVito v. Chicago Park District* (2001), a park laborer who had been on light duty for four years due to a reported back injury was caught on videotape while off duty twisting, bending, and climbing in stressful and physically demanding tasks. The light-duty job he was performing involved answering phones at an office near his home. He had been told that he could leave work whenever he felt pain or stress, which was typically after two or three hours, although he was paid the full wages of a regular employee. After being caught on tape and fired, he sued, claiming his employer failed to accommodate his disability in violation of the ADA. At trial, he professed that he was ready, willing, and able to work full-time in a light-duty assignment, but the courts found otherwise. The plaintiff had not worked full-time for thirteen years at the time of his appeal hearing, ostensibly because of his disability, and testified that he felt no better than he had felt when he first injured his back. These two factors justified a finding that the plaintiff was unable to work full-time and therefore was not qualified to work a full-time job. The court also took aim at his attempt to first obtain accommodation for his total disability for work full-time, and then seeking damages for the employer's failure to accommodate the disability, which the employee later claimed was not total after all.

Seniority and ADA

The Supreme Court held that, under the ADA, requests for an accommodation that conflict with the terms of a contractual seniority provision are unreasonable and will be permitted only when the employee can demonstrate special circumstances that make the requested accommodation reasonable (*US Airways Inc. v. Barnett,* 2002). Robert Barnett injured his back in 1990 and again in 1992 while working for US Airways and was transferred to a position in the mailroom. Shortly after Barnett's injury, all of US Airways' cargo and mailroom positions were opened to seniority-based bidding. Barnett then submitted a request to avoid the seniority system by an accommodation under the ADA. He asked US Airways to create an exception to the seniority bidding system to allow him to remain in his current position. US Airways rejected Barnett's accommodation request, placing him instead on limited-duty status. After being placed on injury leave, Barnett subsequently requested that US Airways accommodate him by modifying the cargo position to permit him to perform desk work only. US Airways rejected the request and terminated Barnett, who then sued under the ADA.

The district court ruled that Barnett had established he was disabled under the ADA, but determined that US Airways was under no obligation to make an exception to its seniority policy. The Ninth Circuit reversed and ruled that a bona fide seniority system was not a bar to a reasonable accommodation. The Supreme Court agreed to hear the case. Justice Stephen Breyer concluded that, as a general rule, a requested accommodation that conflicts with a seniority system is not a "reasonable" accommodation as a matter of law. This principle applied in the nonunion context as well as in the unionized/collective bargaining agreement context. The court ruled that the plaintiff must bear the burden of showing special circumstances that make an exception from the seniority system reasonable in the particular case.

Light Duty

A few general rules seem to apply to the question of light duty. The employer must maintain confidentiality for mental illness conditions, as is the case for all medical illnesses. Light-duty assignments are temporary and may be refused if the employee's impairments are permanent. Be alert to the claim that an extended light-duty assignment means that the employer considers the employee to be suffering a disability (the *"regarded as"* issue). It is recommended that employers create a written light-duty policy for all employees and work out the details of pay, hours, and regulations of work before action needs to be taken—a matter that may involve the civil service board, the union, and other stakeholders.

Disciplining or Discharging Difficult Officers

In general, the courts have maintained that the department has an overriding right to inquire into the mental stability of an officer, and that other presumed rights, such as the right of privacy, are of secondary importance when a police officer is involved. The need for a fitness-for-duty evaluation can be very clear in some cases. For example, in *Watson v. City of Miami Beach* (1999) a police commander noticed that a patrol officer was unusually offensive and antagonistic toward co-workers and supervisors. In a three-year period, eleven grievances had been filed by or against this officer. The officer, who was relieved of duty pending a fitness-for-duty evaluation, brought suit under the ADA. The appeals court rejected his claim of being psychologically disabled because the department had shown that he had serious personality conflicts, a problem not covered by ADA. The panel said that these characterizations merely show he had serious personality conflicts with co-workers, and that such conflicts do not rise to the level of a mental impairment under the ADA. Further, the rules of the department had demonstrated a business necessity to remove him and not to wait until perceived threat became real or questionable behavior resulted in injuries. The court ruled that no evidence existed that management acted improperly by ordering the officer to undergo a fitness-for-duty evaluation.

Personality Disorders under ADA

A youth counselor was referred for an FFDE following a period of disagreeable and explosive incidents involving his loss of personal temper control. An examining psychiatrist determined that the employee was subject to episodic temper outbursts that posed "serious limitation" on his ability to serve in a sensitive occupation. In response, the employee claimed that the complaints about his behavior were "profoundly offensive," and he exhibited his resistance to rehabilitation by avoiding therapy sessions. After his termination, he sued for relief under the ADA. A three-judge appellate panel noted that a personality disorder does not affect a major life activity, especially if the "disability" is relevant only to a specific job (*Duncan v. Wis. Dept. of Health,* 1999).

Even when a recognized disability exists, the law enforcement agency is not required to place unrealistic stress on the supervisory process when the officer is unable to perform basic duties, such as competently using a weapon. If armed employees are found to be psychologically disabled, the agency is not required to reinstate officers who are in need of close supervision or must be relieved of their firearms (*Penn. St. Troopers' Assn. [Kornguth] v. Pa. St. Police,* 1994). In an earlier Pennsylvania case, an appellate panel upheld the demotion of an officer to an unarmed civilian position. They found his claim of psychological recovery to be irrelevant (*Herman v. Cmwlth. Dept. of Gen. Services,* 1984).

Accommodation of Employee Demand for Reduced Hours

A public health care employee, who worked up to seventy hours per week, began to experience chest pain, shortness of breath, numbness in her arms, and dizziness. Her physician diagnosed a left arterial enlargement and directed her not to work more than forty hours per week. Her supervisors agreed that she could not perform the job while working only forty hours per week, and she was terminated. She sued under the Rehabilitation Act of 1973 (29 U.S.C. §791), the ADA, the FMLA, and similar state laws. The U.S. district court dismissed all claims, and a three-judge appeals panel affirmed the ruling. In her deposition, the health care employee conceded that long hours were "part of the job" and that she needed to work part of all three work shifts. The panel ruled that an individual's ability to perform only one job is not a handicap (*Tardie v. Rehabilitation Hosp. of Rhode Island,* 1999).

Permanent Physical Limitation Status and ADA

Four Seattle corrections officers sued to stop the initiation of an officer rotation policy. The officers argued that they could not have direct contact with inmates (as was required of all officers periodically) because of the possibility of physical confrontation that would aggravate their medical conditions. The officers had each suffered one of a series of disparate difficulties.

The U.S. district court and a three-judge appellate panel found that the officers were not "qualified" for their employment because of their "no inmate contact" medical restrictions. The court found that the ability to restrain inmates during an emergency is critical to jail security. The court ruled that jail safety would be jeopardized by the officer's inability to deal with emergencies. The panel noted that the bargaining agreement provided that corrections officers were expected to rotate among several positions, most of which require inmate contact (*Kees v. Wallenstein,* 1998).

Rejection in Screening is not Equal to Disability

In the mid-1990s, a veteran Texas police officer relocated to Missouri and applied to work as a police dispatcher. In a preemployment screening, she received a marginally elevated score on one scale of the MMPI-2 (see Chapter 8), suggesting depressive concerns. She sued under the ADA, challenging the MMPI as not job related and claiming that management perceived her as being disabled (the "regarded as" standard). The appellate court held that (1) she presented no evidence that she was disabled and (2) the fact that she was hired as a dispatcher meant the city did not perceive her as disabled. The court ruled that, regarding the use of the MMPI, appropriate psychological screening is job related and consistent with business necessity where the selection of individuals to train for the position of police officer is concerned (*Miller v. City of Springfield,* 1998)

Suicide Attempts and the ADA

Police Officer Spades attempted suicide by shooting himself in the head. Because this was considered a violent use of a firearm, and the department has a legal liability in employing such an officer, he was terminated. After receiving a variety of mental and medical treatments for his injuries and mental condition, Spades attempted to be reinstated. When his application was not accepted, he claimed a violation of the ADA and the FMLA. He alleged he was fired because of his depression and/or that management refused to grant him federally required medical leave. Citing *Murphy v. United Parcel Service* (1999) a three-judge panel recognized that his depression had been corrected and he no longer suffered a federally recognized disability. Moreover, increased potential liability associated with an employee's past activities was ruled a legitimate concern of the city, particularly when there is known violent behavior. Spades' FMLA claim was likewise rejected, because civil liability is a nondiscriminatory reason for his termination (*Spades v. City of Walnut Ridge*, 1999.).

Police and HIV

An HIV-positive police candidate brought suit against the city of Chattanooga alleging that refusal to hire him violated the ADA. The ADA specifically lists AIDS and HIV as covered conditions. The examining physician had concluded that the plaintiff was not physically fit to perform the duties of a police officer because he was not strong enough to withstand the rigors of the position. The city's personnel director then informed the plaintiff that he would not be hired because he had not passed the physical examination and the city could not put other employees and the public at risk by hiring him. The appellate court reversed the district court's grant of summary judgment for the city, finding that the city had not conducted an individualized inquiry and that the plaintiff produced sufficient evidence that he was qualified to perform the functions of a police officer.

This case illustrated that even if an employer follows medical guidelines, the courts have indicated a reluctance to uphold "direct threat" findings that rely on fixed standards, absent some consideration by the employer of the individual's condition and circumstance. Further, the courts are reluctant to uphold an employer's decisions based on a direct threat, in which the employer is unable to support such a decision with documentation that the medical evidence encompasses an individualized assessment of an applicant or employee (*Holiday v. City of Chattanooga*, 2000).

Direct Threat and Business Necessity

It is generally the employer's prerogative to formulate and rely upon safety-based job qualifications, even though such standards may screen out individuals with disabilities. However, when challenged, an issue exists as to what defense an employer may use to justify the qualification standard. The court (*EEOC v. Exxon Corp.*, 2000) examined the employer's policy of permanently removing employees who had undergone treatment for substance abuse from certain safety-sensitive, little-supervised positions. The U.S. District Court for the Northern District of Texas held that the employer's only available defense to an employment standard that screens out disabled individuals was to prove that employees subject to the policy posed a direct threat. The court of appeals reversed partial summary judgment for the EEOC in its enforcement action against Exxon. In reversing the decision, the Fifth Circuit held that an employer could also defend the selection standard as a business necessity.

Exxon adopted its substance abuse policy after the Exxon Valdez incident, because of concerns that the tanker captain's alcoholism, although treated previously, might have contributed to the accident. The court examined the legislative history of the ADA and concluded that the direct-threat provisions apply to situations in which an employer might impose a safety standard in an individual case. A safety-based qualification standard that applies across the board for a position is a standard no different from other requirements defended under the ADA's business-necessity provision. The court noted that in evaluating whether the risks addressed by a safety-based qualification standard constitutes a business-necessity, the court should consider the magnitude of possible harm and the probability of occurrence.

Adverse Impact and Scientific Preparation

Usually, ADA employment exclusions that have an adverse or unfair impact on a protected subgroup (e.g., Hispanics, African Americans, women) are impermissible. A federal district court in Pennsylvania ruled that an employer of transit police officers, who are part of a foot-based patrol unit, may require applicants to maintain a minimal aerobic capacity to qualify for employment. The court sustained the requirement based upon business necessity, even though the standard was shown to have a disparate impact on female applicants. According to the court, deterring crime and assisting fellow officers in emergency situations are critical components of the job. Any officer's failure to perform such tasks in an efficient manner would lessen the effectiveness of the transit unit and compromise the safety of officers and the public (*Lanning v. Southeastern Pennsylvania Transp. Authority,* 2000). Note that the court relied heavily upon the testimony of the employer's expert that the job in question required a higher-than-normal aerobic capacity based upon the expert's empirical data and considerable experience in developing tests for law enforcement agencies. As reviewed previously (*Daubert* triad), the better qualified the expert in the specific scientific issues of the case, the greater the likelihood of judicial acceptance.

It is fair to reflect that the ADA is among the most influential of the recent civil rights acts upon police fitness-for-duty applications. This is the case both because police administrators have a long-standing obligation to protect the public from the misuse of police authority (including those behaviors connected to mental illness), and because the medical/psychological illness model that underlies FFDEs appears to be in conflict with many protections introduced by the ADA. This apparent conflict of values is evident in the many court cases that have been brought in the years since the ADA's passage, and by increasing the proportion of law enforcement departmental resources that must be devoted to managing claims that stem from ADA regulations and interpretations. Emphasis within this chapter has been on the careful and informed use of the FFDE method to assist in compliance with ADA intent and with public safety issues. The following section continues the exploration of federal rules and regulations upon law enforcement agencies within an FFDE context.

Chapter 15

The Family Medical Leave Act, the Fair Credit Reporting Act, and Fitness-for-Duty Evaluations

Bureaucracy is the epoxy that greases the wheels of progress.

Jim Boren

THE FAMILY MEDICAL LEAVE ACT

The **Family Medical Leave Act** (Public Law 103-3) of 1993 was meant to allow eligible employees of a covered employer to take job-protected, unpaid leave, or to substitute appropriate paid leave if the employee has earned or accrued it, for up to a total of twelve work-weeks in any twelve months. Reasons for leave include the birth of a child and care for the newborn child, placement of a child with the employee for adoption or foster care, care for a family member (child, spouse, or parent) with a serious health condition, or because the employee's own serious health condition makes the employee unable to perform the functions of his or her job. This leave may be taken on an intermittent basis rather than all at once, or the employee may work a part-time schedule if the job permits. All public agencies are covered by FMLA regardless of the number of employees.

In general, an employee has a right to return to the same position or an equivalent position with equivalent pay, benefits, and working conditions at the conclusion of the leave. The employer generally has a right to thirty days advance notice of leave from the employee where practicable. In addition, the employer may require an employee to submit certification from a health care provider to substantiate that the leave is due to the serious health condition of the employee or the employee's immediate family member. Pursuant to a uniformly applied policy, the employer may also require that an employee present a certification of fitness to return to work from the medical service provider when the employee applies to return to work. The employer may delay restoring the employee to employment without such release certificate relating to the health condition that caused the employee's absence (60 FR 2237, January 6, 1995; 60 FR 16383, March 30, 1995).

The Family Medical Leave Act was meant to protect the employment of persons who have need for short-term emergency medical leave to arrange for treatment for themselves or for family members. FMLA regulations provide that only limited medical information may be required of an employee as a condition of granting leave. If the employer needs additional information from the employee's health care provider for FMLA leave, the employer must have its consultant, with the employee's permission (see Chapter 13), contact the employee's health care provider for purposes of clarification and authenticity of the medical certification.

Requiring an FFDE on a Released FMLA Employee

As a general rule, an employer cannot require a fitness-for-duty examination if the employee has been certified by a physician or psychologist to be able to return to work. This rule is not absolute. For example, the employer may be allowed to demand an FFDE if the employee's behavior continues to reveal indications of impairment or dysfunction. If a return-to-work certificate is confusing, unclear, or otherwise not understandable to the employer, and the employer has a policy of past practice requiring independent examinations in such cases, the employer may be allowed to demand an FFDE. Finally, an FFDE can be demanded if the reason for the FFDE can be shown to be independent of the medical or psychological reason for the leave from which the employee is returning. In general, even if the treating physician or psychologist has no idea about the requirements of law enforcement work, the LE executive may have to allow the officer to return to work without an FFDE until the department has recent or independent reasons to suspect that the officer is unfit.

FMLA and Substance Abuse

FMLA leave is allowed for purposes of treatment for substance abuse disorders provided that the normal FMLA application conditions are met. An employee may also take FMLA leave to care for an immediate family member who is receiving treatment for substance abuse. The employer may not take action against the employee only because the employee has exercised his or her right to take FMLA leave for treatment. However, merely submitting for substance abuse treatment leave does not shield an employee from otherwise justifiable employment action taken by an employer. If the employer has an established policy which is applied in a nondiscriminatory manner and has been communicated to all employees, providing that under certain circumstances an employee may be terminated for substance abuse, the employee may be terminated whether or not the employee is taking FMLA leave

FMLA Leave for Impermissible Personal Business

A worker who uses FMLA leave for personal business rather than strictly for medical purposes may be dismissed properly from his or her employment. Following an investigation, New York University Medical Center terminated an employee for fraudulently misusing his sick leave. The employee sued, claiming that he had been fired in violation of the FMLA because he had taken leave for shoulder surgery. The court noted that the employee's sick leave had begun a week before the surgery was scheduled and that the employee had admitted he had used that time for personal matters, including attending traffic court and his daughter's christening (*LeBoeuf v. N.Y. Univ. Med. Ctr.,* 2000). The court found for the employer.

Serious Health Condition

A "serious health condition" entitling an employee to FMLA leave means an illness, injury, impairment, or physical or mental condition that involves (1) medical care (e.g., an overnight stay or the like) in a hospital or clinic or (2) continuing treatment by a health care provider. A serious health condition includes any one or more of the following:

1. Any period of medical or psychiatric incapacity (e.g., inability to work, attend school, or perform other regular daily activities due to the serious health condition, treatment, or recovery) of more than three consecutive calendar days
2. Any period of incapacity due to pregnancy or for prenatal care or incapacity due to a chronic serious health condition
3. Any period of absence to receive multiple treatments (including any period of recovery) by a health care provider after an injury or for a condition that resulted in a period of incapacity of more than three consecutive calendar days

However, conditions for which cosmetic treatments are administered (such as most treatments for acne or plastic surgery) are *not* usually considered "serious health conditions." Also, an employee may take FMLA leave for treatment for mental illness or substance abuse, but not for absence *because* of the employee's use of the substance.

All employers should be comfortable in reviewing the specific conditions of an employee's FMLA leave and return circumstances, particularly as they apply to FFDE procedures and policy.

THE FAIR CREDIT REPORTING ACT

The relationship between police psychology and the FCRA appears to be an example of the **Law of Unintended Consequences.** The FCRA affects law enforcement agencies by making the collection of medically related evidence somewhat more difficult than it has been and by introducing complications into the reporting of FFDE results by external providers to LE executives. The proponents of the law, who were interested in making the search for credit worthiness information fair and truthful, contemplated no such outcomes.

To begin to understand the effect of this law, the LE executive must consider its intent. Companies that gather and sell this information are called **consumer reporting agencies (CRAs),** of which the credit bureau (a company that tracks payment records for various consumer debt) is the most prevalent type. The information that most CRAs sell, such as whether a person has filed bankruptcy, to creditors, employers, landlords, and other businesses, is called a **consumer report.** In the past, complaints have been made that incorrect information has been included in consumer reports, resulting in problems when the consumer wants to raise a loan, rent an apartment, or transact business. The **Fair Credit Reporting Act** (15 U.S.C. §1681 et seq) or FCRA, as enforced by the Federal Trade Commission (FTC), is intended to promote accuracy and ensure the privacy of the information used in consumer reports. All businesses that supply information about persons to CRAs and those that use consumer reports may be affected under the law. Since external law enforcement FFDE providers, in a sense, supply information to the contacting departments, although credit information is almost never the focus of the report, the law may cover them inadvertently.

FFDEs involve an examination of the officer and his or her background for purposes that may impact upon his or her employability, which may affect his or her creditworthiness if the officer is eventually dismissed. The FTC had indicated that external providers may be technically considered to be consumer reporting agencies, even though the clear purpose and goal of FFDEs is very different from that of consumer reports, for which the FCRA was unquestionably intended. In the FCRA, a consumer report includes criminal and civil records, driving records, civil lawsuits, reference checks, and any other information obtained by a consumer reporting agency. Similar information subsets are necessary to determine certain aspects of the liability risk presented by an impaired officer in some FFDEs. Intent on preventing misuse of this credit information, the act covers all likely parties to such investigations, such as **private investigators.** Although FFDEs may touch on such questions, most of the FFDE information that is obtained from other than direct psychological testing and interviewing with the officer, comes from departmental records that are almost always known to the officer in some form (e.g., complaints, reprimands).

When an employer receives a consumer report and intends not to hire the applicant or to move to discharge or discipline an employee based upon the report in any way, the applicant may have a right to an unedited copy of the report that was sent to the department. As previously discussed, excellent reasons exist not to reveal to officers the basis upon which the psychological testing arrived at conclusions that are reflected in the recommendations. If the officer becomes aware that certain responses are seen as dangerous (for example, expressions of sexual interest in children), the officer may be able to manipulate or defeat the testing process meant to detect this behavior. Psychological tests require years of validation and cannot be changed at each administration. The public may be exposed to an armed officer who may be a positive or negative risk, and but who has escaped detection by maneuver and subterfuge, such as by concealing or manipulating meaningful verbal or written responses. In such a scenario, the inclusion of **minimal possible information** in the psychological report is desirable, just as it is for reasons of confidentiality under the ADA and HIPAA. In the case of LE agencies, the decision to release a consumer report should rest solely with the LE department, and not with the consumer reporting agency (such as the FFDE provider).

Additional Concerns for Law Enforcement Employers

The Fair Credit Reporting Act is designed to promote accuracy, fairness, and privacy of information in the files of every consumer reporting agency. Although never meant for public safety agencies, the following FCRA conditions may be required in regard to FFDEs by a police psychologist:

- The officer must be given a chance to dispute inaccurate information. In law enforcement terms, this may mean that if the officer suffers an adverse outcome because of specific information (such as a false report of a drug arrest), he or she has a right to challenge the information.
- Outdated information may not be reported. In most cases, a CRA may not report negative information that is more than seven years old or ten years old for bankruptcies.
- Access to the file is to be limited. A CRA may provide information about an officer only to people with a need recognized by the FCRA.
- Consent is required for reports that are provided to employers.
- The applicant may seek damages in regard to violators.

In most cases, the proper FFDE should meet the conditions of the FCRA as a normal procedure that is useful in meeting other federal regulations and professional standards.

Problems in Law Enforcement FFDEs

The formal mechanism of the FCRA is not problematic so long as the issue is factual information, such as whether the applicant declared bankruptcy or was arrested. However, psychological examinations may be based upon professional constructs that are not tangible or concrete. Statistical indicators in psychometric testing can measure important information, such as propensity to violence or misconduct, just as medical abstractions (blood pressure, urinary glucose) are used as predictive measures of medical tendency to illness (see Chapter 8). Some impaired officers may claim that findings of clinically paranoid or psychotic behaviors on testing or interviewing are unrelated to police duties. In other words, they may seek to contest the *validity* of standard clinical or psychometric findings, as they would contest a claim that they did not pay their rent in a certain year. If permitted to challenge such professional finding as a matter of their own personal opinions, a practical obstruction to the use of the FFDE in law enforcement would result and inhibit the ability of the LE agency to provide for public safety and the business necessity of the police operation.

Transactions or Experiences

When a company (e.g., a laboratory) provides the results of its testing directly to the employer (drug lab test), the report is *not* a "consumer report" under the FCRA. Drug tests are said not to bear on an individual's character, general reputation, personal characteristics, or mode of living, although clearly such information may accomplish precisely that when illicit drug appear in the person's blood. Section 603(d)(2)(A) of the FCRA excludes from the definition of consumer report any report containing information *solely* as to transactions or experiences between the consumer (employee) and the person making the report. Since illicit drug test reports constitute communications based on the experience of the laboratory in applying scientific methods to urine obtained directly from the employee, such correspondences are not "consumer reports" covered by the FCRA when they are provided directly to the employer by the laboratory (*Hodge v. Texaco, Inc.,* 1992).

Where a report is from a drug counselor, and the results of a lab test are included in the report, the product now is transformed into a consumer report covered by Section 603(d) because it includes information other than obtained from transactions or experiences. The transactions-or-experiences exception does not apply to the drug counselor's evaluation because he or she did not perform the analysis, and only reported on what others had done. Section 603(f) of the FCRA indicates that party which regularly engages in the practice of assembling or evaluating information on consumers for the purpose of furnishing consumer reports to third parties is a CRA under that definition. If a drug test report is provided by a party that is indisputably a CRA because of the general nature of its business (e.g., a credit bureau), the report would be a consumer report. Interestingly, an examination of the transactions or experiences exemption would seem to imply that a psychological firm that reported *only* technical findings from their own scientific testing (analogous to the drug testing lab) would not be a CRA as long as other information was not combined with this information.

The Case of Officer Johnson

Officer Johnson of the Anytown Police Department has been reported for what appeared to be sexual harassment within the department, which he has reportedly directed primarily toward female clerical staff and dispatchers. However, because of his violent nature, his victims are reluctant to file formal complaints. The chief received an anonymous tip alleging that this officer physically abused a female dispatcher and threatened her if she told of his violent assault. Many departmental members observed the dispatcher's facial contusions, and some employees believe they originated during a incident between the officer and the dispatcher at work in which the officer was overheard threatening violence. Because the officer had been careful not to be observed directly in such actions, the chief had an external audiovisual consulting firm install a videotape system to covertly record the interaction between Officer Johnson and the dispatcher. Once threatening and abusive conduct was observed and recorded, Officer Johnson was discharged.

Shane Salazar v. Golden State Warriors

The Officer Johnson incident would seem to have been resolved with the application of common sense. Unfortunately, a ruling in 2000 *(Shane Salazar v. Golden State Warriors)* illustrates the complexity introduced by the FCRA as it is applied to situations of this sort. In *Salazar,* an employee was reported by other company members to be selling illicit drugs in and near the workplace. Without the employee's permission (the FCRA normally requires employee permission to conduct investigations), a private investigator was retained by the employer to conduct an investigation of suspected drug use. The investigator electronically recorded a drug transaction at the workplace, the employee was discharged, and he later sued under FCRA and other laws.

The plaintiff's original complaint included seven causes of action:

1. Violation of the Fair Credit Reporting Act
2. Invasion of privacy
3. Breach of the covenant of good faith and fair dealing
4. Defamation
5. Wrongful termination in violation of public policy
6. Intentional infliction of emotional distress
7. Negligence

Upon motion of the defendant, the court dismissed the second, third, fifth, sixth, and seventh claims for failure to state a reason upon which relief may be granted. Following the dismissal, the plaintiff amended his complaint to include a number of labor code/unpaid overtime claims, and then both parties agreed to dismiss the defamation claim. This left the overtime issues and the alleged FCRA violation. The defendant moved for partial summary judgment on the grounds that the FCRA did not apply as a matter of law to the videotape and report that the investigator submitted to the employer because they fell within the transactions-or-experiences exception to the definition of a consumer report.

The court ruled that although the investigative agency was considered a CRA, the videotape and report contained information solely as to the experiences been the consumer (the plaintiff) and the person making the report (the investigator). The court held that the fact that the plaintiff was unaware that the transaction or experience was taking place did not remove the report from the exception. The court then granted summary judgment to the employer as to the FCRA violation.

Of particular interest is that the investigative agency obtained three other types of information during the investigation: (1) the listing of the registered owners of automobiles encountered by the investigators, (2) a criminal background check on the plaintiff, and (3) a printout from a public information database regarding the plaintiff. The agency provided only the vehicle information to the employer, and since the motor vehicle information did not include information about the plaintiff by itself, it did not constitute a consumer report. Had the agency included the other items in its report, it would have been deemed a consumer report *outside* of the transaction or experience exception, and the plaintiff might have prevailed.

Following *Salazar* and other FCRA considerations, it would appear that actual psychological test results taken from the applicant by the FFDE provider and interpreted in standard ways (such as a drug test) by that same party is covered by the transactions and experiences exception, as is any information collected directly from the employee. Materials that are supplied by the LE employer (say a report of excessive force) may be included without changing the status of the report, since its contents are already known to the employer, and not new information. The employee is allowed to respond to reports of excess force, and his or her responses may be included in the FFDE report in an even-handed manner for the employer to consider. Materials received by the FFDE provider from others (such as medical reports) may not violate the rule *if not included* in the content of the report to the employer, as occurred with the criminal check and the public database information in *Salazar.*

Permissibility Considerations

When investigators conduct surveillance of facilities in which employees are committing thefts, it is clear that the reports of such direct observations would not be considered consumer reports. The information contained in these observation reports could be reported to the employer without violating FCRA regulations. A third-party surveillance of an employee who leaves the workplace without authorization to go bowling on company time would also not be subject to FCRA restrictions. However, if this observer were to report on any inquiries made of others at the bowling alley or provide the employer with shoe-rental records, such a report would constitute a form of consumer reporting activity and be subject to the FCRA regulation.

In regard to consent, a properly worded blanket authorization signed by employees at the time of initial employment (prohibiting being absent without leave) would probably serve as adequate written authorization for investigation at any time in the future, should conditions warrant such action. In law enforcement, the FCRA further strengthens the need for a published uniform code of employee regulations, including FFDEs, in which the new officer is trained, and with which the officer authorizes his or her consent to investigate in the presence of evidence of violations. In any event, the employer would be required to advise the employee of the investigation within three days of the date it was ordered and comply with other FCRA requirements.

Unedited Copies of Reports

Employers who use **investigative consumer reports** have certain obligations under the FCRA to supply a copy of the report to the employee. Information cannot be redacted in those instances in which the FCRA requires that the consumer (employee) be provided a copy of a consumer report, as in §604(b)(3)(A). The FCRA mandates that unedited copies of "investigative reports" must be given to employees who request such materials. This is a difficulty in FFDEs and psychological screenings, which were never meant to be credit services, for reasons of test security and other purposes discussed elsewhere in this book. In *Hartman v. Lisle Park District* (2001), a federal court in Chicago held that a law firm that investigated employee misconduct was not a credit reporting agency and that the employee under investigation for misconduct was not entitled to receive a copy of the report.

THE FAIR AND ACCURATE CREDIT TRANSACTIONS ACT

President George W. Bush signed the Fair and Accurate Credit Transactions Act (also known as the "Fact Act") into law on December 4, 2003 (H.R. 262), amending the Fair Credit Reporting Act. The Fact Act was a response to the Federal Trade Commission's opinion that an outside attorney investigating sexual harassment (or other misconduct) for a company was a CRA under the 1996 amendments to the FCRA. The ability of most public employers to investigate incidents of employee misconduct seemed to be impossible under this interpretation, since few departments had the internal resources to conduct investigations (such as FFDEs). In effect, if an employer failed to inform the alleged harasser about the investigation in advance, obtain his or her consent to proceed, and disclose the complete investigation report to the employee, the employer would be in violation of the FCRA. The privacy rights and safety of victims and witnesses could be compromised if an employer acted in such a manner.

The Fact Act excludes from the definition of "consumer report" all communications made to employers in connection with an investigation of suspected employment misconduct that is in compliance with federal, state, or local laws and regulations; the rules of a self-regulatory organization; or any preexisting written policies of the employer. Employers may hire outside consultants who investigate workplace issues without having to notify the target of the investigation or obtain consent. The privacy of both the targets of the investigation as well as potential victims and witnesses is protected. Such reports can be given only to the employer; federal, state, or local officers and agencies; or as otherwise required by law. If an employee is disciplined or discharged as a result of the report, a summary of its contents must be made available to the employee.

Although little has changed when real questions of credit are involved, the Fact Act is a step in the right direction regarding public safety and business necessity connected with the misconduct of certain employees. It encourages the use of experts and sophisticated outside consultants to achieve the goals of a safer workplace and better control of destructive conduct. The legal effect of this change is not yet fully understood, and there will certainly be some unanticipated effects upon the workplace and upon FFDEs as time passes. As a correction of the abuses within the FCRA, the Fact Act appears to be a model for ways in which other well-intended laws and regulations that appear to intrude into the LE executives' authority to protect the public may be amended to allow for needed supervision and examination. This is not quite as clear with larger agencies, which cover this risk by self-funding or through industry-pooled risk schemes, even if such programs are managed by third-party administrators. However, since managing workers' compensation claims is a statutory insurance function, it may be argued successfully that the FCRA restrictions do not apply. Since the purpose of workers' compensation investigations is not to "evaluate a consumer for employment, promotion, reassignment or retention as an employee," little difference appears to exist between an independent insurance carrier and a business that self-funds the risk.

COMMENTARY

Any review of the history of the FMLA and the FCRA will reveal a set of unintended consequences that arose out of well-intentioned laws which complicated the responsibilities of LE executive management duties and of law enforcement FFDEs providers. When combined with earlier discussed federal laws (e.g., ADA, HIPAA), there appears to be an ever-growing need for a detailed and sensitive understanding of regulatory issues for all stakeholders. Not every labor rights law is equally applicable to or appropriate for armed and minimally supervised law enforcement officers. Special authority and great power demand special scrutiny and control. The rights to privacy and concealment that may apply to a secretarial worker or sales clerk may not be appropriate for a patrol officer or detective. It seems unlikely that the drafters of the FMLA intended that fully armed and empowered police agents were to be immune from departmental examination when they returned from medical leave with nothing more than a doctor's release to duty. Such a policy may be fine for a carpenter or computer operator, but those persons are not vested with the power to command obedience and deprive others of life or liberty. Equally, it seems doubtful that the authors of the FCRA intended to hobble the work of outside consultants in the investigation of criminal behavior and sexual harassment, but such appeared to be the consequence of that legislation until it was amended by the Fact Act.

In the final chapter, an overview of the interaction of FFDE methodology and the universe of federal laws is addressed and some attempt is made to argue for a balance of rights and interests in the professional management of law enforcement officers. The safety and protection of the society as a whole is presented to the reader as the proposed primary value of law enforcement.

SECTION V:
CONCLUSIONS

Chapter 16

Reflections and the Future of Law Enforcement Fitness-for-Duty Evaluations

> When we walk the streets at night in safety, it does not strike us that this might be otherwise. This habit of feeling safe has become second nature, and we do not reflect on just how this is due solely to the working of special institutions. Commonplace thinking often has the impression that force holds the state together, but in fact its only bond is the fundamental sense of order which everybody possesses.
>
> Georg Wilhelm Friedrich Hegel

Psychological FFDEs can be a methodology that is meant to preserve the economic and personnel resources of an agency or corporation by allowing the employer to have an expert FFDE provider inquire into the possibly impaired behavior of an employee. The proper use of this procedure also demonstrates an employer's interest in protecting the public, other employees, and supervisors from the potential harm that may be connected with deviant behavior exhibited by an employee, an obligation under tort laws. The FFDE methodology is of particular importance in law enforcement personnel work, where a desire exists to retain the agency's investment in recruitment, training, experience, and supervision of its officers, while recognizing the risks of impairment when they occur in armed and frequently unsupervised law enforcement officers. FFDEs can also be used as a tool to address acute problems, such as difficulties connected with a departmental trauma (such as a shooting) or a chronic problem, such as dealing with an officer who is losing control of his or her temper.

FFDEs can be of great benefit to a depressed or anxious officer who may require protection for his or her employment status while he or she receives treatment for the condition in question. The FFDE methodology may best be seen as a part of a larger administrative system that includes criminal inquiries (internal affairs), medical certification (heath and safety division), personnel management (human resources), training, field supervision, and overall policymaking. Each component of the system provides some element within the mosaic of protections for both the community and members of the law enforcement agency.

The police executive should use only accomplished and qualified police psychologists for the FFDE task, working in concert with available in-house or independent, contractual mental health therapy providers. Not only should the police psychologist (FFDE provider) be a capable clinician, but he or she should also have training and experience in legal issues, police culture, and the ethical problems of the FFDE. The reasons for referral and the goals of an FFDE must be developed and codified before the first referral is made. A firm, official agency FFDE policy should be acknowledged by all stakeholders (civil service commission, union, internal affairs, city government, etc.) as well as a clear, predetermined, and uniform method of referral, examination, and eventual recommendation. A published and authorized code of conduct that addresses the rules of universal officer deportment, as well as the FFDE conditions and uses, should be a part of every department's policy mechanism. Appropriate preparation and execution of an FFDE policy can be invaluable to the well-prepared LE executive, and inferior methods and procedures can be an unnecessary burden in managing law enforcement personnel responsibilities.

THE FUTURE OF THE LAW ENFORCEMENT FFDE

Maintaining the Vital Balance

The central problem of the FFDE procedure is that of balancing the rights of the examined officer with those of the department, fellow officers, and the public. Every law enforcement officer has the same right to dignity and privacy that is common to all persons. At the same time, the demand for sound and rational conduct or behavior is much greater for an officer than for the ordinary citizen, because of the officer's legal capacity to command obedience, immediately deprive others of liberty, and use force, even if fatality results.

Society offers qualified confidentiality to substance abusers in the treatment of that condition, for example, because it is assumed that they are more likely to seek out and comply with the treatment if they feel that they are not at risk for public exposure of such activities (value of confidentiality). A variety of state and federal laws make access to the records of such treatment very difficult to obtain for similar reasons of confidentiality. Professional societies (such as the licensing boards of some professions) may sanction treaters if a breach of confidentiality occurs. State and federal bureaucracies are staffed with persons who are meant to enforce a large number of privacy, confidentially occurs, communication, health, and commerce laws that involve the rights of those who are thought to be handicapped or are in need of some forms of treatment. Persons who are examined, tested, assessed, treated, or who are defined as disabled are therefore assured not to suffer adverse outcome in employment, health care, access to opportunity, and the like because of their condition.

That same legal system demands that the public, including other employees, be free from mistreatment, harassment, threat, and risk of many types (value of security). Any employer, including governmental employers, may be subject to civil sanctions if that employer negligently hires and/or fails to train, supervise, or examine an employee who injures others, especially if it can be shown that the officer was impaired in some manner connected to the injury-causing behaviors. The penalties for employer failure to inquire into impaired conduct may be severe when that employee wears a uniform, carries a gun, and is said to contribute to the avoidable deprivation of constitutionally or federally guaranteed rights under color of law. Consider the following example:

The Case of Officer Lynn

Officer Lynn of the Anytown Police Department takes a leave of absence to be treated for what she described as a "prescription drug dependency." After several months, she presented her department with a brief release to return to duty in the form of a memo or note from her treatment provider (a free-standing substance abuse program), which mentions nothing of the reason for treatment, treatment goals, risk assessment, or what was accomplished during the treatment. It is not clear whether the treater was aware that the patient was a police officer. The memo essentially read that the officer was "released to return to work" without further comment. Does the department have the right or duty to require that its police psychologist (or consultant) review Officer Lynn's treatment record or communicate with the treating staff, with or without the patient's permission? Can Officer Lynn be evaluated independently for fitness for duty, or must the department accept the opinion of her treatment provider? Does it matter which party treated her (e.g., a psychiatrist, substance abuse counselor, family doctor, or hypnotist) in regard to the credibility of the report that Officer Lynn is ready to return to work or is free from current substance abuse? Should the record, if available, be reviewed for substance abuse treatment issues only, or should incidental or collateral problems noted by treaters (e.g., a predatory sexual problem) also be subject to review? Should information other than a simple statement of the fitness of the employee to return to armed police work be conveyed to nonpsychologist departmental personnel, and if so, in what way? What can be done if the treatment provider and the department's police psychologist disagree about the officer's readiness to return to duty? What should be done with information obtained from the treatment record that indicates that the officer had misled or deceived her departmental representatives by hiding a history of misconduct (e.g., extensive illicit substance abuse) in current treatment or at the time Officer Lynn applied for her job?

Unfortunately, there are no simple and incontestable responses to any of the questions posed in the Officer Lynn example. Protecting disability and treatment information of the officer while ensuring complete trust in the judgment and behavior of uniformed officers are values that are clearly in conflict in such cases. As this review makes clear, legislative and judicial authorities have not as yet clearly signaled a preferable resolution regarding this balance. For example, proponents' attempts to improve confidentiality for clinical patients as contained in the HIPAA do not appear to have considered the public safety issues that are presented in the Officer Lynn example. In general effect, the HIPAA, ADA, and FMLA will likely make it progressively more difficult in the future to obtain the sort of medical and psychological information needed to answer public safety and business necessity questions. Society will have to solve these enigmas if FFDEs are to remain a useful service for law enforcement executives who are attempting to protect the public from impaired officers.

Policing the Police

The Case of Officer Arthur

Officer Arthur of the Anytown Police Department stops motorists regularly and demands identification, conducts searches, and makes arrests for infractions in his position as a traffic officer. He expects cooperation and submission from the errant motorist, even if the motorist does not believe that he or she has done anything wrong. Even the slightest verbal resistance may provoke Officer Arthur to flashes of anger and muttered threats to take the motorist to jail. Several persons who were said to have "touched" the officer have found themselves in the hospital to treat wounds that they "accidentally sustained" in the struggle that followed. When Officer Arthur was ordered to report for an FFDE, he declined to answer the police psychologist's questions, indicating that he thought it was "none of [the FFDE provider's] business." When asked to respond to structured psychological testing, he refused again, claiming he knew the task was simply to "find me crazy" and to appease those who hated him and conspired to make him seem ridiculous. Although he had taken medical leave from his department some time earlier to be treated for "stress," a call from the departmental medical consultant to the provider indicated that Officer Arthur had forbid the transfer of any information about such treatments. Only after he had been suspended from his department and exhausted administrative appeals did he agree to be examined, although in a gruff and resistant fashion only.

It is a remarkable paradox that some persons who expect others to submit to their authority without hesitation or complaint are often themselves the least likely persons to comply willingly with a lawful inquiry into their own conduct. Police academies and field-training departments must do a better job at making it clear to young officers that they are subject to the same rules of cooperation and submission that apply to others. The need for commissioned and supervising officers to recognize the principle that all persons, including police officials, must allow a reasonable attempt to ensure that their conduct conforms to acceptable rules cannot be overemphasized. The contempt and resistance that some officers may show when examined by a qualified police psychologist will inevitably create obstacles to proper evaluation that will result in the loss of community confidence in the propriety and correctness of officer conduct. Nothing can be more damaging to the reputation of professional law enforcement than when the public at large suspects that individual officers believe that they are above the law. This difficulty may be seen in many court-rooms around the country in which the suspicion and mistrust of the police by the juries is translated into a rejection of officer testimony and a decline in public security.

Surrender of Autonomy

In many law enforcement organizations, great resistance exists among LE executives to the idea that officers should be selected or re-tained in any manner other than at the pleasure of the command staff. Although the essential concept of objective personnel procedures (e.g., nonpsychological testing) dates back to the introduction of the civil service systems of the late nineteenth century, many LE execu-tives view objective methods as only supplemental to the personal methods of hiring officers. Over time, many larger and wealthier de-partments, which are approached by many more applicants than they can hire, have embraced the idea of some type of psychological en-trance examination as a step to selecting law enforcement personnel, mainly because of public and judicial pressures. In smaller or less wealthy departments, resistance has occurred to the placing of any obstacles in the path of an interested candidate because there have of-ten not been enough qualified applicants for all open positions, even without such hiring obstacles. In the long run, the absence of a rea-sonable preemployment and postemployment (FFDE) psychological inquiry is never a good idea.

As a matter of policy, many LE executives avoid employing an FFDE methodology because they fear risking the loss of an officer for reasons over which the department may have little control, such as the officer's state of mind. It may also be difficult for a chief to allow an officer to be examined if that officer has been recruited for per-sonal or political reasons (e.g., the officer's family is involved so-cially with the chief). In other cases, it may be believed that the FFDE may increase, rather than decrease, the department's vulnerability to lawsuits. The chief may fear that information about the difficulties in his department might be revealed to an aggressive plaintiff's attorney or that knowledge of any form of misconduct might become a public embarrassment. In some cases, LE executives have informed this book's authors that they did not wish to institute an FFDE program (or participate in a fitness research project) because such a program would imply that the departmental leadership "thought" that they had problems and this revelation would hurt morale. As noted previously, although FFDE information is likely to be kept confidential by the courts, no absolute rules exist to ensure such an outcome.

Despite the ebb and flow of national and local politics, an overall trend exists in the direction of greater public transparency, judicial review, and bureaucratic regulation of FFDEs. The "vest-pocket" management of public resources by a small number of politically active persons appears, as a long-term issue, to be a thing of the past. The closed, tightly controlled world of the early twentieth century law enforcement agencies appears to be archaic in the light of endless federal intrusion and litigious turmoil. Methods of law enforcement administration that are examinable, fair, and unbiased must become the standard operating practices of the twenty-first century. The pressures generated by the courts, mass media, and federal administrative agencies are simply not compatible with the older, refractory methods of law enforcement administration.

Financial Issues and Fairness

It may be easier for an LE executive to find federal grant money to buy bulletproof vests or special sirens than to obtain money to support an FFDE program. Financing a complicated FFDE program of specialized professional work at the same time that officer salaries are low and a need exists to buy patrol cars may require a good deal of political courage. Not only do the commanders need to see that intangible services, such as inquiry into the questionable behaviors of officers, is necessary, but that they may actually save money for patrol cars when such methods reduce liability risk and subsequent costs.

In some cases, LE executives are dissuaded from creating a system of FFDE service provision by the incorrect belief that the cost of legal settlements and judgments comes from the state, municipal, or county general fund, an insurance company, or other "far away" financial pockets. In other words, some LE executives see no reason to stress their budgets to forestall expenses that are someone else's financial problem. Common sense should inform the behavior of every adult that indirect departmental expenses are eventually going to be paid out of the operating budget. The department or agency must, directly or indirectly, pay for legal defense, judgments, and settlements, usually by a "risk-management" deduction from the agency's annual budget prior to fiscal-year distribution. The money is usually held in a reserve account to pay attorneys, court costs, depositions, court reporters, experts, and actual judgments and settlements with plaintiffs. In the rare event that monies are not paid out, money may be restored to next year's budget for that agency, but in other cases, it may be returned to the general fund. If costs increase, a larger percentage of the budget is normally withheld in the subsequent fiscal year in anticipation of growing costs in the risk management area. In cases of private or pooled municipal insurance, the next year's premium will certainly increase. At times, the process may seem remote and may convey the impression that no financial benefit exists in improving departmental efficiency regarding risk and liability, but the money that is spent in officer and departmental legal defense is always a cost to the agency in some way.

Another twist in the liability picture for public agencies is the sometimes-encountered claim that the department does not have to pay its legal judgments because of some form of sovereign immunity or constitutional regulation that shields the department or agency. This is a complex topic that dates back to the common-law concept that the "the king can do no wrong." In other words, to preserve public funds, the sovereign authority is not compelled to pay a judgement without consent. In some jurisdictions, the state constitution or legislative acts may make the collection of a judgment against an agency or a subdivision of state possible only if the legislative arm of that governmental entity votes to allow the payment. This situation may be based upon the idea that the judicial branch of the government is coequal to the executive and legislative branches, and therefore none is superior to the other. Thus, if the court-ordered judgment is resisted by the executive branch (where the police authority resides), the result is a stalemate, which can be broken only by action of the legislative branch. Where this circumstance exists, it applies only to state or municipal courts, and not to the federal bench, which may order the collection of judgments against most governmental agencies without difficulty. Moreover, even at the state level, a chronic attitude of indifference to injuries sustained by local citizens, even where court-ordered redress has been "neutralized," is likely to contribute to a politically and socially unstable circumstance and bring contempt upon the government's institutions.

On the other hand, a storm of discrimination and civil rights litigation has been generated in recent years. According to the Department of Justice, plaintiffs filed more than 250,000 civil rights complaints in federal court in 1998. The proportion of all civil cases that were civil rights-related increased from 9 percent in 1990 to 17 percent in 1998. Between 1990 and 1998, median jury awards to plaintiff winners in civil rights trials were more than twice the amount of damages awarded in bench trials. In 1998, juries awarded a median of $129,000 to plaintiff winners compared to $87,000 among bench trials. Award amounts of $10 million or more increased from 2 to about 10 percent from 1990 to 1998. Although no one would wish to have a law enforcement agency in violation of common rules of civil conduct, the judicial system should not become a lottery in which persons with questionable claims may indifferently attempt to leverage money from public service personnel and departments.

FFDE Treatment Mandates

The use of the FFDE's mental health treatment recommendation option has unwittingly become problematic in recent years. On the one hand, it would appear to be a humane and respectful matter to suggest that an officer's difficulties can be remedied in standard forms of treatment, with the officer, his or her department, and community all benefiting from this process. Such a view may even appear to be consistent with the intent of laws such as the ADA, in providing a method of addressing the disability and allowing the officer to proceed with his or her career. On the other hand, the department has a responsibility to ensure that the noted emotional or mental problems of an officer are addressed effectively, and that reasonable results have followed treatment before the officer is returned to duty.

The seemingly reasonable process of treatment may be complicated when some officers deny the validity of the FFDE findings and reject subsequent recommendations. The officers may simply insist that nothing is wrong with them, and may spend time and money seeking "independent evaluations" with local (usually without training in police psychology) professionals, many of whom are willing to find the officer mentally "perfect." Despite evidence to the contrary, such officers may now claim proof that they have no need for assistance. Other officers agree to treatment, but insist on determining the type and frequency of treatment personally, for example by insisting that their clergyman or family practitioner, who may have very limited mental heath training, provide the recommended "counseling" on a very infrequent basis. Some officers may reject part of the treatment recommendations (e.g., for psychotherapy or counseling) and insist that psychotropic medication use (often prescribed by a family doctor with no special psychiatric training) is adequate to prepare them to return to duty. Even when the officer complies superficially with treatment ("I had to go see a shrink!"), there may be no apparent change in any aspect of his or her observable conduct, and the treating therapist may note a lack of cooperation or effort on the officer's part. In such cases, officers may appear to comply with a limited number of treatment visits, often with no real investment in the therapy process, and then insist upon a release to duty.

To make matters worse, regulatory law and its related case findings (as in the Age Discrimination in Employment Act [ADEA], the Fair Labor Standards Act [FLSA], the Employee Retirement Income Security Act of 1974 [ERISA], the Occupational Safety and Health Administration Act [OSHA], as well as the ADA, FMLA, HIPAA, FCRA, etc.) may make a departmental determination of the effectiveness of treatment impossible by actually blocking access to medical records. For example, the ADA and HIPAA rules may restrict access by the FFDE provider to complete therapy notes or objective reports of the officer's treatment providers, and FMLA regulations may prohibit follow-up evaluations. Many community-based therapy providers do not care that the department may have serious liability problems regarding an impaired officer. Community-based therapy providers are often compelled to deal with a patient who demands a release to duty or an insurance carrier who refuses to pay for continued therapy. The therapy provider may be concerned about the actions of the licensing board if the patient complains that he or she has not been released to work by the therapist, in spite of total self-determined improvement. The officer's community-based therapy provider may feel pressure to provide a simple, one-sentence letter of release describing the officer as fit to return to duty, and then refuse further inquiries behind a shield of confidentiality. The department now has a dilemma. If the officer is returned to duty and someone is harmed because of irrational behavior on the part of the officer, the department is open to charges of deliberate indifference to the danger posed by the officer. On the other hand, if the department resists accepting that the officer is entirely recovered on the strength of a release note, expensive and time-consuming litigation, union grievances and administrative (civil service, personnel, federal monitoring, etc.) hearings may follow.

Some departments, to preserve their resources, may consider ignoring the treatment option and falling back on strict disciplinary rules, in which the officer's behavior is always seen as volitional and the officer as responsible for his or her conduct. In these schemes, impaired conduct equals demotion, suspension, fine, or discharge. The burden of claiming and proving disability then falls on the officer. These procedures are unfortunate, both because of the loss of many recoverable officers and because impaired officers may suffer unnecessarily in cases in which their problems may be treated successfully. A clear need exists for special federal legislation that protects all well-meaning parties in the law enforcement FFDE procedure and acknowledges that some of the rules and safeguards in ordinary labor, civil rights, or disability law simply are not compatible with public safety values.

A MODEL BILL

A **model bill** is a general outline of a proposed law that may be submitted in some form (usually with modifications to fit both the styles of the legislative body and political accommodations) to a lawmaking body to reduce the need to create the same law in every venue. Model laws may originate in professional, political, or advocacy organizations, and may be useful in reducing the need to reproduce the basic or fundamental principals that submission agents consider to be essential to address an important issue through legislation.

The following is a model bill for the **Public Safety Assurance Act (PSAA),** a proposed law to correct some of the deficiencies in law enforcement administration and the police psychological service methods that have been considered throughout this book. The PSAA is included to illustrate a method of moving the FFDE procedure into the mainstream of public law enforcement service administration.

The model is phrased as a federal bill, which may be altered to apply to any state legislative body, although the reference to modifications in federal acts could not be introduced validly in nonfederal legislation. Detailed definitions and clauses, sometimes a part of model bills, are omitted in the PSAA for reasons of simplification.

PUBLIC SAFETY ASSURANCE ACT (PSAA)
Preamble

It is acknowledged that only commissioned law enforcement officers have the legal authority to suspend personal liberties and to use deadly force in the course of their authorized and appropriate duty within civilian settings. The need for respect for and submission to the lawful and proper commands of the law enforcement officer, with confidence in the proper nature of his or her actions, is vital in a free society. Deviations from lawful, rational and proper conduct, whether the product of mental disorder or defect or for other reasons, are serious problems that damage the public order and injure the reputation of courageous and dedicated officers throughout our nation. Irrational officer behaviors that threaten the public safety or degrade the ability of law enforcement agencies to protect the public are of special concern. Law enforcement duties may be stressful and demanding at times, creating a need to offer humane and scientific services to those officers who may require relief from mental difficulties that may affect the performance of law enforcement responsibilities. All law enforcement officers should be free from the burden of mental disorder, especially those difficulties that may impact upon the officers' central and customary roles as commissioned officers. All law enforcement supervisors and commanders **(responsible designated authority)** must be responsible to monitor subordinate officer conduct and behavior and to intercede in such conduct by appropriate means. All officers should have access to resources that should reasonably be expected to assist such officers in the amelioration of medical, substance abuse, or psychological difficulties. All U.S. law enforcement officers who are commissioned to carry firearms and make lawful arrests shall be subject to employment regulations that emphasize subordination to command authority, respect for the civil rights of the public, and the competent and effective capability to perform law enforcement tasks in a safe manner. Such officers shall show personal and emotional stability consistent with public safety and the business necessity of their role.

Standards

The Public Safety Assurance Act sets forward definitions of officer impairment and reasons to find the officer unfit for active duty as a commissioned officer. It is declared to be the policy of the Congress to improve public safety and the standard of commissioned officer conduct and to provide for the mental health of officers. It is further declared to be the policy of the Congress to encourage greater and continuing uniformity of fitness-for-duty laws and regulations among the several states and within the federal government, as well as closer cooperation and assistance between the state and the federal government in developing, administering, and enforcing federal and state laws and regulations pertaining to fitness-for-duty examinations.

Application

The PSAA shall apply to all federal, state, municipal, county or other law enforcement or police agencies that receive federally derived financial support or payments of any sort, either directly or indirectly through public or private parties.

Responsible designated authority (RDA): All law enforcement agencies, with fifteen or more full- or part-time commissioned officers, defined as those tax-supported organizations that function in whole or in part to enforce the laws of any governmental entity, who have the power of arrest and/or are authorized to use weapons in the commission of their duty, shall appoint a responsible designated authority, which may be the chief or any person(s) appointed by the chief or most senior commanding officer, to oversee officer misconduct or inappropriate behavior. The RDA shall have the power to command an officer to undergo a fitness-for-duty evaluation by a fitness-for-duty provider, as allowed through the code of conduct of the department, and to receive and act upon the recommendation derived therefrom, with the participation of the departmental director, chief, or commanders or other authority as allowed by the legal and official structure of the department or agency. The RDA may be a part of the internal affairs officer (IAO) or health and safety officer (HSO) (see Instruments of Departmental Action) or other officer or appointee.

Fitness-for-duty evaluation (FFDE): All law enforcement agencies with fifteen or more full- or part-time commissioned officers in their service shall create a method by which officers are monitored by supervisory personnel (RDA) for the purpose of determining the degree to which officer behaviors, in reasonable connection with their duties as armed law enforcement officers, may represent a danger to the public, fellow officers, and others, as well as to determine the capability of the officers to perform the necessary duties of their assignments. Reasons for referral may include, but shall not be limited to, any threatening or dangerous conduct, unreasonable use of force, sexually, racially, or ethnically inappropriate behavior, failure to meet the minimal demands of the role of officer to which the officer has been assigned, or suspected substance abuse, excess force, or brutal disregard for the well-being of others. The FFDE shall be defined as a scientific inquiry into the officer's conduct, behavior, or mental functioning using professional and legally defendable instruments and methods conducted by a fitness-for-duty evaluation provider (FFDE-P).

Fitness-for-duty evaluation provider (FFDE-P): A licensed psychologist or psychiatrist practicing within the limits of his or her professional competence and capability, who possesses advanced training and experience in law enforcement assessment and culture and is knowledgeable in the forensic issues of law enforcement FFDEs, shall perform this function. The professional methods employed in any FFDE shall be focused upon the complaints and events that precipitated the referral for the FFDE (although other observations and inquiries may be necessary) and where the FFDE-P is well prepared by training and experience to employ instruments (psychometric tests) that can be shown to reasonably indicated psychological fitness for purposes of the evaluation. The FFDE-P may obtain records from physicians, psychologists, social workers, institutions, programs, and other medical or mental heath providers or facilities for the purpose of inquiry into the officer's capability to meet the demands of his or her law enforcement role in a manner that is safe and competent regarding the well-being of the public, fellow employees, and the officer.

Mandatory referral for evaluation: Any officer referred for an FFDE by the proper responsible designated authority of his or her department shall submit and cooperate fully with this procedure. Failure to submit or comply with any part of the FFDE is to be considered insubordination and good grounds for dismissal of the officer from any commissioned law enforcement employment or the officer shall be referred for disciplinary proceedings at the option of the RDA or as indicated by the operations code of similar regulations of the department.

Liability and immunity and indemnification: The FFDE-P, his or her associates or corporations, and the referring law enforcement or public agency and its employees shall be immune from any federal or state civil legal action in connection with the good-faith provision of any aspect of the FFDE service, notwithstanding malice or malpractice. If it can be demonstrated that the FFDE-P has not committed any wrongful or wanton act associated with an FFDE, the costs of defending against such suits as may arise will be indemnified by the department for whom the FFDE was conducted.

Recommendations: The FFDE-P shall produce recommendations within the body of the FFDE that included one of the following:

> **Not fit for duty with little chance of recovery:** The officer suffers a degree of mental illness or disability in his or her job-related conduct that is of sufficient magnitude so that the FFDE-P finds the officer **im-**

paired and unlikely to be restored to duty in a reasonable period of time (six months or otherwise noted in the departmental regulation).

Not fit for duty with possibility of recovery, requiring leave: The officer suffers a degree of mental illness or disability in his or her job-related conduct that is of sufficient magnitude that the FFDE-P finds the officer impaired and requiring leave for the treatment of the disability, but is likely to respond to interventions that would restore the officer to duty in a reasonable period of time. The officer may reapply for duty at such time that his or her condition allows for a return to work in the opinion of one or more of the treating providers, with concurrence of the departmental FFDE-P.

Not fit for duty with possibility of recovery and capable of accepting accommodation as a law enforcement officer: The officer suffers a degree of mental illness or disability in his or her job-related conduct that is of sufficient magnitude that the FFDE-P would find the officer impaired but likely to respond to interventions that would restore the officer to duty in a reasonable period of time. The officer may be offered modified law enforcement duty during the period of recovery if such is available, and the officer is otherwise qualified for such assignment. Officers who are suspended, take or are placed on leave, or provided with accommodations or reduced duty positions may not be returned to full duty without the approval or both the FFDE-P and the RDA, regardless of the opinions of outside medical or mental health providers. The FFDE-P and RDA are mandated to develop a reasonable posttreatment or leave examination procedure for each department to ensure the safe return of impaired officer to full duty.

No mental health issues: No evidence has been produced to the satisfaction of the FFDE-P that indicates that the officer suffers the burden of mental illness or disability, and therefore all reports or observations of inappropriate or undesirable conduct should be considered to be volitional and subject to ordinary criminal or disciplinary proceedings.

Refusal to submit to examination: Any significant omission, distortion, or misrepresentation in interview or written documentation or psychometric testing that represents, in the opinion of the FFDE-P, an attempt to defeat, ignore, or avoid the purpose of the FFDE shall be considered a refusal to submit or comply with the FFDE.

Instruments of Departmental Action

A fitness-for-duty evaluation system shall be created by the department either through salaried employees or by contracting with independent, qualified professionals to conduct FFDEs as needed within the department. Associated departmental or agency sections or divisions may be created as follows in connection with the FFDE process. Since a need exists to develop a mechanism to administer the FFDE procedure, all departments with fifteen or more commissioned officers will appoint or designate senior officers or create divisions or responsible designated authority within the agency to perform the following functions:

1. *Internal affairs officer(s)* (full- or part-time) to investigate and support the prosecution of criminal and corruption behaviors among law enforcement officers within that department. FFDE referrals may originate with this officer.
2. *Health and safety officer(s)* to conduct required administrative tasks that involve illness and medical leave issues, benefits, and administrative tasks connected with commissioned officers. FFDE referrals may originate with this officer.
3. *Citizen complaint officer(s)* to provide the department with an objective, fair method by which civilian complaints may be processed and reviewed for referral to the IA officer or other appropriate agencies of the department. FFDE referrals may originate with this officer.
4. *Employee assistance program officer(s)* or related systems director to arrange for short-term counseling, such as may be needed in critical incident debriefings or survivors' counseling. FFDE referrals may originate with this officer.
5. *Health insurance officer(s)* to arrange for necessary public or private insurance or other health service payment system services to provide for the treatment of officers to restore them to duty where such is recommended by the FFDE.

Public Safety Administrative Override

The Public Safety Assurance Act supercedes other federal or state regulations regarding health, confidentiality, commerce, disability, and employment as may be deemed appropriate to meet the rationale of the act in regard to commissioned law enforcement personnel. All union agreements, negotiated employment contracts, and consent decrees must be consistent with the intent of Public Safety Assurance Act.

FINAL THOUGHTS

An obligation exists for all law enforcement agencies to consider rehabilitation for the officer who has experienced an impairment of some area of employment-connected behavior that can be approached reasonably as a medical or psychological treatment issue. Current

FFDE recommendations of treatment, a matter that is mired in a legal and ethical miasma of contractions and official nondisclosure, are underemployed because of the ambiguities in contemporary FFDE treatment systems.

Critical questions remain. When is an officer recovered adequately so as to assume official duties? Who is responsible if the expert (treater, examiner) is wrong and someone is injured or not protected by that officer? Can the focus or direction of therapy with a serving officer be mandated to the provider of clinical services, and if the provider does not agree, what can be done? What happens if the officer cannot afford treatment, or the **managed care organization** refuses to fund what the examiner or treater believes to be adequate treatment? To whom does the department owe loyalty, the "odd" officer or the citizens and supervisors who complain about him? Does the union owe responsibility to any member/officer who wishes to continue employment in spite of his or her risky behavior, or to the other members/officers who may depend upon the impaired officer for their lives?

These and other questions will constitute the core intellectual and practical challenge of the LE executive, the police agency attorney, and the police psychologist in the twenty-first century. There are no simple answers, only a constant striving to do better and to meet the responsibility that the agency owes the community in an unflinching and honest manner.

APPENDIXES

Appendix A

Fitness-for-Duty Evaluation Guidelines

The Internal Association of Chiefs of Police (IACP), Police Psychological Services Section, adapted the following description in 1998 as the general guidelines for FFDEs.

Introduction

Law enforcement officers must be mentally and emotionally stable from the time of hire throughout employment. When this stability comes into doubt, agencies may turn to a psychological fitness-for-duty evaluation (FFDE). These guidelines are designed to provide specific guidance to law enforcement agencies in monitoring the psychological fitness-for-duty evaluation process with the primary goal of improving the quality of this police psychological activity. Ideally, all agencies and their evaluators would approach these evaluations similarly so that administrators can count on consistency, both internally and externally. Toward that end, the Police Psychological Services Section has developed guidelines for law enforcement agencies that reflect a range of commonly accepted practices of the section membership. No collection of guidelines can anticipate future changes or all possible eventualities, and there is no intent to limit other reasonable practices by qualified evaluators. The guidelines do not represent an official statement of the American Psychological Association.

Qualifications

1. A psychological fitness-for-duty evaluation is a highly specialized activity within the discipline of police psychology. As such, these evaluations should only be conducted by a qualified mental health professional. At minimum, the evaluator should do the following:
   a. be a licensed or certified psychologist or psychiatrist with experience in the diagnosis and treatment of mental and emotional disorders;

    b. possess training and background in psychological test interpretation and law enforcement psychological assessment techniques;

    c. have familiarity with the literature in police psychology and the essential job functions of a peace officer; and knowledge of case law and other legal requirements related to employment and personnel practices (e.g., the Americans with Disabilities Act);

    d. have devoted part of his or her practice to police psychology or worked under the supervision of a police psychologist; and

    e. be prepared by training and experience to qualify as an expert for any proceeding that might arise from the evaluation.

Who Is the Client

1. The client in an FFDE is the referring agency and not the officer being evaluated. At the same time, a duty of care to the officer may be expected as the recipient of a professional service, to be defined by professional ethical standards, pertinent state and federal laws, and/or judicial decisions. Advisements and admonishments identifying the client should be clear to all parties, and their representatives, before the FFDE commences.

2. Evaluators should make every effort to avoid conflicts of interest such as an incompatible dual relationship (e.g., conducting an FFDE on an officer who had previously been a confidential counseling/therapy client, evaluating an officer with whom there has been a social or business relationship, etc.) Where a conflict may be unavoidable or deemed to be of minimal impact, the conflict should be disclosed and documented before the evaluation goes forth, and all vested parties should concur, with appropriate consents and releases of information obtained. In addition, if confidential counseling/psychotherapy is a recommendation of the FFDE, the evaluator, or someone closely aligned, should not be the provider of the recommended service.

The Referral Process

1. An FFDE is not a substitute for supervision or a mode of discipline. When possible, agencies should be encouraged to develop comprehensive FFDE policies that define such matters as conditions leading to referral. Such a process encourages including adequate documentation of problematic behaviors, attempts to remediate (or reasons why remediation is inappropriate), and a clear, job-related question regarding the officer's psychological suitability. Usually a written referral from the agency to the evaluator is desirable. This document could identify the reason for the referral, and might detail the agency's attempts, if any, to remediate the problem (e.g., training, tailored supervision, discipline, mentoring, reassignment and/or referral to EAP ser-

vices), or why such interventions were deemed inappropriate (e.g., the precipitating behavior was so egregious or the need so immediate).
2. In conducting an FFDE, it is usually desirable to collect background and collateral information regarding the officer. To capture the officer's pattern of conduct, this information might include performance evaluations, commendations, testimonials, internal affairs investigations, pre-employment psychological screening, formal citizen/public complaints, use-of-force incidents, officer-involved shootings, civil claims, disciplinary actions, incident reports of any triggering events, medical/psychological treatment records, or other supporting or relevant documentation related to the officer's psychological fitness-for-duty (e.g., some evaluators may ask the subject of the evaluation to submit documents and other data for the evaluator to consider). The evaluator should consider neither less nor more than that which is necessary to answer the referral question.

The Evaluation Process

1. No FFDE should be conducted without either the officer's informed written consent or a reasonable alternative. The officer should be informed of the purpose and scope of the FFDE, that no privilege exists to prevent disclosure of any or all information observed or reported during the evaluation to the client agency, and to whom the report(s) is being provided. If the request for a written consent from the officer is declined, the evaluator should adopt a suitable option (e.g., the evaluator can provide a formal written notification to the officer that includes all informed consent advisement and admonishments, witnessed and signed by a third party and/or captured on tape; or, the failure to gain a written consent from the officer can be referred to the agency for resolution before the evaluator commences the FFDE; or, the evaluator may choose to decline to proceed without a written, informed consent from the officer).
2. Depending on the referral question and the evaluator's clinical judgment, an FFDE is customarily a multi-method evaluation of the examinee. To that end, the examination should usually bring different assessment strategies and techniques to bear on developing a clear understanding of the psychological issues in the case. Ordinarily, the following methods make up this battery of techniques (although not all cases will require all methods):
   a. review of the requested background information
   b. psychological testing using objective, validated tests appropriate to the referral question(s) (personality, psychopathology, cognitive, specialized). The selection and number of assessment instruments should be sufficient to address the referral issue(s)
   c. a face-to-face, comprehensive clinical interview that includes a mental status examination

    d. a biopsychosocial history (e.g., family, education, employment, marital, medical, legal, financial, substance use, attitudes reflecting bias and prejudice, history of psychological problems and treatment, etc.)

    e. third-party collateral interviews with relevant individuals, if deemed necessary and appropriate by the examiner

    f. referral to, and/or consultation with, a specialist if the presenting problem goes beyond the expertise of the evaluator.

The Report and Recommendations

1. An agency is not entitled to any more psychological information regarding an employee than is necessary to document the presence or absence of job-related personality traits, characteristics, disorders, propensities, or conditions that would interfere with the performance of essential job functions. Thus, the written report provided to the agency should be restricted to only the presence or absence of these functional, job-related limitations with any pertinent psychological problems then linked with the essential job functions expected to be affected (e.g., an officer has a documented pattern of citizen complaints for rude and discourteous behavior. Training, counseling, mentoring, and discipline have failed to prevent yet another serious citizen complaint of officious behavior. The FFDE findings include test and interview signs of characterological hostility and lack of interpersonal sensitivity expected to lead to continued abrasive contact with the public). The report should contain a clear opinion if the officer is presently fit for unrestricted law enforcement duty, fit for duty with optional time-limited accommodations, temporarily unfit for duty pending a proposed intervention, or unfit for duty with little likelihood of remediation. Each of these opinions should include adequate reasoning to support the judgment. If the officer is found fit for duty, examiners should assume that duty will be unrestricted. If fit for unrestricted law enforcement duty, the written report requires little psychological information provided to the agency.

2. If information deemed necessary for review by the evaluator cannot be obtained, any recommendations might include the comment that the evaluation is based on available data and could be affected by specific additional information requested, but not obtained by the evaluator. Furthermore, the evaluator may want a disclaimer that indicates the need to reconsider the evaluation opinions if it is determined that the provided information proved misleading, deceptive, incomplete, distorted, or untrue.

3. If temporarily unfit for duty, recommendations should be offered regarding counseling, modified job assignment, mentoring, training, or other remedies by which the officer can be helped to regain his or her psychological suitability, to include a schedule for re-review for return

to duty. Any intervention recommendations should be consistent with available resources within the client agency so as not to create an untenable position for the officer or the agency (e.g., if an agency has no light-duty assignments, the examiner should not recommend a light-duty assignment). If the officer is found unfit, with a poor prognosis for recovery, or after remediation efforts have failed, the opinion should include the evaluator's view that further efforts to correct the condition are likely to be ineffective. Reasoning should be clearly articulated for all conclusions.

4. Evaluators are under no obligation to explain the FFDE results to the officer. If the agency wants feedback from the evaluator to the officer, the department and evaluator could decide this issue before the evaluation begins, and the evaluator could be asked to provide the requested response. If this alternative is inadvisable or undesirable to the agency or evaluator, the evaluator could suggest another qualified mental health professional be made available to the officer to assure the accurate interpretation of the contents of the agency's report. If a special report is to be provided to the officer or the officer's legal representative, the evaluator should be mindful to take reasonable steps to ensure explanations are given in a manner understandable to the officer.

Legal Considerations

1. The evaluator should document and be prepared to make available all data, subject to legal requirements, that form the basis for his or her findings and opinions. The standard to be applied to such documentation anticipates that the detail and quality of such documentation may be subject to reasonable scrutiny within an adjudicative venue.
2. Evaluators are expected to safeguard the confidentiality of the written report, and law enforcement agencies should share this responsibility.
3. The evaluators should be aware of the legal requirements for a psychological FFDE in his or her jurisdiction, and evaluators should stay abreast of changing case law. Many pertinent psycholegal issues may already be regulated by law, but absent legal requirements, evaluation procedures can be decided by the professional judgment of the qualified evaluator.

Appendix B

Fitness-for-Duty Evaluation Regulation Model

This appendix contains a model for a departmental or agency policy to be included in the operational manual, bylaws, or regulations of the law enforcement agency, civil service code, union agreement, or other appropriate body of rules such that it makes the policy enforceable and useful. A division or section of a medium-sized or larger department should be responsible for implementing the FFDE procedure; in smaller departments, a designated official agent (such as the chief) may have this duty. The responsible departmental section is generally the *health and safety division, internal affairs division,* or the *personnel department,* and in very large departments, *the psychology division* or *medical services division.*

REGULATION OF PSYCHOLOGICAL FITNESS-FOR-DUTY EVALUATION (FFDE) POLICY

Anytown Police Department
Anytown, USA

Purpose. To establish a departmental policy and define responsibilities, regarding psychological fitness-for-duty psychological examinations for law enforcement personnel, including all commanding officers, commissioned officers, and employees who are armed or whose responsibilities may place other persons at risk.

Definition. Psychological fitness-for-duty evaluations (FFDEs) are necessary for the safety and welfare of the community and of department personnel, and to ensure compliance with federal, state, and local laws [*cite appropriate laws*] that require that commissioned and serving law enforcement officers, be free from any physical, emotional, or mental conditions that might adversely affect the exercise of the duties of a peace officer in any way. The purpose of this policy is to establish consistent procedures for ordering and implementing psychological fitness-for-duty evaluations (FFDEs) of sworn personnel and of other personnel involved in public safety functions.

Power of the chief. The chief or his or her proper designee shall require a psychological fitness-for-duty psychological evaluation of any law enforcement personnel under his or her command for purposes of public safety and the business necessity of the department, such that the chief shall be advised as to the ability of any law enforcement employee to properly fulfill his or her duties as established by custom, regulation, or law.

Observational mandate. Because the public is required to comply with commands by law enforcement personnel and submit to the authority of a law enforcement officer, a public policy mandate exists that such employees not engage in behaviors that are potentially harmful to self or others, or exhibit behaviors that may reasonably be believed to impair operational efficiency and the capability of performing assigned duties.

1. All observations of potential misconduct, reported as civilian, co-worker, or supervisory complaints, and subsequent hearings, warnings, letters of counseling or guidance, and the like shall be documented and recorded in support of any FFDE referral.
2. Any employee shall be subject to and comply with an order for a fitness-for-duty psychological evaluation when observed or credibly reported behavior, in the sole opinion of the chief or his or her proper designee, raises reasonable questions regarding an employee's ability to function as an officer as follows:
    a. The officer appears to exhibit behavioral problems that suggest a collapse of integrity, motivation, effectiveness, or judgment.
    b. Following a good history of conduct and behavioral control, the officer exhibits the sudden onset of forgetfulness, hostility, depression, withdrawal, irrational speech, or any inability to meet the minimal demands of his or her assignment.
    c. The emergence of prejudicial, bigoted, or overbearing written or spoken conduct or behavior, especially when it is connected with threats of the violation of the rights of citizens.
    d. Credible allegations of the excessive, inappropriate, and unexplained use of force are supported by reasonable evidence.
    e. Threats, insinuations, or actual use of violence by the officer, particularly when associated with unjustifiable aggressive displays toward colleagues, superiors, or the public.
    f. Complaints of debilitating medical conditions associated with excessive sick leave and absenteeism that are not verified in repeated, standard medical examinations.
    g. Complaints by family, relatives, friends or associates of threatening or bizarre off-duty behavior, frequently in the form of spousal abuse or substance abuse.
    h. When the officer proceeds with any lawsuit against any party in which he or she alleges significant mental, emotional, or behavioral injury of any type.

i. If signs of emotional instability appear following a shooting incident or traumatic, job-related incident, even if the officer was in no way at fault in the event.
j. Sexual inappropriateness or acting out, especially in regard to unwanted sexual advances, harassment, or implications of the misuse of police authority further a sexual action or interest by the officer.
k. Following a traumatic or injurious event, such as a motor vehicle accident or any such event in which the officer had experienced or observed an event of horror, fear, or dismay that, in the sole opinion of the chief, may be considered harmful emotionally.
l. Any form of behavior prohibited and circumscribed by the civil service or personnel rules.

Control of evaluations and reports. Psychological reports are to be kept confidential and stored in a secure location that is not accessible to any personnel not authorized by the chief. The professionally prepared reports are to inform the police chief and authorized departmental personnel of the police psychologist's consultation findings. The reports are to contain minimally necessary information, in the police psychologist's sole opinion, in order to maintain appropriate privacy of the officer while departmental authorities address the issues of evaluation. The reports are advisory only and shall not be the sole basis for administrative decisions. They shall address:

1. the employee's ability to carry out duties in regard to psychological or mental factors;
2. the advisability of mental health intervention for an employee whose performance places the operation of the department at risk; and/or
3. in the absence of the burden of mental illness or defect, the apparent need for further administrative or disciplinary inquiry.

Referral for fitness-for-duty evaluations. The police chief may authorize a mandatory evaluation based on a request from any senior law enforcement administrator, the internal affairs division commander, the health and safety division commander, or the personnel division manager as part of an administrative action for any of the general reasons listed previously. The commander/manager must document incidents of questionable behavior, as well as counseling and/or disciplinary measures that have been employed previously to the police chief in memorandum form.

Where the employee's immediate supervisor initially solicited the voluntary cooperation of the employee to seek psychological help from internal or external resources, the officer's responses to this solicitation shall be documented.

In the event the division commander/manager is unable to secure voluntary compliance, then the commander may request that the chief order a psychological evaluation for an employee showing behavioral signs of distress or impairment or when mental instability is reasonably suspected by obtaining an order from the chief.

SCHEDULING OF EVALUATIONS

1. The evaluator shall be a qualified clinical psychologist or clinical neuropsychologist licensed and in good standing in the state who, in the sole opinion of the chief, can demonstrate reasonable training and experience in police psychology and is on contract to provide FFDE services for the department. The fee will be assessed to the department as per contract.
2. For FFDEs, the employee shall be served with an order from the police chief to undergo an evaluation. Failure by the employee to report for an evaluation, or failure to show reasonable compliance, effort and forthrightness in responding to the interview and test components of the FFDE, shall result in disciplinary action.
3. The employee's division commander (or the chief) shall effect service of the chief's order and inform the employee about the reason(s) for the evaluation.
4. The assistant police chief of the administrative bureau shall be responsible for scheduling the evaluation with the contractually authorized police psychologist.
   a. The evaluation shall be scheduled, as much as possible, during the employee's workday.
   b. Should the evaluation be scheduled during an employee's off-duty time, the employee shall be compensated for his or her time accordingly.
5. The employee evaluated shall incur no expense for the evaluation and shall be reimbursed for all personal costs associated directly with the evaluation in accordance with departmental reimbursement guidelines.
6. An evaluation normally requires a half workday to a full workday to complete. In exceptional circumstances, more time may be required, necessitating additional appointments.

EVALUATIONS

1. The police officer or employee shall be asked to read and sign a consent form advising him or her about the purpose of the evaluation and the limits of confidentiality.
2. The police officer or employee shall be advised by the evaluator that the evaluation is the property of the referring authority, the office of the

police chief, and that confidentiality does not exist in the context of the applicant's/employee's relationship with the evaluator.

3. If the police officer or employee being evaluated does not agree to the conditions of the evaluation or declines to respond to tasks and questions in a credible and honest manner in the sole opinion of the police psychologist, the referral source will be so informed. The employee may be viewed as having failed to obey a lawful order, resulting in disciplinary action.

4. The FFDE evaluator shall use multiple data sources, to include standardized psychological tests, structured psychological interview techniques, and behavioral observations, and combine them in a professional manner. Data sources may also include:

   a. Interviews with relatives and/or supervisors, as advisable;
   b. Police records, to include previous evaluations and reports;
   c. Investigative background reports, including all available documentation.
   d. The police officer or employee directed to undergo a mandatory evaluation may request a copy of the evaluator's report from the department in order to arrange for an evaluation from another source, paid for by the employee. This does not relieve the employee from the duty of undergoing the mandatory evaluation ordered by the department.
   e. For all evaluations in which a potential disability is indicated, the referring authority shall consult with the chief and/or legal counsel to determine what steps should be taken to determine whether state or federal law requires a reasonable accommodation or other action.

REPORTS AND RETENTION

1. Fitness-for-duty evaluation reports and recommendations shall be directed to the police chief for review.
2. Upon completion of the chief's review, the assistant police chief of the administrative services bureau shall secure the report in a special locked file.
3. The record will be kept for a period of seven years after the last data entry, after which time basic information will be retained and the report will be destroyed except in the event of pending litigation.
4. The police chief shall notify the evaluated employee that his or her report is available for optional review in the presence of the evaluator, who will answer the employee's questions about the report. The evaluated employee may waive the right to review the report.
5. No information pertaining to any evaluation shall be released without the consent of the police chief.
6. Retention and release of information shall be subject to applicable state and federal law.

APPEAL AND REEVALUATION

1. The police officer or employee may forward to the police chief a copy of an independent evaluation obtained from other qualified sources that was conducted at the employee's expense.
2. In the case of a possible conflict of interest, the police chief may order a reevaluation by a psychologist not connected with the department at no cost to the employee.
3. After completion of therapeutic intervention (treatment), the employee may be required to undergo another departmentally funded posttreatment evaluation to determine current fitness-for-duty.
4. It is not the intention of this policy to interfere with either officer-initiated or supervisor-suggested counseling efforts, the function of the employee assistance program (EAP), or to alter or replace confidential counseling provided by the department as a result of critical incidents or emergencies. This policy is intended to provide a procedure for the assessment of an employee's mental and emotional ability to perform the essential functions of his or her position, when the employee's conduct, in the sole opinion of the FFDE examiner, may be considered a threat to public safety, the safety of the employee or other employees, or, may interfere with the agency's ability to deliver effective police services.
5. Where appropriate, a supervisor and employee may discuss reasonable, informal accommodations to a mental or emotional problem that may enable the employee to perform the essential functions of his or her position while any problem is being resolved. However, an employee is not required to disclose a disability to a supervisor. The failure to achieve a mutually satisfactory accommodation shall result in the matter being referred to the health and safety division by the supervisor with a written recommendation for an FFDE.
6. In circumstances when an employee's conduct immediately or directly threatens anyone's safety, a supervisor may relieve the employee of duty immediately pending further investigation. In other cases, employees may be relieved from duty or reassigned as necessary for reasons of public safety or the efficient operation of the department, pending completion of an evaluation. The supervisor may seize weapons or other department property (including identification materials or objects, such as badges or identity cards), and, where appropriate, the employee may be ordered not to exercise peace officer or other official powers. Nothing in this policy is intended to prevent or limit a supervisor from taking any emergency action that he or she deems to be reasonably necessary to protect life or property or the proper administration of department function.
7. The chief or the health and safety division commander may determine, in the exercise of his or her discretion and with or without additional investigation, that a fitness-for-duty evaluation is or is not

warranted. If an examination is warranted, it should be scheduled within forty-eight hours or otherwise as soon as possible under the prevailing circumstances. The agency shall be vested with authority to make any such decision based upon any reasonable cause.

8. The employee shall receive a written order for the evaluation. Such an order should include a brief description of the reasons for the evaluation. It should also specify the date, time and place of the evaluation, and include the name of the psychologist conducting the evaluation, directives to cooperate with the psychologist's and/or staff's requests and to answer any questions posed by the psychologist or staff completely and honestly; and a notice that the evaluation is being conducted for use by the department.

9. The evaluator will be designated by the chief and must be credentialed as a licensed psychologist with appropriate training and experience in the diagnosis and treatment of mental disorders and use of psychometric testing, and have special training and experience as a police psychologist. The referred employee shall follow all instructions and participate actively in all activities and tasks prescribed by the evaluator, the refusal of which is to be considered insubordination. The evaluator shall be instructed by the department to release only that information that is allowed under this policy or is otherwise required by law.

10. The chief and his or her proper designee have a right to information that is necessary to achieve any legitimate employment or public safety purpose. The report is not for the purpose of treatment, but to determine fitness-for-duty from the prospective of liability and threat or risk of harm to the public, fellow officers, supervisors, or the efficient operation of the department—a requirement for public safety. The limited verbal and/or written results of the evaluation will be provided to the chief and his or her proper designee as a confidential personnel record. The FFDE provider must maintain all information in confidential files that are owned by the department, and for which he or she is the custodian. No diagnosis or unnecessary information is to be transmitted to the chief and his or her proper designee, although medical, psychological and technical information may be transmitted to potential treatment providers, as long as a proper release for such information is secured from both the department and the officer.

11. The report and information received by the chief and his or her proper designee shall be limited to:
    a. Conclusions regarding the determination of fitness-for-duty
    b. Descriptions of whether or not the officer must be relieved of duty or may function in a limited capacity (accommodated) within his or her agency

    c. The need for treatment for the officer, irrespective of whether the officer continues to serve in an active capacity

    d. Where feasible, a reasonable opinion as to the likelihood of recovery or behavior change

    e. Where appropriate and requested, a statement of medical cause (worker's compensation or other legitimate purposes) may be requested by the chief or his or her proper designee of the FFDE evaluator, and the department, where appropriate to the specific case, may make administrative arrangements to permit the following:

       1. The need for a posttreatment FFDE, where treatment has been recommended.

       2. Where the employee has initiated a lawsuit, arbitration, grievance, worker's compensation, or other claim or challenge involving his or her medical history, mental or physical condition, or treatment, the FFDE report may contain any information that is relevant to any such action.

       3. An employee may voluntarily waive in writing any or all confidentiality and privacy restrictions on any medical or psychological information reported to the chief by any medical or psychological treatment provider.

       4. The chief and his or her proper designee shall establish appropriate procedures to protect the information from unauthorized use or disclosure. The FFDE report and any associated material or documents shall be retained in the employee's secure medical file, held separately from the general personnel or internal affairs files. The report may be used or disclosed only in a legitimate and appropriate proceeding to the extent authorized by regulation, law or agreement.

       5. Statements made by the employee shall be considered compelled and may not be used in a criminal proceeding against the employee.

       6. Depending upon the results of the evaluation and the recommendation of the evaluator, and in conjunction with other information, reports and observations of peers, supervisors, and credible witnesses, the chief may:

         a. Return the employee to full duty,

         b. Place the employee on temporary light or modified duty,

         c. Remove the employee from any duties pending treatment and reevaluation,

   d. Conditionally allow full or modified duty concurrent with the employee receiving approved and appropriate treatment at the sole discretion of the chief after consultation with the chief's qualified experts,

   e. Institute or resume disciplinary proceedings as appropriate,

   f. Institute proceedings to medically terminate employment, or when appropriate, offer an alternative position, for which the employee may be competitively qualified at the sole discretion of the chief.

Appendix C

Fitness-for-Duty
Evaluation Letter of Guidance

The following is useful as a letter to be sent to law enforcement executives for the purpose of guidance and instruction following referral of an officer for a fitness-for-duty examination.

Commander Smith
Anytown Police Department
Anytown, USA

Thank you for referring your officer for a fitness-for-duty evaluation. As you know, a fitness-for-duty evaluation is not a psychological examination meant for diagnosis or treatment, but rather an assessment of the liability or risk posed by the officer to himself or herself, the department, fellow workers, and the public in general.

Preparation for a fitness-for-duty examination

Since a fitness-for-duty evaluation is always in response to a public or supervisor complaint, sets of complaints, stressful events, or observations made by the police executives, fellow officers, the general public, or others, the following is necessary as part of the evaluation:

Please deliver the essential personnel records for the officer or deputy to my office to be reviewed before the examination date. Include the documents connected to the complaints or observations that pertain to the reasons for the referral request. Complaints made against or by the officer, histories of traumatic or objectionable behaviors or events, past medical or disciplinary records, and the like are particularly welcome. Avoid narratives that tend to "medicalize" the complaint (e.g., "He is acting paranoid") since this is neither a useful nor a direct observation (i.e., it is a conclusion).

It is recommended that you inform the officer of the reasons for the FFDE in general terms, such as to assist in explaining the reasons for events covered in complaints of certain dates or to certify that the officer is fully recovered from a shooting or accident of a certain date. Do not discuss the officer's personal issues with him or her, nor inquire into his or her mental or physical health prior to the FFDE. Do not inform staff of the FFDE referral if they have no sound administrative reason to possess such information. Do not generally announce to fellow officers or clerical staff that the officer is unavailable because he is undergoing a psychological examination.

What should the officer take to the examination?

The officer should be aware of the *location, date and time* he or she is to appear for the examination and must allow sufficient time to make the trip under all reasonable weather and traffic conditions. The officer should appear at the examination site fifteen minutes before the actual appointment to allow for initial paperwork. If he or she arrives late for any reason, he or she may be refused examination. He or she should expect to sign an authorization to send the report to his or her supervisor, police chief, sheriff, or other authorized superior. Our police psychologists perform professional *consultations* and your department has a right to accept, partly consider, or reject the fitness report. The department is the client for whom the work is performed, as well as the owner of the report and all of its associated data. If the officer indicates that he or she will not cooperate for any reason whatsoever, he or she will be returned to your law enforcement agency with a report that he or she refused the examination. If he or she does not cooperate in the actual completion of the examination (for example, distorting his or her responses), the report will reflect that observation as well. Telephone and other contacts directly between the officer and our agency are *strongly discouraged,* and communications, including the contents of the report, should pass through a supervisor or other departmentally nominated person to the officer in summary form at your option. Unless other arrangements have been made, it is the responsibility of your department or agency to provide appropriate documentation or notices as may be required under the Fair Credit Reporting Act, the Americans with Disabilities Act, or other state of federal legislation or case law.

The officer must bring an *official ID with a picture* (such as a driver's license), and his or her *DD 214 (military discharge document)* if he or she has been discharged from any military service *within the past ten years.* If he or she is to bring medical or administrative documents, they must be *sealed* in an official envelope. It is preferable for the officer to have his or her medical, psychological, or other documents mailed or otherwise transmitted *directly to Matrix, Inc.,* by the record holder before the exam date (c/o Dr. J. Doe, 890 Main Street, Anytown, USA). At the very minimum, the officer should have the names, addresses, and dates connected with any important psychological or medical treatment or procedure. *He or she must bring a list of medications used in the most recent three months, and psychiatric medications used over the last year* (and prescribing physicians' names).

The officer should be aware that physicians and hospitals often keep separate records, and separate releases of information signed by him or her to *each party* may be necessary to obtain needed records. He or she should bring information about the dates, locations, and charges connected with any court appearance, citation, arrest, or conviction related to his or her own *personal legal history,* no matter how long ago. He or she should have information about any prior psychological or psychiatric evaluation or assessment taken in connection with his or her employment application, whether or not he or she was successful in the application, including dates, names, and locations of examiners or providers. *Remind him or her to bring his or her eyeglasses* and any other appliances that might be necessary for extended interview and written examination.

Under no condition is the officer to bring family, friends (other than for transportation), or legal or union representatives to the examination, unless required in our contract with your agency. If he or she is accompanied by unauthorized persons who insist upon participation in the examination, the examination shall be canceled. Our agency will withdraw its participation and refer the officer back to his or her department for appropriate action. The officer may bring individual portions of nonperishable food, *since the evaluation may continue throughout the day.* Except where unavoidable, the officer should not bring a weapon of any kind to the evaluation.

No report will be produced based on fractional or incomplete information. The officer is expected to complete extensive paperwork and related questionnaires and tests, as well as submit to verbal examination and otherwise appropriately complete all documentation. Incomplete documentation will result in a statement that the officer has failed to complete the requirements of his or her evaluation and no report will be submitted beyond that fact.

Further instructions

Please feel free to contact me if I may be of further assistance.

John Doe, PhD
Clinical Psychologist

Appendix D

Fitness-for-Duty Letter for Officer to Report for Examination: Mandatory and Optional Programs

The following is a general outline of a letter that may be sent to an officer who has been ordered to report for an FFDE under a *mandatory* regulation.

Anytown Police Department
1234 Any Street
Anytown, USA
OFFICIAL DIRECTIVE

Officer John Q. Public
Badge No. 5678
Downtown Division

You are hereby ordered by the chief to appear at the offices of Dr. John Doe, police psychologist, 890 Main Street, Anytown, USA (121-123-1234) at 9 a.m. December 1, 2004, for purposes of undergoing a fitness-for-duty evaluation. **You are relieved of all official duties until you are restored to duty by order of the chief.** Following completion of the evaluation, you are to report to your sergeant for further instructions.

Dr. Doe and his organization are the contractual consultants for the Anytown PD regarding matters of psychological fitness. You are ordered to submit to the requirements of this evaluation by extending your full cooperation with all requested tasks.

The purpose of the evaluation is to obtain a specialized, professional opinion concerning your current capability to offer armed, independent law enforcement duties. Departmental concerns stem from reported violations of regulations XX (behavior unbecoming an officer) and XZ (use of excess force), about which you have received earlier notice.

You are ordered by the chief to appear in civilian dress and without any weapons. You are to bring eyeglasses if needed, as well as any objects or materials (including a bag lunch if you wish) that you will need to engage in written and verbal tasks for a full day. **If you are more than fifteen minutes late, you may forfeit the opportunity to be examined,** which will be considered a refusal to participate. Other persons, such as family, fellow officers, union representatives, and attorneys will not be allowed to observe or participate in the evaluation. Any misrepresentations, omissions, or distortions in your verbal or written communication with the examiner will be considered to be a form of a refusal to participate.

If you refuse to participate fully in the evaluation or decline to cooperate in any way, your behavior will be considered insubordination. In such a case, the chief will order that the department proceed with a disciplinary hearing regarding both insubordination as well as other violations of regulations that pertain to your conduct as an officer.

The evaluation is being conducted for use by and will be the property of the department, but is confidential regarding all others ("limited confidentiality") as permitted by (cite state law) departmental regulations. Statements given under departmental orders to submit to examination may not be used in a criminal proceeding against you. Other limits and conditions of evaluation and regulations regarding this procedure will be discussed at the examiner's office prior to the beginning of the procedure.

Captain James Smith
Commander
Downtown Division

Following is a general outline of a letter that may be sent to an officer who has been ordered to report for an FFDE under an *optional* regulation.

Anytown Police Department
1234 Any Street
Anytown, USA
OFFICIAL DIRECTIVE

Officer John Q. Public
Badge No. 5678
Downtown Division

You are hereby requested by the chief to appear at the offices of Dr. John Doe, police psychologist, 890 Main Street, Anytown, USA (121-123-1234) at 9 a.m. December 1, 2004, for purposes of undergoing a fitness-for-duty evaluation. **You are relieved of all official duties until you are re-**

stored to duty by order of the chief. Either following completion of the evaluation or awaiting your election to undergo a disciplinary review, you are to report to your sergeant for further instructions.

Dr. Doe and his organization are the contractual consultants for the Anytown Police Department regarding matters of psychological fitness. You are requested to submit to the requirements of this evaluation by extending your full cooperation with all requested tasks.

If you decline to participate fully in the evaluation in any way, you will be ordered to submit to a disciplinary hearing regarding the cited regulatory violations. In such a case, you must report to your sergeant immediately and the chief will order that the department proceed with a disciplinary hearing regarding the violations of regulations that pertain to your conduct as an officer.

If you elect to undergo the fitness evaluation, you should know that the purpose of the evaluation is to obtain a specialized, professional opinion concerning your current capability to offer armed, independent law enforcement duties. Departmental concerns stem from reported violations of regulations XX (behavior unbecoming an officer) and XZ (use of excess force), about which you have received earlier notice.

You must appear in civilian dress and without any weapons. You are to bring eyeglasses if needed, as well as any objects or materials (including a bag lunch if you wish) that you will need to engage in written and verbal tasks for a full day. **If you are more than fifteen minutes late, you may forfeit the opportunity to be examined,** which will be considered a refusal to participate. Other persons, such as family, fellow officers, union representatives, and attorneys will not be allowed to observe or participate in the evaluation. Any misrepresentations, omissions, or distortions in your verbal or written communication with the examiner will be considered a refusal to participate.

The evaluation is being conducted for use by and will be the property of the department, but is confidential regarding all others ("limited confidentiality") as permitted by (cite state law) departmental regulations. Statements given under departmental orders to submit to examination may not be used in a criminal proceeding against you. Other limits and conditions of evaluation and regulations regarding this procedure will be discussed at the examiner's office prior to the beginning of the procedure.

Captain James Smith
Commander
Downtown Division

Appendix E

Sample Fitness-for-Duty Evaluation Report

Following is a typical FFDE report. Note that many acceptable forms of the FFDE report exist, and each syntax should be developed to meet the needs of a given department within general guidelines:

Fitness-for-Duty Evaluation

Name: John Q. Public
        1 Main Street
        Anytown, USA 00000

Race/Sex: White/Male
Marital status: Single
Age/date of birth: 29/01-01-75
SSN: 111-11-1111

Employer: Anytown City Police
           1 Elm Street
           Anytown, USA 00000

Date of evaluation: 01/01/04

Place of evaluation:
FFDE provider
890 Main Street
Anytown, USA 00000

Evaluator: J. Doe, PhD Clinical Psychologist

Referral source: Lt. Jim Jones, Internal Affairs

Reason for Evaluation

John Q. Public, a twenty-nine-year-old single white male, Anytown City Police Officer, was referred by Lt. Jim Jones of the Internal Affairs Unit for a fitness-for-duty evaluation (FFDE), secondary to a series of complaints involving a number of documented sexual and violent incidents. The evaluation was conducted for fitness-for-duty purposes, which predominantly involved the health, safety, and welfare of the officer, his department, fellow employees, and the public in general, but the report is not considered a general clinical examination.

Background Information and Observations

Officer Public appeared for the evaluation in a timely manner. Prior to the beginning of the evaluation it was explained to Officer Public that, from the perspective of the police psychologist, the evaluation was *voluntary* (irrespective of the order from the officer's employer) and that he had a right to discontinue the evaluation or discontinue permission to distribute the evaluation any time prior to its actual distribution. This offer extended to any period of time prior to the actual distribution of the fitness-for-duty report. It was explained that the evaluation was *not confidential* and that it was conducted primarily for purposes of determining whether Officer Public represented any form of threat to the health, safety, and welfare of himself, his co-workers, supervisors, or the public in general. It was explained that such threats could involve a number of issues, including but not limited to his inability to function properly in the role of police officer, any form of insubordination, inappropriate or bizarre conduct, irrational acts, or uninviting or fantastic behavior in action or words. It was explained that the results of the evaluation would be transmitted to him through his departmental supervisors, or by whatever means allowed for by the personnel and/or civil service codes of his department. It was explained that the FFDE provider considers the evaluation to be a form of *consultation only* (not treatment or a clinical service) to be taken into account by his employer with other facts, information, and regulations to determine appropriate subsequent actions. All communications are, therefore, to be directed by Officer Public to his employer only and not to the FFDE provider. The ultimate actions taken by his department are not within the control of the FFDE provider, and it was explained that any concerns the officer may have had in that regard should be directed to his supervisor and/or police chief. It is the responsibility of the officer's employer to inform the officer of other rights that the officer may have and to take such rights into account before taking any action. The officer understood and agreed to all conditions of the evaluation before it took place. The officer was given the instructions for Officers Undergoing Fitness-for-Duty Evaluations form, which explained the rules governing the evaluation in writing.

Officer Public was dressed in civilian clothing and demonstrated good hygiene and grooming. At times he appeared to be moderately anxious. He acknowledged that he felt the referral for fitness for duty was inappropriate because it was based "solely on the opinions" of certain supervisors, yet he also indicated he was "not certain" why he had been referred for evaluation. He denied any difficulty in regard to psychological problems or in his relationships with others, particularly women. He took a generally defensive position with the examiner, denying common weaknesses or problems. Reliability is considered to be below average. No obvious disturbances of motor activity were noted. Eye contact was deemed poor. Memory appeared to be in the low-average range, although at times, Officer Public reported minor memory difficulties in reporting problems that he had experienced in the past. His mood appeared to be mildly downcast. Insight appeared to be below average. Intellectual functioning and physical health appeared to be in the average range.

Fitness-for-Duty Examination Intake Report and Interview

When asked in writing why he had been sent by his agency for an evaluation, Officer Public wrote, "I'm not 100-percent sure. The only thing that I was told was that I had received too many complaints from women on various issues." When asked to elaborate, he responded that he had once used loud, vulgar language with a woman motorist at a traffic stop. She accused him of being rude. At another time, he was accused of punching a car at a football game. More recent, however, he reported that he had been accused of "sexual battery," although he indicated that the female who filed the report was unreliable. He admitted that he had been sexually active with this woman in the past. However, he had reportedly separated from her. Recently, the woman invited him to her home to use alcohol and watch pornographic movies. After he left, she called the police and reported that he had committed a sexual battery upon her (see departmental memo of *date*).

When asked for the "real reason" that he had been referred for the evaluation, he indicated in writing that, "I feel that my being here is solely on the misguided opinions of my supervisors and not on the facts. I don't feel that there is a problem or a need for me to be here." He admitted that he didn't "read women very well," and seemed to become involved with them in ways that resulted in his further difficulties.

When asked if he had any other complaints, he said that he could not remember any. When prompted about the "young girls incident," he admitted that he had "contact" with two girls who "like" his company but their mother complained to his department that the girls were uncomfortable with his presence.

In regard to other incidents of misconduct, he indicated that he had been called to a location when a suspect reportedly became verbally hostile. "I took action, handcuffed him, and made him sit down." The storeowner (apparently based on videotapes of the event) filed a complaint that he had choked and kicked the helpless suspect, resulting in Officer Public receiving a fifteen-day suspension.

Officer Public indicated that he has never been sued, nor has he sued anyone. He denied a history of bad temper, domestic violence, or the commission of a felony. He indicated that he did not hold grudges and he does not have bad credit.

Officer Public has been with the Anytown Police Department since 1998. Before that, he was a corrections officer at a county jail, where he had been named in a civil rights lawsuit for beating a handicapped prisoner.

Officer Public indicated that he has never resigned from a LE position under pressure of discharge, and has never had a sexual relationship with anyone that he has worked with or met through his law enforcement work. He indicated a fair relationship with his supervisors and an excellent relationship with his fellow officers.

The officer denied any history of illicit drugs or use of any kind. He indicated that he consumed alcohol at the rate of about one ounce of pure alcohol (one drink) per week. This is usually in the form of wine, beer, or mixed drinks. He admitted an earlier period (mid-1990s) of heavier alcohol use.

Available Documentation

The Anytown City Police Department forwarded documentation prior to the evaluation. This included, but was not limited to, the following:

A departmental memo from Sgt. Melvin York to Captain Robert E. Lee, dated 09/11/02, which Officer Public punched the passenger side of a female suspect's car. Eventually, Officer Public twisted the female suspect's arm behind her back and placed her in handcuffs.

Interdepartmental correspondence to Officer Public from Chief Tough Leader, dated 02/02/02, indicated that Officer Public had been suspended for two days due to his untruthfulness in an investigation. This stemmed from a complaint from a Mrs. Nobody concerning the nature of his unwanted relationship with her teenage daughters.

Interdepartmental correspondence, dated 08/27/00, from Chief Tough Leader that Officer Public reportedly restrained a female associate in her apartment while he removed articles of her clothing.

Interdepartmental correspondence from Chief Tough Leader to Captain Robert E. Lee indicated that Officer Public was recorded on a security camera choking and kicking a suspect for no understandable reason.

Psychological Testing

The Shipley Institute of Living Scale, the Minnesota Multiphasic Personality Inventory—Second Edition (MMPI-II), the Millon Clinical Multiaxial Inventory—Third Edition (MCMI-III), and the Personality Assessment Inventory (PAI) were all administered as part of this evaluation. The results were reviewed and are consistent with the recommendations offered here:

Discussion

It is clear that Officer Public appeared to take a defensive position by denying common human frailty on testing. He appeared to become involved with various forms of interpersonal conflict and difficulty, especially related to psychosexual behavior and aggressive conduct. The instances of violations of departmental rules and the absence of what appears to be realistic acceptance or regret appeared to bode poorly for the possibility of future behavior change.

Recommendations

The FFDE provider acts in the consulting role only. This report may be subject to change, as further information becomes available. The recommendations that are offered are based upon an understanding of the needs of the law enforcement agency as they are made known to the evaluator as well as specific claims made in regard to Officer Public. Certain information, as indicated previously, was obtained from Officer Public directly.

The FFDE provider does not provide clinical services for officers nor does he determine the ultimate outcome of these recommendations. These recommendations are meant to be part of an overall review of Officer Public's behavior and to be used by the department to provide additional information that may be useful in the operation of the agency, the protection of the officer, his co-workers, and the general public. This report is not a replacement for a criminal or internal affairs investigation, or other such inquiry. This report is not meant to be used in isolation of other important sources of information.

The following recommendations are offered as consultation to the Anytown Police Department in regard to Officer John Q. Public. Given the information from all sources, the following recommendations are offered:

1. *Officer Public evidenced limited participation in the fitness-for-duty evaluation.* Although there is evidence that he attempted to minimize his personal difficulties in both interview and psychological testing formats, he revealed sufficient information that, with additional external documentation, he appears to suffer from a significant behavioral difficulty.
2. *It is recommended that Officer Public be considered unfit for unrestricted duty.* Given that he is operating as a minimally supervised, armed police agent, and given that many of the difficulties demonstrated through historical reports, psychological testing, and interview seem to touch directly upon his work, he does not appear to be currently fit for unrestricted duty. Of course, the department and the officer himself will have to make individual decisions about the details of such

treatment, but it is recommended that a basic attempt at a treatment intervention precede any consideration of return to duty.

3. Upon completion of therapy, his therapists may release Officer Public for a second FFDE when they believe he has made maximum medical or psychological improvement. This information should be conveyed to Officer Public's department, and Officer Public should then be asked to submit to a posttreatment fitness-for-duty evaluation, at which time an independent judgment concerning evidence of recovery may be examined.

J. Doe, PhD
Clinical Psychologist
FFDE Provider

Appendix F

Statement of Understanding

In the office of the FFDE provider, the officer should be informed of his rights and the nature of the procedure in both written forms. Following is a sample statement of understanding that should immediately precede the FFDE. Refusal to agree with the conditions outlined in such a document should result in termination of the FFDE and a referral of the officer back to the referring law enforcement executive.

STATEMENT OF UNDERSTANDING MODEL

Please read the following statement and sign below to indicate that you understand the conditions of this examination and are submitting to a liability assessment voluntarily.

You are about to complete a set of tests and questionnaires and undergo an interview as part of a fitness-for-duty evaluation. The purpose of this evaluation is to inquire into your thoughts, feelings, and behaviors as they apply to your fitness to perform armed police duties under minimal supervision. Some of the questions you will answer will be of a personal nature. Your pattern of responding on the evaluation will be subjected to professional analyses, which will compare your pattern to officers that have taken the same evaluation. These analyses produce estimates of the risk or liability you may pose to the department or public safety and security in many different categories.

It is important to be completely forthright and honest in answering all questions. Since this process is part of your overall application to work as an authorized police agent, misrepresentations, distortions, or omissions may be considered grounds for disciplinary action.

This procedure is being performed at the request of your employer. Several days after the administration of these tests, a brief outline of the findings will be conveyed to your department. This is not a clinical evaluation, and you will receive a feedback summary of findings through your departmental supervisor in whatever manner is allowed for by your department, civil service rules, or other regulations. There is no right of confidentiality, and information obtained may be provided to your department.

You may refuse to take this examination or answer any questions, but those questions you answer must be truthful, or you may be subject to disciplinary action. If at any time you do not wish to proceed, please notify the examiner, return all materials, and you will be free to leave. Your department will be notified that you have declined examination and will give you further instructions.

STATEMENT OF HANDICAP OR IMPAIRMENT

Some people may suffer from special physical or mental problems, that would keep them from being able to work in the same manner as those without problems. Such people, with the help of special equipment (e.g., wheelchair, special working conditions, medications, or machinery), can engage in useful work.

Are you claiming to be mentally or physically disabled and in need of special accommodations under the Americans with Disabilities Act either for purposes of this evaluation or any aspect of employment as a law enforcement agent?

_____Yes _____No

If yes, please list the disability from which you believe you suffer and the special accommodations that you will require: _____

_____

_____

I understand the above statements and instructions and I have answered the above question truthfully and to the best of my ability.

Signature _____ Date _____

Witness _____ Date _____

Glossary

42 U.S.C. 1983: A modern administrative regulation that allows federal civil complaints to be brought against persons who violate the legally or constitutionally guaranteed rights of any person under the color of law. Also called SECTION 1983.

Abel Assessment for Sexual Interest: A psychometric test technique for evaluating the deviant sexual interest of sex offenders. *See U.S. v. WHITE HORSE.*

accommodation: An adjustment or addition in equipment, procedure, or work environment that would reasonably allow a qualified disabled person to perform certain essential job duties under the ADA.

acute stress disorder (ASD): An anxiety-based psychological disorder that may follow a traumatic physical or emotional event. ASD may partially or totally resolve or worsen with time. *See* POST-TRAUMATIC STRESS DISORDER.

administrative conflict of interest: In the law enforcement fitness-for-duty methodology, a circumstance in which the subordinate status of an internal provider gives the appearance that the professional's opinion may be improperly influenced by superiors and is not objective. *See* CLINICAL CONFLICT OF INTEREST.

American Psychological Association (APA): A nonprofit association whose membership represents all branches and areas of academic and applied psychology. Division 18 (Public Service) contains psychologists who are interested in police psychology.

Americans with Disabilities Act of 1990 (ADA): The federal law that makes it illegal for employers to discriminate against a qualified disabled individual within job application procedures; the hiring, advancement, or discharge of employees; employee compensation; job training; or other terms, conditions, and privileges of employment.

Association for the Treatment of Sexual Abusers (ATSA): A nonprofit, interdisciplinary organization that fosters research, facilitates information exchange, furthers professional education, and provides for the advancement of professional standards and practices in the field of sex-offender evaluation and treatment.

astrology: A prescientific belief system in which human behavior and other events are supposedly predicted from the location and movement of the stars.

authorization: A specific written document that allows for the use and disclosure of personal health information for purposes other than treatment, payment, or health care operations.

bad guys: In police culture, all persons thought to be inclined to commit criminal acts.

behavior unbecoming an officer: A term of administration regarding misconduct by law enforcement officers that usually applies to distasteful, fantastic, and undesirable conduct that is not clearly criminal or corrupt.

Bendectin: An antinausea drug that was thought to cause birth defects. The failure to scientifically prove this claim contributed to establishment of the *Daubert* standard.

Binet-Simon scale: An early cognitive intelligence or IQ test: a forerunner to the Stanford-Binet Intelligence Test. *See also* TERMAN.

bipartisan commissions: Gatherings of qualified, distinguished persons who are appointed equally by both dominant political parties, usually on a temporary basis, to address a governmental administrative question, usually by an official report.

Boston police strike of 1919: The first U.S. public employees strike, it was associated with widespread disorder and forced the use of the state militia to break both the strike and the riots that followed.

bullshit: Jargon term for the bureaucratic regulations and rules that are seen as busywork and a means of controlling street-level police officers.

Bureau of Internal Revenue: An early federal tax enforcement agency created to collect revenue to finance the Civil War.

business necessity: A general exemption to the requirements of hiring persons with disabilities in the ADA in which the disability unavoidably interferes with the essential requirements of a particular job (e.g., blindness for an airline pilot).

caveats: Warnings or formal notices filed by an interested party with a court, requesting the postponement of a proceeding until a hearing is conducted.

Civil Rights Act of 1871: Codified under the title of 42 U.S.C. 1983 or simply Section 1983; this reconstruction-era law provides civil penalties for state and local officials who violate federally protected rights UNDER THE COLOR OF LAW.

civil rights movement: The increase in political and social resistance within the United States to the traditions, laws, and policies that discriminated against racial and cultural minorities, especially African Americans, primarily in the 1960s.

civil service: A merit-based system meant to provide for the hiring of qualified persons in government service. It was part of the professionalization movement in American police history.

civilian review boards (CRBs): Boards composed of non-LE persons who examine officer conduct, sometimes including complaint processing, officer discipline decisions, policy changes, and the operation of mediation centers.

clinical conflict of interest: An ethical standard in which the human service provider appears to hold two incompatible or conflicting roles (e.g., a treater and evaluator), implying a contamination of objective professional judgment.

clinical evaluation: Any combination of interviews and/or tests that are used to diagnose and treat a person who submits themselves for clinical services.

clinical interview: A specialized interview conducted by a mental health professional for the general purpose of diagnosis and treatment of a mental or emotional disorder.

cognitive testing: Intelligence testing.

color of law: An action taken within the official purview of a public or governmental institution, such as a police officer making an arrest.

community-based model: A theory of police goals and functions based upon the notion that the views and needs of the community being served must be a strong influence in police actions.

complaint review boards: Any group or committee composed of police executives and/or prominent citizens that receives and processes (judges, refers, and documents) citizen complaints regarding the behavior of law enforcement officers.

Comstock laws: Any laws derived from the Comstock Act (1873), which restricted the transport of pornography, contraceptives, or information regarding them through the mail. *See also* U.S. POSTAL INSPECTION SERVICE.

concurrent validity: The degree to which a psychological test yields the same underlying information as another tests (e.g., the degree to which the tests measure the same concepts).

confidentiality: The maintenance of written or verbal information in a manner from which other persons or institutions are excluded.

conflict of interest: A situation in which a person, such as a public official, an employee, or a professional, has a private or personal interest sufficient to appear to influence the objective exercise of his or her official duties. *See also* CLINICAL CONFLICT OF INTEREST.

consent: A specific written document that allows for disclosure of personal health information for purposes of treatment, payment, and health case operations.

constable: Officer of the king and of the individual communities throughout many English-speaking countries; a law enforcement officer.

consumer report: A report that includes criminal and civil records, driving records, civil lawsuits, reference checks and any other information obtained by a CRA as defined by the FCRA.

consumer reporting agencies (CRAs): Companies that gather and sell information, such as a person has filed bankruptcy, to creditors, employers, landlords and other businesses.

corruption: A term referring to the misuse of law enforcement or other public office, in which money, goods, or services are unlawfully exchanged for favorable official treatment.

covered entities (CE): In the HIPAA, any of three basic groups of corporate entities that are regulated by the law: health plans, health care providers, and health care clearinghouses.

criterion measure: A measure of outcome or of performance against which a test score is compared.

cultural diversity: A social or political movement in which an active attempt is made (such as with preferential hiring rules) to include racial and cultural minorities in an organization or institution where they have been underrepresented.

culture: A connected system of acquired values, beliefs, and rules of conduct which defines accepted behaviors, goals, and material and intellectual skills in any given social group, whether formally or informally structured. *See also* POLICE CULTURE.

cyclical pattern: The tendency for a law enforcement reform or change to revert to the prereform pattern after a period of time; the loss of the benefit of an earlier reform movement.

***Daubert* triad:** A term given to the three cases (*Daubert, General Electric Co. v. Joiner,* and *Kumho*) that established the current use of FRE 702 regarding the admission of expert evidence in court.

***Daubert v. Merrell Dow Pharmaceuticals, Inc.* (1993):** The first of three Supreme Court decisions that defined FRE 702, affecting the admission of experts in the federal court system. It ended the primacy of the *Frye* standard of general acceptance by the profession and replaced it with concern for the adequacy of the scientific method on which the testimony is based (the *Daubert* standard).

defamation: A statement that tends to injure the plaintiff's reputation and expose the plaintiff to public hatred, contempt, ridicule, or degradation, which is communicated to third parties, and which the speaker or publisher knew or should have known was false.

deliberate indifference: In civil rights litigation (as in 42 U.S.C. 1983), part of the concept that a policy maker can be held liable for the civil rights violations of subordinates because such actions resulted due to a failure to supervise, select, train, or control officers under their command.

Denny, Reginald: White truck driver assaulted in the Los Angeles riots following the acquittal of the officers who assaulted RODNEY KING.

Department of Justice (DOJ): A division of the executive branch of the U.S. federal government responsible for enforcing a wide variety of federal laws, especially those touching upon law enforcement agencies, criminal law, and civil rights law.

direct threat: A person who shows a significant risk of harm to the health or safety of others according to the ADA.

disability: An incapacity, restriction, or disadvantage, usually of physical or mental origin, that affects the ability to perform some forms of work and other aspects of daily life.

discretion: The freedom to act or refrain from acting vested in an officer who must decide that a law has been broken and some official action must be taken. Discretion is the opposite of a mandatory regulation (such as a legal requirement to arrest under some circumstance).

doctor-patient relationship: A relationship in which a special, legally enforceable agreement is established between a provider of health services and a patient, usually involving patient confidentiality and compliance with the doctor's directions.

documentary examination phase: In FFDE procedure, the collection of official documents from the appointing authority (LE executive) that provides details concerning the complaint or complaints that form the reasons for referral and which precedes the actual FFDE itself.

draft riots of the Civil War: An uprising and violent attack by recent European immigrants against public authorities and African Americans in New York City in 1863. It was an important event in the development of American policing.

dragnet: A general term for the systematic search for a criminal suspect using all police resources; also a popular television series of the 1950s and 1960s, based loosely on the operational style of the LAPD under Chief WILLIAM PARKER.

duty to mitigate: A legal responsibility to take steps to minimize the loss or injury from some adverse event. For example, following the transmission of an FFDE report to the wrong supervisor, the FFDE provider must attempt to recover it immediately.

duty to warn: In mental health professions, the ethical and legal responsibility to warn any party in imminent danger of harm because of a patient's threats or actions; an exception to the RULE OF CONFIDENTIALITY and doctor-patient relationship. *See also* TARASOFF RULE.

employee assistance program (EAP): Employer-sponsored, short-term administrative and clinical program of counseling and related support that is designed to address behavioral problems noted in or affecting the workplace.

employment examinations: Structured tests of cognitive skill or basic education used as a criterion for employment. In early use, an attempt to reduce the employment of illiterate or unprepared persons under the SPOILS SYSTEM approach to public employment.

enforcement-priority model: A view of police goals and functions based upon the notion that the views and needs of crime suppression must be the primary consideration in police actions and decisions.

Equal Employment Opportunity Commission (EEOC): The federal agency established by Title VII of the Civil Rights Act of 1964 which enforces the Age Discrimination in Employment Act (ADEA), the Equal Pay Act (EPA), Title I and Title V of the AMERICANS WITH DISABILITIES ACT (ADA), Section 501 and 505 of the Rehabilitation Act, and the Civil Rights Act of 1991.

Ethical Principles of Psychologists: A set of ethical rules and aspirational goals of the AMERICAN PSYCHOLOGICAL ASSOCIATION (APA) meant to aid professional psychologists in decisions regarding proper conduct.

examinee-only rule: In FFDE procedures, the rule that the referred employee must submit to examination without others present to influence the examination in any way.

exclusionary rule: The rule that requires the suppression of evidence (disqualifies its use at trial) that has been obtained illegally by the government in the prosecution of criminal case (a Fourth Amendment issue).

executive immunity: The legal standard by which certain executive branch government officials are immune from civil liability for all official actions taken in good faith.

expert witness: A person who is a specialist in a subject or discipline, often scientific or technical, who may assist that judge or jury by presenting his or her expert opinion.

external provider: In the law enforcement fitness-for-duty methodology, a specially trained mental health provider who contracts independently (not an employee) with a law enforcement agency to conduct FFDEs of officers.

eyewitness: A person who may give testimony in a court of law based upon the direct experience (what he or she saw or heard) that is of importance in a legal proceeding.

Fair Credit Reporting Act (FCRA): A federal law meant to promote accuracy and fairness of information transmitted in credit-reporting circumstances.

fake good: Unreasonable claims of perfection and lack of common life difficulties as reported in psychometric test profiles; a reason to suspect that test results are invalid.

Family Medical Leave Act (FMLA): A federal law that provides unpaid, job-protected leave to eligible employees to care for their families or themselves for medical conditions.

Federal Bureau of Investigation (FBI): The best-known federal law enforcement agency, established in 1908. It has held a broad mandate including the enforcement of espionage, interstate commerce, tax, and racketeering laws. *See also* HOOVER, J. EDGAR.

Federal Rules of Evidence (FRE): A code of rules that have governed the introduction of evidence in proceedings since 1975, both civil and criminal, in federal courts.

FFDE provider or FFDE-P: The specially prepared mental health professional who provides examining services in the FFDE context but does not provide treatment services to that same officer.

field training officers (FTO): Supervisory police officers that train recruits or inexperienced officers in actual policing situations (in contrast to police academy training); thought to be a major influence in the transmission of police culture.

first American police reform movement (militarization): In the United States, a transformation of police department organizations into military-style units, including ranks, uniforms, divisions, and command methods; the first of three reform movements.

fitness-for-duty evaluation (FFDE): A specialized inquiry conducted by a specially qualified mental health professional in response to complaints of an officer's reported inability to perform official duties in a safe and effective manner because of mental illness or defect.

forensic: Related to the application of any science to issues of law or service to the courts.

forensic evaluation: Any combination of interviews and/or tests that are used to examine (often involuntarily) a person for purposes of rendering a report of that person's mental or medical condition to a court of law, an authorized attorney, or an administrative agency, such as a workers compensation organization.

four-fifths rule: A DOJ "rule-of-thumb" by which any administrative procedure may not be considered legal if it adversely impacts upon disadvantaged communities greater than majority communities more then four-fifths of the time.

fruit-of-the-poisoned-tree doctrine: A legal standard by which criminal evidence collected in impermissible or illegal ways may not be used in court against the accused.

***Frye* standard (1923):** The rule in federal courts that expert witnesses are permitted to testify based upon their acceptance by the their profession and peers. *See DAUBERT v. MERRELL DOW.*

Garrity Statement: Information given to examiners in an FFDE, in which the examinee is told that information obtained may not be used as evidence in a criminal prosecution against them because the examination is mandatory (not voluntary). *See* LYBARGER ADMONISHMENT.

General Electric Co. v. Joiner: The second (1997) of the *Daubert* triad defining the admissibility of expert testimony in the federal court system. *See DAUBERT v. MERRELL DOW, KUMHO TIRE.*

Gompers, Samuel: The president of the American Federation of Labor in the early twentieth century and a key figure in the U.S. labor organization movement.

good guys: Innocent civilians, often the victims of the criminal acts of the BAD GUYS. Persons deserving of the assistance and protection of police officers.

grunt: A term referring to the basic combat soldier who is thought to be incapable of making independent decisions, but does the "dirty work." Also a low-ranking urban street officer.

Health Insurance Portability and Accountability Act of 1996 (HIPAA): A federal law meant to improve efficiency in health care delivery by standardizing electronic data interchange and the protection of confidentiality and security of health data through enforceable standards.

health maintenance organization (HMO): A form of health insurance in which only visits to professionals within the HMO network are covered by the policy. The HMO must approve all services for coverage, often limiting the number and type of services available.

hearsay: An out-of-court statement offered to prove the truth of what it asserts. The general rule is that hearsay is inadmissible.

Hoover, J. Edgar: Founder and long-term director (1924-1972) of the FEDERAL BUREAU OF INVESTIGATION; a key figure in the development of training and investigative techniques in the United States.

hybrid entities: Defined as those entities within HIPAA whose primary (as compared with ancillary) activities are not covered under the general act (not heath service related).

impaired: A general term used in the FFDE sense, to describe any law enforcement officer who is unable to perform official duties because of behavior, medical, or conduct reasons.

incumbent officers: Any officer who has successfully completed his basic training and probationary requirements and is currently active in a law enforcement capacity.

independent treatment review service: A set of tasks in which the FFDE provider reviews the treatment records of an officer when the officer applies to be reinstated for full duty. *See* POSTTREATMENT RE-EVALUATION.

index scores: Psychometric or statistical values that are derived from the combination of more basic or fundamental scores, scales, or outcomes in order to improve the validity of the test.

individualized assessment: In the ADA, a general requirement that the determination that a disabled person is not employable because he or she poses a direct threat is supported by an examination of that particular person, and not by a blanket rule that all persons with a particular disability be considered unsafe.

informal justice: Rough treatment meted out to BAD GUYS by police because the criminal justice system has failed to punish them adequately for their criminal conduct.

innocent and vicious: A street-level theory of police work that separates persons into those who need and deserve protection (GOOD GUYS) and those that are wrong-doers and require rough handling (BAD GUYS), even if they are not currently committing crimes.

internal affairs (IA) division: The section of a law enforcement agency that investigates problem behaviors (such as corruption, misconduct, and criminal actions) among members of that agency. In some cases, IA has the power to bring cases before the personnel division, a civilian review board, a public prosecutor, or a disciplinary committee.

internal provider: In the law enforcement fitness-for-duty methodology, a specially trained mental health provider who is an employee of a law enforcement agency and who conducts FFDEs of officers.

International Association of Chiefs of Police (IACP): A nonprofit association of senior law enforcement executives that promote interest in all aspects of security and law enforcement areas. The IACP Psychology Section is active in police psychology issues.

investigative consumer report: A consumer report in which information on a consumer's character, general reputation, personal characteristics, or mode of living is obtained through personal interviews with neighbors, friends, or associates of the consumer.

Inwald Personality Inventory: An objective personality test that was intended for use with public safety personnel (Inwald, 1980, 1984).

***Jaffee v. Redmond* (1996):** An important legal case in which the Supreme Court upheld the confidentiality of psychotherapy notes.

Kansas City Preventive Patrol Experiment: A 1972 study that addressed police efficiency and effectiveness by varying types of police patrol systems and scientifically measuring the outcome.

King, Rodney: An African-American motorist whose beating by Los Angeles Police Department officers was videotaped, leading to the trial and exoneration of the officers involved, which in turn contributed to subsequent riots because of the minority community's perception of unfairness.

***Kumho Tire v. Carmichael* (1999):** The last of three Supreme Court *Daubert* cases, in which the requirement for a scientific basis in expert testimony was extended to professional areas based upon experience and training.

LAPD: Los Angeles Police Department.

laterally promoted: A rank or assignment change, within or between law enforcement agencies, of police members to positions of command or authority ahead of less well-educated but more "experienced-in-rank" officers. *See* SENIORITY SYSTEM.

Lautenberg Amendment: A federal law that restricts the ability of a person to carry a firearm after a conviction for the misdemeanor crime of domestic violence.

law enforcement (LE): Any form of policing or security occupation or professional activity meant to detect and prevent violations of law, as in police, security, or investigative agencies.

Law Enforcement Assistance Administration: Defunct federal agency (c. 1970s) that provided discretionary monies that were set aside for psychologists and other mental health professionals to develop police psychology programs, predominantly EAPs.

Law of Unintended Consequences: A major effect or outcome caused by some rule, action, or law that was not anticipated by its originators.

life-and-death incident: In police culture, a situation of extreme emergency in which the immediate willingness to use deadly force is required to protect innocent lives.

Lybarger Admonishment: Information given to examiners in an FFDE, in which the examinee is told that information obtained may not be used as evidence in a criminal prosecution against them because the examination is mandatory instead of voluntary. *See* GARRITY STATEMENT.

malice: Publication of defamatory material with knowledge that it was false or reckless disregard of whether it was false or not.

managed care organization: *See* HEALTH MAINTENANCE ORGANIZATION (HMO).

mandatory: An administrative model by which officers may be ordered to submit to FFDEs under certain circumstances or face charges of insubordination.

merit hiring: Any system for new officer selection based in part on some standard of educational or experiential achievement; the opposite of patronage.

Metropolitan Police Force (Bobbies): The London police force established by Sir Robert Peel in 1829. An influential agency in establishing methods and procedures that became a model of law enforcement throughout the English-speaking world.

minimal possible information: A general rule in which professional medical/psychological reports prepared for employers and personal managers avoid detailed and unnecessary medical and personal information that may embarrass the person about whom the reports were written.

minimum necessary rule: The principle in HIPAA that no more information than is necessary for a permissible purpose may be conveyed to a receiver of personal health information.

Miranda warning: A verbal or written statement given to suspects at the time of arrest, informing them that they have the right to remain silent and to be represented by an attorney before questioning (a Fifth Amendment issue).

mission: A cultural view of certain police officers that assumes that their fundamental purpose is to serve as guardians of morality and to protect civilized society against "the scum of the street."

model bill: A general outline of a proposed law that may be transmitted in some standard form to fit the needs of any particular legislative body's consideration.

moral integrity: A construct or proposed behavioral trait of psychologist LEWIS TERMAN and his associates of the early twentieth century, which, when combined with sufficient intelligence, was meant to predict who would become a good police officer.

M-PULSE: Matrix Psychological Uniform Law Enforcement Selection Evaluation—an actuarial method of officer candidate selection.

municipal liability or **police executive liability:** The liability of police executives or policy makers within a governmental organization when they have tolerated the civil or constitutional rights violations by their subordinates.

myth: In the ADA, an unsubstantiated, but widely held belief that a disabled person is unable to perform the essential duties of a job or set of jobs without direct evidence.

narcissistic entitlement: In mental health work, an excessive belief in one's infallibility or correctness and in one's comfort and convenience above all other concerns.

National Advisory Commission on Civil Disorders (1968): A U.S. commission that determined that a need existed to develop methods to detect and avoid the selection and retention of police officers whose duties would be hampered by their personal prejudices.

National Labor Relations Act (NLRA): Enacted in 1935, this law guaranteed workers the right to join unions. It created the National Labor Relations Board (NLRB) to enforce this right and prohibited employers from discouraging the organizing of labor unions or from preventing workers from negotiating a union contract.

negative risk: Any increase in law enforcement liability brought about by the inability or unwillingness of an officer to perform required tasks in law enforcement, such as may occur as a result of dereliction of duty, officer substance abuse, or insubordination to command.

negligent retention: Allowing of persons to continue in employment that the employer knew or should have known to represent an unacceptable risk to the health, safety, or welfare of the public, fellow workers, or supervisors.

nepotism: The preferential and unjustified hiring of family members as employees over better qualified applicants; considered a form of corruption or malfeasance in public service.

neuropsychological testing: A set of motor, cognitive, and sensory psychometric tests that have been developed to measure behavioral changes due to injury or disease of the brain.

normative group: The body of data collected from prior test takers against which a particular person is compared for purposes of decision making in psychometric situations.

NYPD: New York City Police Department.

objective personality testing: Any of a number of psychological tests of personal adjustment and mental illness in which the respondent endorses statements or questions as applying to him or her in some way, and the results are subjected to statistical analysis.

occupational alcoholism programs (OAPs): Early employee assistance programs that focused on alcohol abuse reduction in the workplace; replaced by the EAP concept, which addressed a broader array of problem behaviors.

officer-involved shooting board (OISB): A police department administrative board that investigates instances of the use of deadly force.

optional: An administrative model by which officers may be asked to submit to FFDEs under certain circumstances or select to face disciplinary charges as an alternative.

paradox of policing: In democratic societies, the tension between the desire to be protected by police agencies from crime and mayhem, while also seeking to restrict police power from becoming abusive and oppressive.

Parker, William: Chief of the LAPD (1950-1966) and a major contributor to the mid-twentieth-century development of the professional police department.

patronage: The political appointments or jobs that are at the disposal of those in power, often used to increase political power by exchanging jobs for votes. *See* SPOILS SYSTEM, MERIT HIRING.

PCBs (polychlorinated biphenyls): A mixture of cancer-causing chemicals that are no longer produced in the United States. *See GENERAL ELECTRIC CO. v. JOINER.*

Peal, Sir Robert: Founder and first commander of the Metropolitan Police Force, the model of many police organizations in the English-speaking world.

peer counselors: An EAP term in which fellow workers with limited training, rather than professionals, offer counseling to employees in a particular workplace.

peer review: In science or profession, a review of the research or publications of an expert by a body of professional colleagues; one standard of that professional's acceptability to peers.

penile plethysmograph (PPG) testing: A device used in the assessment of sexual arousal in males by physically measuring penis size.

perceptual rigidity: A psychological term to describe difficulty in changing an established assumption or understanding in the face of contrary evidence.

personal health information (PHI): Individually identifiable health information that is explicitly linked to a particular individual, and includes health information with data items, that could be expected to allow individual identification.

Personality Assessment Inventory (PAI): An objective personality test that may be used in law enforcement assessments (Morey, 1991).

personnel division (or **human resource services**): The subdivision of any administrative organization that deals with employment, hiring, firing, pensions, and sick leave.

police culture: Socially transmitted behavior patterns, beliefs, institutions, and general understandings that are common to most law enforcement organization members. *See* CULTURE.

police executive or **law enforcement executive:** Any commanding or policy making member of a law enforcement agency.

police psychologist: A professional, licensed psychologist with special training and qualifications in aspects of the specialized delivery of psychological services to law enforcement agencies or law enforcement officers.

police psychology: The application of the science and techniques of the discipline and profession of psychology to law enforcement issues and problems.

political machines: Political organizations run by "bosses" or a group of politically influential persons, which arrange for the exchange of votes for professional politicians in return for jobs, favors, and help with problems, such as assistance when arrested.

politically correct: A concept in which any word or action of a person must conform to the tenets of political liberalism. In police culture, a willingness to sacrifice justice and crime suppression to extend special privileges to persons deemed disadvantaged.

poll tax: A fee or charge connected with the right to vote. It was a method to both reduce the political participation of racial and cultural minorities following the Civil War and degrade their participation in the political process.

positive risk: Any increase in liability brought about by the irrational misconduct of a law enforcement officer, such as threats of harm against others or explosiveness and aggression. *See* NEGATIVE RISK.

post-traumatic stress disorder (PTSD): A psychological or psychiatric disorder that may occur following the experiencing or witnessing of aversive events. PTSD sufferers often relive the experience through nightmares and flashbacks, have difficulty sleeping, and feel detached or estranged and are unable to perform certain life tasks.

posttreatment reevaluation: A follow-up FFDE that occurs when an impaired officer requests a return to full duty, usually following an episode of psychological treatment. *See* INDEPENDENT TREATMENT REVIEW SERVICE.

predictive validity: The extent to which a psychometric instrument or test is able to forecast an intended outcome (e.g., the degree to which a college entrance test predicts later college grades or successful completion of the degree program).

prefect: Commander of the Roman *VIGILES*, an early form of police.

President's Commission on Law Enforcement: A 1973 federal commission that recommended that police officers develop professional discretionary methods that addressed the basic causes of crime in communities, rather than the crimes themselves.

primary activities: In the HIPAA, the central or main function of an organization (such as health care); its fundamental service or product. *See* HYBRID ENTITIES.

privacy: The right of an individual to control his or her personal information and to not have it divulged or used by others against his or her wishes.

Privacy Act of 1974: A federal law that, among other protections, prohibits disclosure of an individual's health record without prior written consent within certain settings.

private investigators: Licensed, nongovernmental investigators who may become involved in the collection of information regarding fraud, personal misconduct, and criminal activities.

Prohibition Era: The period during which the Eighteenth Amendment to the Constitution, which prohibited the manufacture, sale, and distribution of alcoholic beverages, was law (1920-1933). *See* VOL-STEAD ACT OF 1920.

promotion by merit: Any system in which promotion within a public agency to a higher level of responsibility is a based on objective standards of achievement or accomplishment.

psychology records repository: A secured records area in which psychologically sensitive and usually inaccessible documents are kept separately from other documentation (e.g., personnel, IA, health records).

psychometric tests: Objective (standardized and normed) psychological tests.

psychometrics: The science of mental test construction and use or the practice of psychological testing by structured and standardized methods and interpretation. The branch of psychology that deals with the design, administration, and interpretation of tests for the measurement of psychological variables such as intelligence, aptitude, and personality. *See* STANDARDIZED TESTS.

psychotherapeutic privilege: A mental heath term that expresses the patient's right to have written or verbal information that is collected or revealed in psychotherapy kept confidential.

psychotherapy: Any guidance, counseling, or verbal psychosocial approach to the treatment of mental illness or inappropriate behaviors.

Public Law 91-616: A 1970 federal law that established alcohol treatment programs for public employees; now expired.

Public Safety Assurance Act (PSAA): A model legislative act that enhances the authority of police psychologists and law enforcement executives to protect the public through the examination and disposition of impaired officers.

rate of appearance: The speed with which behavioral, emotional, or mental problems seem to have appeared and affected the occupational performance of an officer.

reason for referral: A clear statement of the reasons to believe that the conduct or behavior of an officer is the result, in whole or in part, of any form of mental illness or defect, and therefore the officer is in need of an FFDE to inform LE executives of the nature of the difficulty.

reasonable accommodation: Any modification or adjustment to a job or the work environment that will enable a qualified applicant or employee with a disability to participate in the application process or to perform essential job functions.

Reconstruction Era: The period in American history (1865-1877) at the end and immediately after the Civil War in which the governments of states that had been in rebellion were largely controlled by the federal government, and former slaves were granted full rights of citizens.

"regarded as" standard: Under the ADA, an individual may be defined as having a qualifying disability if he or she is considered to be or *regarded as* being disabled by their employer.

release of information: A document in which a patient directs a clinical provider or institution to send all or part of that patient's available records to another party in compliance with state and federal laws.

responsible designated authority (RDA): The police executive or commander who has the authority to order a law enforcement officer to submit to an FFDE.

Roosevelt, Theodore: The twenty-sixth president of the United States; an early police reformer when serving as a police commissioner in New York City in the 1890s.

roust: To harass, detain, or disturb a group or an individual that a police officer believes may be engaged in some form of criminal or otherwise inappropriate conduct.

rule of confidentiality: The professionally and legally enforceable requirement that no element of a patient's treatment be revealed to others without the patient's express permission.

rules of engagement: The definitions and regulations that control the behaviors allowed of a military force in combat.

second American police reform movement (professionalism): An attempt that was made to "professionalize" police departments by emphasizing the officer's need for education and adherence to an enforceable code of rules and ethics.

Secret Service: A federal law enforcement agency created to protect the president and enforce certain other federal laws.

Section 1983: *See* 42 U.S.C. 1983.

Sections 1985 and 1981 of Title 42 of the U.S. Code: Federal laws that provide for the criminal punishment of persons who violate the civil rights or constitutionally protected rights of any persons.

security: The spectrum of physical, technical, and administrative safeguards that are put in place to protect the integrity, availability and confidentiality of information, as in the HIPAA.

seduction: In police culture theory, the exciting and profitable opportunity for a law enforcement agent to become part of the underworld; a tendency to take on the values or lifestyle of social groups (e.g., drug dealers) who normally would be the target of police action.

seniority system: A system of promotion within law enforcement agencies that is generally based upon the officer's length of time in service.

sequestration: A legal procedure in which a witness is removed from the courtroom to prevent undue influence resulting from observing other witnesses. Expert witnesses are usually immune to this rule.

serious health condition: In the FMLA, a medical condition (injury or illness) that justifies leave, and involves a period of incapacity of more than three consecutive calendar days and extended hospitalization or clinic-based care.

sheriff: Originally an official appointed by the English crown at the county (shire) level to enforce English law; among the earliest law enforcement authorities in the United States, still the primary law enforcement officer at the local level in many states.

special records center: A method of securing FFDE reports within police departments such that it is inaccessible to most employees. *See* PSYCHOLOGY RECORDS REPOSITORY.

speculation: In the ADA, a supposition or presumption that a disabled person is unable to perform the essential duties of a job without direct evidence.

spoils system: A governmental employment scheme, in which the winners of political office award jobs under the control of that office to friends, family, and political supporters; from the expression "to the victors go the spoils."

standardized tests: A scientifically designed psychological test, usually based on a normative group.

state control: The assumption of control by a larger political unit (a state government) over an agency of a lower-level governmental unit (the police department of a municipality) to improve operation or reduce mismanagement of the local agency.

stonewall: In the law enforcement fitness-for-duty methodology, a strategy in which an examinee claims a complete and incredible personal absence of common weaknesses or problems; a form of noncooperation with examination.

stratification: Division or arrangement into social classes, as in a stratified sample (representative of the levels of society) in research. A hierarchy of command in police work.

systolic blood pressure test (SBT): An early form of the lie detector, invented by William Moulton Marston. Testimony concerning this method was rejected as admissible as a basis for expert testimony because it lacked general professional acceptance in *Frye v. U.S.* (1923).

Tarasoff rule: A duty of mental health professionals to warn the intended victims of violence threatened in therapy by a patient. Tatiana Tarasoff, a female student at the University of California at Berkley, was murdered in 1969 by a fellow student, who had confided his intentions to kill her to a psychologist (*Tarasoff v. Regents of the University of California,* 1976).

Terman, Lewis: An early twentieth-century psychologist and researcher who was among the primary figures in the development of the theory and measurement of intelligence; an early theorist in the application of psychological testing to police selection.

Texas Rangers: A paramilitary force raised for frontier protection in 1842 and primarily used to protect settlers in various conflicts. The modern Texas Rangers came into being in 1935 as a general law enforcement arm of the Texas Department of Public Safety.

therapeutic alliance: The working agreement between the patient and counselor or therapist in which the patient agrees to be open and honest in expressing his or her feelings and the therapist agrees to offer the best, unbiased assistance that he or she can.

third American police reform movement (community policing): A movement in which police activity involves an interactive relationship between the police and patrolled neighborhoods, so that crime and disorder (gangs, vacant buildings, drug use centers, etc.) could be challenged at its source.

Title 18 of the U.S. Code, Section 242: The criminal liability for deprivation of civil rights that provides for a fine and imprisonment for any person who under color of law, statute, ordinance, regulation or custom, willfully subjects an inhabitant of any state to the deprivation of any right protected by the Constitution of the United States.

transactions or **experiences:** An exclusion to the Fair Credit Reporting Act's definition of a consumer report in which information obtained solely between the consumer and the person making the report is not considered to be covered by the act.

treatment provider or **treating professional:** The mental health professional who provides standard treatment, usually in a confidential or doctor-patient relationship regardless of whether an FFDE has been conducted: The treating professional should not be the examining professional or FFDE PROVIDER.

under the color of law: Actions in the official capacity of a government agent.

undue hardship: An action requiring excess difficulty or expense out of proportion to reasonably expected benefits.

unpredictability and uncertainty: In police culture theory, the attractions of many to police work based upon the changeable and exciting nature of active law enforcement.

Untouchables: A popular culture term applied to federal agents of the Prohibition Era under the direction of Eliot Ness in Chicago, Illinois, who were described as immune to bribery and underworld influence; the title of a television series of the late 1950s and early 1960s and a movie 1987.

U.S. Marshals Service: The oldest U.S. federal law enforcement service.

U.S. Postal Inspection Service: A federal law enforcement arm of the U.S. Postal Service. *See* COMSTOCK LAWS.

U.S. v. White Horse: A 2001 federal case in which expert testimony about a psychometric test was rejected employing the *Daubert* standard.

validity scales: Scores or scales developed as part of objective psychometric tests that indicate forms of bias, error, or distortion that may invalidate the test's outcome for interpretive use.

Vigiles: Early Roman watchmen, ancient predecessors of modern police.

Volstead Act of 1920 or **National Prohibition Act:** The Eighteenth Amendment to the Constitution that prohibited all elements of the production, distribution, and sale of alcohol. Repealed in 1933 by the Twenty-First Amendment. Seen by many as a contribution to the rise of organized crime and the corruption of police departments.

Weingarten rule: The right for a union representative to be present during the interview of an employee under certain circumstances if the employee may be disciplined as a result.

Wickersham Commission (1931): A historically important independent commission that published its revelations of police brutality and "third-degree" interrogation methods, such as hanging a suspect out of a high window until he confessed.

Bibliography

Abel, G. G., Jordan, A., Hand, C. G., Holland, L. A., and Phipps, A. (2001). Classi-fication models of child molesters utilizing the Abel Assessment for sexual inter-est. *Child Abuse and Neglect: The International Journal 25* (5): 705.

Alpert, S. (1998). Health care information: Access, confidentiality, and good prac-tice. In Goodman, K.W. (Ed.), *Ethics, computing, and medicine: Informatics and the transformation of health care* (pp. 75-101). Cambridge, UK: Cambridge University Press.

Albert v. Runyon, 6 F. Supp. 2d 57 (D. Mass. 1998).

American Educational Research Association, American Psychological Associa-tion, and National Council on Measurement in Education (1999). *Standards for educational and psychological testing*. Washington, DC: American Educational Research Association.

American Managed Behavioral Healthcare Association (1998). *AMBHA statement on clinically appropriate access to medical records*. Washington, DC: American Managed Behavioral Healthcare Association.

American Medical Association (1996). *Code for medical ethics: Current opinions with annotations*. Available online: at <www.ama-assn.org>.

American Medical Association (1998). Report of the board of trustees: Patient pri-vacy and confidentiality. Paper presented at the meeting of the American Medi-cal Association, Chicago, September.

American Psychiatric Association (1998). *Principles for medical records privacy legislation*. Washington, DC: APA Division of Government Relations.

American Psychological Association (1992). Ethical principles of psychologists and code of conduct. *American Psychologist 47:* 1597-1611.

American Psychological Association (2002). Ethical principles of psychologists and code of conduct. *American Psychologist 57* (12): 76-89.

American Psychology-Law Society and Division 41 of the APA (1991). Specialty guidelines for forensic psychologists. *Law and Human Behavior 15* (6): 655-665.

Americans with Disabilities Act, 42 U.S.C. §12112 (c) (3) and (4), (1990).

Americans with Disabilities Act of 1990, 101-336, §2, 104 Stat. 328 (1991).

Banks, C. W. (1992). Validity of the Fairfax County Police Department psychologi-cal test battery. Draft report.

Barker, T. (1978). An empirical study of police deviance other than corruption. *Journal of Police Science and Administration 6:* 264-272.

Barnes v. Gorman, 536 U.S. 181 (2002).

Bartol, C. R. (1982). Psychological characteristics of small-town police officers. *Journal of Police Science and Administration 10:* 58-63.

Bartol, C. R. (1991). Predictive validation of the MMPI for small-town police officers who fail. *Professional Psychology Research and Practice 22:* 127-132.

Bell, L. (1988). The unfair family affair. *Police 4:* 29-31.

Berberich, J. (1986). Managing the direct referral. In Reese, J. and H. Goldstein (Eds.), *Psychological services for law enforcement.* Washington, DC: U.S. Government Printing Office.

Blau, T. H. (1994). *Psychological services for law enforcement.* New York: John Wiley and Sons, Inc.

Board of County Com'rs of Bryan County, OK v. Brown, 520 U.S. 397, 117 S. Ct. 1382, 137 L.Ed.2d (1997).

Board of Trustees of University of Alabama v. Garrett 531 U.S. 356, 121 S. Ct. 955, 148 L.Ed.2d 866 (2001).

Bohl, N. K. (1991). The effectiveness of brief psychological interventions in police officers after critical incidents. In Reese, J. T., J. M. Horn, and C. Dunning (Eds.), *Critical incidents in policing,* Revised edition (pp. 31-38). Washington, DC: U.S. Government Printing Office.

Bone v. City of Louisville, 215 F.3d 1325 (6th Cir. 2000).

Bonsignore v. City of New York, 683 F.2d 635 (2d Cir. 1982).

Bopp v. Institute for Forensic Psychology, 227 A.D.2d 363 (N.Y. 1996).

Brewster, J. and Stoloff, M. L. (1999). Using the good cop/bad cop profile with the MMPI-2. *Journal of Police and Criminal Psychology 14* (2): 29-34.

Brown County Sheriff's Dept. v. Brown County Sheriff's Dept. Non-Supervisory Employees Association., 533 N.W.2nd 766 (Wis. 1995).

Brown v. Bryan County, OK, 219 F.3d 450 (5th Cir. 2000), *Rehearing and Rehearing en Banc Denied* 235 F.3d 944, *Certiorari Denied* 532 U.S. 1007, 121 S. Ct. 1734, 149 L.Ed.2d 658 (2000).

Burke, K. (1969). *A grammar of motives.* Berkeley, CA: University of California Press.

Burnett, R., Johns, E., and Krug, S. (1981). Law enforcement and development report (LEADR). Champaign, IL: Institute for Personality and Ability Testing, Inc.

Butcher, J., Dahlstrom, W., Graham, J., Tellegen, A., and Kaemmer, B. (1989). *Manual for the restandarized Minnesota Multiphasic Personality Inventory: MMPI-2.* Minneapolis: University of Minnesota Press.

Campbell, J. (2000). The consumer perspective. In Gates, J. and Arons, B. (Eds.), *Privacy and confidentiality in mental health care* (pp. 5-32). Baltimore, MD: Brookes Publishing.

Cattell, R. B., Cattell, A. K., and Cattell, H. E. P. (1993). *Sixteen personality factor questionnaire,* Fifth edition. San Antonio, TX: Harcourt Brace.

Caver v. City of Trenton, 192 F.R.D. 154 (2000).

Center for Substance Abuse Treatment (1994). *Confidentiality of patient records for alcohol and other drug treatment* (Technical Assistance Publication Series, No. 13). Washington, DC: Center for Substance Abuse Treatment.

Chapa v. Adams, U.S. Dist. Lexis 10599 (N.D. Ill. 1997).

Chevigny, P. (1995). *Edge of the knife: Police violence in the Americas.* New York: The New Press.

Chevron U.S.A., Inc. v. Echazabal 536 U.S. 73, 122 S. Ct. 2045, 153 L.Ed.2d 82 (2002).

Chin, G. J. and Wells, S. C. (1998). *The blue wall of science as evidence of bias and motivation to lie: A new approach to police perjury,* 59 *University of Pittsburgh Law Review* 233.

City of Boston v. Boston Police Patrolmen's Assn., Inc., 392 N.E.2d 1202 (Mass. App. Ct. 1979).

City of Canton, Ohio v. Harris, 489 U.S. 378, 109 S. Ct. 1197, 103 L.Ed.2d 412 (1989).

City of Greenwood v. Dowler, 492 N.E.2d 1081 (Ind. App. Ct. 1st Dist. 1986).

Code of Federal Regulations (Office of Personnel Management, Medical Qualification Determinations, Authority to require an examination) 5 C.F.R. 339.301

Conroy v. Township of Lower Merion, 2001 WL 153631 (E.D. Pa. 2001).

Conte v. Horcher, 365 N.E.2d 567 (Ill. App. Ct. 1st Dist. 1977).

Corcoran, K. and Winsalde, W. (1994). Eavesdropping on the 50-minute hour: Managed mental health care and confidentiality. *Behavioral Sciences and the Law 12:* 351-365.

Crank, J. P. (1997). Celebrating agency culture: Engaging a traditional cop's heart in organizational change. In Thurman, Q. and E. McGarrell (Eds.), *Community policing in a rural setting* (pp. 49-57). Cincinnati, OH: Anderson Publishing Co.

Cremer v. City of Macomb Bd. of Fire and Police Com'rs, 632 N.E.2d. 1080 (Ill. App. Ct. 3rd Dist. 1994).

Critchley, T. A. (1972). *A history of police in England and Wales,* Second edition, revised. Montclair, NJ: Patterson Smith.

Cullen, F., Link, B., Travis, L. T. and Lemming, T. (1983). Paradox in policing: A note on perceptions of danger. *Journal of Police Science and Administration 11:* 457-462.

Cunningham, M. R. (1986). The prediction of employee violence. *Police Chief 56:* 24-26.

Curtis v. Bd. of Police Com'rs of Kansas City, 841 S.W.2d 259 (Mo. App. Ct. W.D. 1992).

Daubert v. Merrell Dow Pharmaceuticals, Inc. 509 U.S. 579, 113 S. Ct. 2786, 125 L.Ed.2d 469 (1993).

Daugherty v. City of El Paso (5th Cir. 1995) *cert. denied,* 516 U.S. 1172, 116 S. Ct. 1263, 134 L.Ed.2d 211 (1996).

Davis, R. D., Rostow, C. D., Pinkston, J. B., and Cowick, L. H. (1999). An investigation into the usefulness of the MMPI and MMPI-2 in municipal and state police candidate selection. *Journal of Police and Criminal Psychology 14* (1): 100-106.

Davis v. Hennepin County, 559 N.W.2d 117, 120 (Minn. App. Ct. 1997).

DeVito v. Chicago Park District, 270 F.3d 532 (7th Cir. 2001).

Dick, R. S. and Stean, B. (Eds.), Institute of Medicine, Committee on Improving the Patient Record (1991). *The computer-based patient record: An essential technology for health care.* Washington, DC: National Academy Press.

Dierks, C. (1993). Medical confidentiality and data protection as influenced by modern technology. *Medicine and Law 12:* 547-551.

Duncan v. Wis. Dept. of Health, 166 F.3d 930 (7th Cir. 1999).

Dunham, R. G. and Alpert, G. P. (1988). Neighborhood differences in attitudes toward policing: Evidence for a mixed-strategy model of policing in a multi-ethnic setting. *Journal of Criminal Law and Criminology 79:* 504-523.

Durgins v. City of East St. Louis, 272 F.3d 841 (7th Cir. 2001).

EEOC v. Exxon Corp., 203 F.3d 871 (5th Cir.[2000]).

Epilepsy Fdn. of Northeast Ohio v. NLRB, 268 F.3d 1095 (D.C. Cir. 2001).

Flynn v. Sandahl, 58 F.3d 283 (7th Cir. 1995).

Foa, E. B. (1995). *Posttraumatic stress diagnostic scale.* Minneapolis: National Computer Systems.

Fontana v. Haskin, 262 F.3d 871 (9th Cir. 2001).

Freedom of Information Act, 5 U.S.C. §552 (b), (1974).

Friedman, L. M. (1993). *Crime and punishment in American history.* New York: Basic Books.

Frye v. U.S., 293 F. 1013 (D.C. Cir. 1923).

Fuchs, A. L. (2002). The absurdity of the FTC's interpretation of the Fair Credit Reporting Act's application to workplace investigations: Why courts should look instead to the legislative history. *Law Quarterly Review* 118: 339-366.

Garner v. Stone, No. 97A-30250-1 (DeKalb St., filed February 5, 1997).

Garrity v. State of New Jersey, 385 U.S. 493, 87 S. Ct. 616, 17 L.Ed.2d 562 (1967).

Geller, W. A. and Toch, H. (1996). Understanding and controlling police abuse of force. In Geller, W. A and H. Toch (Eds.), *Police violence* (pp. 292-328). New Haven, CT: Yale University Press.

Gellman, R. (2000). Will technology help or hurt in the struggle for health privacy? In Gates, J. and Arons, B. (Eds.), *Privacy and confidentiality in mental health care* (pp. 127-156). Baltimore, MD: Brookes Publishing.

General Electric Co. v. Joiner, 522 U.S. 136, 118 S. Ct. 512, 139 L.Ed.2d 508 (1997).

Gensbauer v. May Department Stores Co., 184 F.R.D. 552 (E.D. Pa. 1999).

Gentz, D. (1986). A system for the delivery of psychological services for police personnel. In Reese, J. and Goldstein, H. (Eds.), *Psychological services for law enforcement* (pp. 257-282). Washington, DC: U.S. Government Printing Office.

Gostin, L. (1995). Health information privacy. *Cornell Law Review 80:* 451-528.

Gough, H. (1991). *California psychological inventory administrator's guide.* Palo Alto, CA: Consulting Psychologists Press.

Gough, H. G. (1996). *California Psychological Inventory Manual.* Palo Alto, CA: Consulting Psychologists Press.

Graham, J. R. (2000). *MMPI-2 assessing personality and psychopathology*, Third edition. New York: Oxford University Press, Inc.

Greenberg, S. A. and Shulman, D.W. (1997). Irreconcilable conflict between therapeutic and forensic roles. *Professional Psychology: Research and Practice 28* (1): 50-57.

Hargrave, G. E., Hiatt, D., and Gaffney, T. W. (1988). F+4+9+Cn: An MMPI measure of aggression in law enforcement officers and applicants. *Journal of Police Science and Administration 16:* 268-273.

Hartman v. Lisle Park District, 158F. Supp. 2d 869 (N. D. Ill. 2001).

Hay, D. and Snyder, F. (Eds.) (1994). *Policing and prosecution in Britain: 1750-1859,* Gloucestershire, UK: Clarendon Press.

Haynes v. Police Bd. of the City of Chicago, 688 N.E.2d 794 (Ill. App. Ct. 1st Dist. 1997).

Health Insurance Portability and Accountability Act of 1996, L 104-191.

Henkle v. Campbell, 626 F.2d 811 (10th Cir. 1980).

Herman v. Cmwlth. Dept. of Gen. Services, 475 A.2d 164 (Pa. 1984).

Hiatt, D. and Hargrave, G. E. (1988). MMPI profiles of problem peace officers. *Journal of Personality Assessment 52:* 722-731.

Hodge v. Texaco, Inc., 975 F.2d 1093 (5th Cir. 1992).

Hodgson v. Dept. of Air Force, 704 F.Supp. 1035 (D. Colo. 1989).

Hogan v. Franco, 896 F.Supp. 1313 (N.D. N.Y. 1995).

Holiday v. City of Chattanooga, 206 F.3d 637 (6th Cir. 2000).

Howland, R. (1995). The treatment of persons with dual diagnoses in a rural community. *Psychiatric Quarterly 66:* 33-49.

International Association of Chiefs of Police (1998). *Fitness for duty evaluation guidelines.* Available online at <www.theiacp.org>.

International City/Council Management Association (IC/CMA) (2000). *Police agency handling of citizen complaints: A model policy statement.* Washington DC: IC/CMA. Available online at <www1.icma.org/main/sc.asp>.

Inwald, R. (1980). *Inwald Personality Inventory.* Kew Gardens, NY: Hilson Research, Inc.

Inwald, R. E. (1984). Psychological screening. *Police Chief 26:* 25-28.

Inwald, R. (1988). *Hilson Personnel Profile.* Kew Gardens, NY: Hilson Research, Inc.

Inwald, R. E. and Shusman, E. J. (1984). Personality and performance: Sex differences of law enforcement officer recruits. *Journal of Police Science and Administration 12:* 339-347.

Iverson, G. L. (2000). Dual relationships in psychological evaluations: Treating psychologists serving as expert witnesses. *American Journal of Forensic Psychology 18:* 79-87.

Jaffee v. Redmond, 518 U.S. 1, 116 S .Ct. 1923, 135 L.Ed.2d 337 (1996).

Jansen v. Packaging Corporation, 123 F.3d 490 (7th Cir. 1997).

Jeffords, J. (1997). Statement of Senator James Jeffords. Hearing on the confidentiality of medical information. Senate Committee on Labor and Human Resources, 105th Congress.

Jensen, J. A., McNamara, J. R., and Gustafson, K. E. (1991). Parents' and clinicians' attitudes toward the risks and benefits of child psychotherapy: A study of informed-consent content. *Professional Psychology: Research and Practice 22:* 161-170.

Juarez, R. (1985). Core issues in psychotherapy with the Hispanic child. *Psychotherapy 22* (25): 441-448.

Kappeler, V. E. (1997). *Critical issues in police civil liability,* Second edition. Prospect Heights, IL: Waveland Press.

Kees v. Wallenstein, 161 F.3d 1196 (9th Cir. 1998).

Kelling, G. (1974). *The Kansas City preventative control experiment: A summary report.* Washington, DC: The Police Foundation.

Kent, D. A. and Eisenberg, T. (1972). The selection and promotion of police officers: A selected review of recent literature. *The Police Chief* (February): 20-29.

Kirkingburg v. Albertson's, Inc., 143 F.3d 1228 (9th Cir. 1998).

Kleinke, J. D. (1998). Release 0.0: Clinical information technology in the real world. *Health Affairs (Millwood) 17:* 23-38.

Kraft v. Police Com'rs of Boston, 629 N.E.2d 995 (Mass. 1994).

Kremer, T. G. and Gesten, E. L. (1998). Confidentiality limits of managed care and clients' willingness to disclose. *Professional Psychology, Research and Practice 29:* 553-558.

Krocka v. Bransfield, 969 F.Supp. 1073 (N.D. Ill. 1997).

Krocka v. City of Chicago, F.3d 507 (7th Cir. 2000).

Kumho Tire v. Carmichael, 526 U.S. 137, 119 S. Ct. 1167, 143 L.Ed.2d 238 (1999).

Kurke, M. I. and Scrivner, E. M. (1995). *Police psychology into the 21st century.* Hillsdale, NJ: Lawrence Erlbaum.

LaChance v. Erickson, 522 U.S. 262, 118 S. Ct. 753, 139 L.Ed.2d 695 (1998).

Lambley v. Kameny, 682 N.E.2d 907 (Mass. App. Ct. 1997).

Lane, R. (1997). *Murder in America: A history.* Columbus: Ohio State University Press.

Lanning v. Southeastern Pennsylvania Transp. Authority 308 F.2d 286 (3rd cir. 2000).

LeBoeuf v. N.Y. Univ. Med. Ctr., No. 98 Civ. 0973, 2000 WL 1863762 (S.D. N.Y. Dec. 20, 2000).

Lefly, H. P. (2000). Perspectives of families regarding confidentiality and mental illness. In Gates, J. and Arons, B. (Eds.), *Privacy and confidentiality in mental health care* (pp. 33-46). Baltimore, MD: Brookes Publishing.

Lewis v. Goodie, 798 F.Supp. 382 (W.D. La.1992).

Louis Harris and Associates. (1993). *Health information privacy survey, 1993.* New York: Louis Harris and Associates.

Lowman, R. L. (1989). *Pre-employment screening for psychopathology: A guide to professional practice.* Sarasota, FL: Professional Resource Exchange, Inc.

Lugar v. Edmondson Oil Co., 457 U.S. 922, 102 S. Ct. 2744, 73 L.Ed.2d 482 (1982).

Machell, D. F. (1989). The recovering alcoholic police officer and the danger of professional emotional suppression. *Alcoholism Treatment Quarterly 6:* 85-89.

Mann, P. A. (1980). Ethical issues for psychologists in police agencies. In J. Monahan (Ed.), *Who is the client? The ethics of psychological intervention in the criminal justice system* (pp. 18-42). Washington, DC: American Psychological Association.

Maplewood v. Law Enforcement Labor Service, 108 LA (BNA) 572, Daly, 1996.

Martin, S. E. (1997). Women officers on the move: An update of women in policing. In R. Dunham and G. Alpert (Eds.), *Critical issues in policing,* Third edition (pp. 363-384). Prospect Heights, IL: Waveland Press.

Mason v. Stock, 869 F.Supp 828 (D. Kan 1994).

May v. U.S. Civil Service Commission, 230 F.Supp. 659 (W.D. La., 1963).

McGuire, J. M., Toal, P., and Blau, B. (1985). The adult client's conception of confidentiality in the therapeutic relationship. *Professional Psychology, Research and Practice 16:* 375-384.

McKenna v. Fargo, 451 F.Supp. 1355 (D.N.J. 1978), *aff'd,* 601 F.2d 573 (3d Cir. 1978).

Meehl, P. E. (1954). *Clinical versus statistical prediction.* Minneapolis: University of Minnesota Press.

Melton, G. B. (2000). Privacy issues in child mental health services. In J. Gates and B. Arons (Eds.), *Privacy and confidentiality in mental health care* (pp. 47-70). Baltimore, MD: Brookes Publishing.

Miller, W. R. (1999). Cops and bobbies: Police Authority in New York and London, 1830-1870, Second edition. Columbus, OH: Ohio State University Press.

Miller v. City of Springfield, 146 F.3d 612 (8th Cir. 1998).

Millon, T., Davis, R., and Millon, C. (1997). *Millon Clinical Multiaxial Inventory-III manual,* Second edition. Minneapolis, MN: National Computer Systems.

Mills, M. C. and Stratton, J. G. (1982). The MMPI and the prediction of police job performance. *FBI Law Enforcement Bulletin 51:* 10-15.

Monell v. Department of Social Services, 436 U.S. 658, 98 S. Ct. 2018, 56 L.Ed.2d 611 (1978).

Monkkonen, E. (1981). *Police in urban America, 1860-1920.* Cambridge, UK: Cambridge University Press.

Moran, D. W. (1998). Health information policy: On preparing for the next war. *Health Affairs 17:* 9-22.

Morey, L. C. (1991). *The Personality Assessment Inventory: Professional manual.* Odessa, FL: Psychological Assessment Resources, Inc.

Murphy v. United Parcel Service, 141 F.3d 1185 (10th Cir. 1999).

National Advisory Commission on Civil Disorders (1968). *National Advisory Commission on Civil Disorders report.* Washington, DC: U.S. Government Printing Office.

National Alliance for the Mentally Ill (1998). *Public policy platform of the National Alliance for the Mentally Ill,* Third edition. Arlington, VA: Author.

NLRB v. Weingarten, Inc., 420 U.S. 251, 95 S. Ct. 976, 43 L.Ed.2d 171 (1975).

Nolan v. Police Commissioner of Boston, 420 N.E.2d 335 (Mass. 1981).

Norman, J. and Rosvall, S. B. (1994). Help-seeking behavior among mental health practitioners. *Clinical Social Work Journal 22:* 449-460.

Nowell, D. and Spruill, J. (1993). If it's not absolutely confidential, will information be disclosed? *Professional Psychology: Research and Practice 24:* 367-369.

O'Harrow, R. (1998). Prescription sales, privacy fears; CVS, Giant share customer records with drug marketing firm. *The Washington Post,* February 15, p. A01.

Olmstead v. U.S., U.S. 438 (1928) 277 U.S. 438 No. 493.

Peck, R. (1994). Results from an Equifax privacy poll on concerns about medical confidentiality. *Medical and Health News 14:* 10.

Pembaur v. Cincinnati, 475 U.S. 469, 106 S. Ct. 1292, 89 L.Ed.2d 452 (1986).

Penn. St. Troopers' Assn. (Kornguth) v. Pa. St. Police, 644 A.2d 1161 (Pa. 1994).

People v. Slaughter, 557 N.Y.S.2d 926 (N.Y. App. Div. 2nd Dept. 1990).

The President's Commission on Law Enforcement and Administration of Justice (1973). *Task force report: The police.* Washington, DC: U.S. Government Printing Office.

Privacy Act, 5 U.S.C. §552 (a) (1974).

Reese, J. (1987). *A history of police psychological services.* Washington, DC: U.S. Government Printing Office.

Reese, J. and Goldstein, H. (Eds.) (1986). *Psychological services for law enforcement.* Washington, DC: U.S. Government Printing Office, Superintendent of Documents.

Resek v. City of Huntington Beach, 41 Fed. Appx. 57 (9th Cir. 2002).

Reuss-Ianni, E. (1983). *Two cultures of policing: Street cops and management cops.* New Brunswick, NJ: Transaction Books.

Risner v. U.S. Dept of Transp. 677 F.2d 36 (8th Cir. 1982).

Roback, H. B. and Shelton, M. (1995). Effects of confidentiality limitations on the psychotherapeutic process. *Journal of Psychotherapy Practice and Research 4:* 185-193.

Robles v. Hoyos, 151 F.3d 1 (1st Cir. 1998).

Roosevelt, T. (1906). *New York: A sketch of the city's social, political, and commercial progress from the first Dutch settlement to recent times.* New York: Charles Scribner and Sons.

Rosario v. City of New Haven, 1998 WL 51786 (D. Conn. Feb. 4, 1998).

Rosenzweig, D. (2000). L.A. seeks to appeal racketeering ruling Rampart: The city asks judge's permission to challenge his decision that the LAPD can be sued under RICO law. *Los Angeles Times,* August 31.

Ross, D.L. (2003). Emerging trends in police failure to train liability. *Policing: An International Journal of Police Strategies in Management* (23): 169-193.

Rostow, C. and Davis, R. D. (2002). Psychological screening. *Law and Order 50* (5): 100-106.

Rostow, C. D., Davis, R. D., Pinkston, J. B., and Cowick, L. M. (1999). The MMPI-2 and satisfactory police academy performance: Differences and correlations. *Journal of Police and Criminal Psychology 14* (2): 35-39.

Roullette v. Department of Central Management, 490 N.E.2d 60 (Ill. App. 1st Dist. 1986).

Rubinstein, J. (1973). *City police.* New York: Farrar, Strauss, and Girox.

Russell, F. (1975). *A City in terror—1919—The Boston police strike.* New York: Viking Press.

Schwartz v. Hicksville Union Free School Dist., 233 A.D.2d 515 (N.Y. App. Div. 2nd Dept., 1996).

Scott v. Edinburg, 101 F.Supp.2d 1017 (ND. Ill. 2000).

Seafield 911 (1991). Signs of developing alcoholism. *Supervisor's training manual.* Davie FL., Seafield 911.

Shane Salazar v. Golden State Warriors, 124 F.Supp.2d 1155 (N.D. Cal. 2000).

Sharkin, B. (1995). Strains on confidentiality in college-student psychotherapy: Entangled therapeutic relationships, incidental encounters, and third-party inquiries. *Professional Psychology, Research and Practice 26:* 184-189.

Shipley, W. C. (1946). *Institute of Living scale.* Los Angeles: Western Psychological Services.

Shulman, D. W., Greenberg, S. A., Heilbrun, K., and Foote, W. E. (1998). An immodest proposal: Should treating mental health professionals be barred from testifying about their patients? *Behavioral Sciences and the Law 16:* 509-523.

Siegler, M. (1982). Sounding boards: Confidentiality in medicine—A decrepit concept. *New England Journal of Medicine 307:* 1518-1521.

Silver, A. (1967). The demand for order in civil society: A review of some themes in the history of urban crime, police, and riot. In David J. Bordua (Ed.), *The police: Six sociological essays* (pp. 12-13). New York: John Wiley.

Skolnick, J. (1994). *Justice without trial: Law enforcement in democratic society,* Third edition. New York: Wiley.

Smith v. U.S. Air Force, 566 F.2d 957 (5th Cir. 1978).

Snow, R. (1992). Civilian oversight: Plus or minus. *Law and Order Magazine* December: 51-56.

Soroka v. Dayton Hudson Corp., 235 Cal. App. 3d 654 (Cal. App. 1st Dist. 1991).

Spades v. City of Walnut Ridge, 186 F.3d 897 (8th Cir. 1999).

State of New Jersey (2000). Directive implementing procedures for the seizure of weapons from municipal and county law enforcement officers involved in domestic violence incidents. New Jersey Department of Law and Public Safety, Division of Criminal Justice (September 19). Available online at <www.state.nj.us/lps/dcj/agguide/9dv34.pdf>.

Stone, A.V. (2000). *Fitness for duty: Principles, methods, and legal issues.* Boca Raton, FL, CRC Press.

Strasburger, H., Gutheil, T. G., and Brodsky, B. A. (1997). On wearing two hats: Role conflict in serving as both psychotherapist and expert witness. *American Journal of Psychiatry 154* (4): 48-56.

Sue, D. and Sue, S. (1987). Cultural factors in the clinical assessment of Asian Americans. *Journal of Consulting and Clinical Psychology 55:* 479-487.

Sujak, D. A., Villanova, P., and Daly, J. P. (1995). The effects of drug-testing program characteristics on applicants' attitudes toward potential employment. *Journal of Psychology 129:* 401-416.

Sullivan v. River Valley School Dist., 197 F.3d 804 (6th Cir. 1999).

Sutton v. United Airlines, 130 F.3d 893 (10th Cir. 1997).

Swidler, A. (1986). Culture in action: Symbols and strategies. *American Sociological Review 51:* 273-286.

Tarasoff v. Regents of the University of California, 551 P.2d 334 (Cal. 1976).

Tardie v. Rehabilitation Hosp. of Rhode Island, 168 F.3d 538 (1st Cir. 1999).

Taube, D. O. and Elwork, A. (1990). Researching the effects of confidentiality law on patients' self-disclosures. *Professional Psychology, Research and Practice 21:* 72-75.

Terman, L. and Otis, A. (1917). A trial of mental and pedagogical tests in a civil service examination for policemen and firemen. *Journal of Applied Psychology 1:* 17-29.

Tollison, C. D. and Langley, J. C. (1995). *Pain patient profile.* Minneapolis, MN: National Computer Systems.

Toyota Motor Mfg. Kentucky Inc. v. Williams, 534 U.S. 184, 122 S. Ct. 681, 151 L.Ed.2d 615 (2002).

Underhill v. Willamina Lumber Co., 1999 WL 421596 (D. Or. May 27, 1999).

US Airways Inc. v. Barnett, 535 U.S. 391, 122 S. Ct. 1516, 152 L.Ed.2d 589 (2002).

U.S. Department of Justice (DOJ) (2003). *Enforcing the ADA: A status report from the Department of Justice*. Washington, DC: DOJ.

U.S. v. City of Pittsburgh (1997).

U.S. v. White Horse, 177 F.Supp.2d 973 (D.S.D., 2001).

Valentin v. Bootes, 740 A.2d 172 (N.J. 1998).

Van Maanen, J. (1978). The asshole. In P. K. Manning and J. Van Maanen (Eds.), *Policing: A view from the street* (pp. 221-238). Santa Monica, CA: Goodyear Publishing.

Vann v. City of New York, 72 F.3d 1040 (2nd Cir. 1995).

Vinson v. Superior Court, 740 P.2d 404 (Cal. 1987).

Waits v. City of Chicago, 2003 WL 21310277 (N.D. Ill. June 6, 2003).

Walker, S. (1977). *A critical history of police reform: The emergence of professionalism*. Lexington, MA: Lexington Books.

Walker, S. (1981). Popular justice. In David R. Johnson (Ed.), *American law enforcement: A history*. Arlington Heights, IL: Forum Press.

Walker, S. (1998). *Popular justice: A history of American criminal justice*, Second edition. Oxford, UK: Oxford University Press.

Walker, S. and Bumphus, V. (1992). The effectiveness of civilian review: Observations on recent trends and new issues. *American Journal of Police 11* (4): 1-26.

Waller, A. (1995). Health care issues in health care reform. *Whittier Law Review, 16:* 15-49.

Watson v. City of Miami Beach, 177 F.3d 932 (11th Cir. 1999).

Wertz v. Wilson, 922 S.W.2d 268 (Tex. App. Ct. Austin 1996).

Westin, A. (1993). Interpretive essay. In Louis Harris and Associates (Eds.), *Health information privacy survey, 1993* (p. 7). New York: Louis Harris and Associates.

Wilson, J. Q. and Kelling, G. L. (1982). Broken windows: The police and neighborhood safety. *Atlantic Monthly 249:* 29-38.

Index